EMERGENCY
NAVIGATION

Pathfinding Techniques for the
Inquisitive and Prudent Mariner

DAVID BURCH

Foreword by David Lewis

INTERNATIONAL MARINE
Camden, Maine

Published by International Marine

3 Hardbound printings
First paperback printing 1990

10 9 8 7 6

Copyright © 1986 International Marine, an imprint of TAB BOOKS. TAB BOOKS is a division of McGraw-Hill, Inc.

Library of Congress Cataloging-in-Publication Data

Burch, David, 1942-
    Emergency navigation.
  Index
  1. Navigation   I. Title
UK555.B837   1985   623.89   85-19846
ISBN 0-87742-260-5

Questions regarding the content of this book should be addressed to:

International Marine
P.O. Box 220
Camden, ME 04843

EMERGENCY *NAVIGATION*

Pathfinding Techniques for the Inquisitive and Prudent Mariner

Contents

List of Figures

Foreword

by David Lewis

David Burch's book is a comprehensive review of emergency navigation at sea that is a pleasure to read. Throughout the book he keeps returning to first principles of navigation which he expounds with admirable clarity. His emergency procedures are explained in terms of natural (often astronomical) laws, so that their rationale is fully comprehensible and their practical applications and limitations clearly defined. The book is a far cry from some emergency handbooks, with their mixed bag of semi-anecdotal advice, and is not intended to serve as such. Yet in an emergency situation, with the sextant overboard and the watch broken, it would be of far more use to the unfortunate mariner.

But this work, despite its title, is far more than an essay on the principles and practice of emergency procedures. It is a particularly well-written account of the principles of navigation in general, and as such, cannot fail to bring fresh insights to all of us. Certainly it clarified for me certain areas of nautical astronomy that I thought I had grasped, but had not.

It is rare to read a book that is equally successful in expounding matters of principle and the practical realities of their application on the real ocean, but David Burch has succeeded in this also.

It is well to be overly conservative in matters of marine navigation — the reefs of the Pacific are littered with the wrecks of the over-confident. I merely want to stress that emergency navigation, as explained by David Burch, is not so very hard. Given this book to study, its practice is within the reach of any of us.

Non-instrumental navigation is often thought of in the context of the tropical Pacific where the feats of the Polynesians and Micronesians have focused our attention. David Burch makes clear that its application is worldwide. After all, the Norse discoverers of America had no more instruments (if we discount the dubious sunstone) than the settlers of New Zealand. When we traversed the South Magnetic Pole in the southern summer of 1981-82, the compass was useless for 600 miles. There was admittedly a SatNav aboard, but for direction between fixes, a sun diagram was constructed much as is explained in this book. Together with swell, wave and wind patterns, it enabled us to steer accurately, except on two occasions when we had to lie-to in calms when falling snow obscured the sun.

Polar and tropical seas are admittedly environmental extremes, particularly the former. Less exotic, but fully as serious navigational emergencies may arise off Maine or California, and readers of this book will be well-armed with the knowledge to deal with them. Dip into its pages then, for pleasure and profit; the stern specter of disaster apart, the book is stimulating, easy to read, and has something to teach everyone.

One last point, but not the least significant: every section and paragraph is permeated with sound practical seamanship. Apart from the work's other virtues, this alone would make it worthwhile.

Acknowledgments

One cannot write on emergency navigation without reaffirming the indebtedness that all mariners owe to Harold Gatty, author of *The Raft Book* and other studies of emergency navigation on land and sea. I have learned much from his work and have been motivated by it.

I am especially grateful to Dr. David Lewis for his review of the manuscript and his foreword to the text. His definitive study of Polynesian navigation, *We, the Navigators,* was my introduction to the topic of no-instrument navigation, which in turn led me to investigate the application of Polynesian methods at other latitudes, and from there to this book.

The initiation of this work in 1979 was made possible by a grant from the Washington Sea Grant Program under NOAA Grant No. NA79AA-D-00054. Their assistance remains much appreciated.

Introduction

Have you ever wondered what you would do if circumstances left you in charge of a boat in the middle of the ocean, without any navigation equipment? Let's say you were wearing a watch, but had no satnav or Loran, no navigation books or tables, no knotmeter or log, no sextant, and no compass. And suppose, on top of that, you had no idea where you were in the first place. Could you figure out where you were from your watch and the stars, and from there steer a course halfway across the ocean without a compass? One goal of this book is to tell you how to achieve such things — and other, less dramatic feats of contingency navigation.

At sea we must accept that everything can get wet, turned upside down, and dropped. Any piece of equipment, no matter how well guarded, can fail or be lost — somehow we could end up without it. There's no way around this; it's part of the challenge we accept when we go to sea. We must be self-reliant. If equipment fails, we must go on or go back, one mile or a thousand miles, without it.

Navigational equipment is no exception. In the worst case, we should be prepared to navigate with none of our customary aids. Skills in no-instrument navigation can't be discounted because the chances we'll ever need them are small. The chances are very small. But we only have to need them once to give new meaning to statistics.

1.1 What Is Emergency Navigation?

This book uses the term "emergency navigation" in a special way. Here it simply means navigation with limited or makeshift instruments, regardless of the circumstances. An emergency in the usual sense is not required. Indeed, one purpose of this book is to show just the opposite: If the only problem at hand is the loss of our customary navigation tools, there need not be an emergency in the usual sense — if we are prepared.

Another goal of this book is to show that any oceangoing navigator can learn the necessary skills to be prepared. You don't have to be a master mariner, born and reared on the sea, or a descendant of an elite line of Polynesian navigators to discover your position at sea and find your way across an ocean without conventional instruments. But you do have to do your homework. The oceans are big and they flow in different directions. And directions of the winds and seas and sun and stars change hourly and daily as we proceed. The waters around us may span some million square miles; the island we may have to find may be visible only from 30 miles off.

Emergency navigation includes the obvious things we might think of: steering without a compass, finding boat speed without a knotmeter, keeping track of position without a sextant. But the meaning of emergency navigation depends in part on what we are used to. It can also mean just plain, basic celestial or coastwise navigation that we haven't used for years, because the radar, Loran, and satnav had served all our navigational needs — until they got wet, or we ran out of power, or their antennas were broken off in a storm.

Set adrift in a life raft without instruments, a thousand miles from land, one obviously must navigate by emergency methods. But this is the extreme case. The navigator of a comfortable, well-equipped yacht, with his only sextant damaged or overboard must also resort to emergency navigation. And a sportsfisherman a mile offshore may not have a compass when the fog sets in. On a hazardous coast, emergency navigation is just as vital to this person.

Emergency methods are approximations and tricks. But some of the tricks are good tricks and the approximations not far from the truth. In many cases, our routine navigation can benefit from these makeshift methods. After all, the way we must ultimately calibrate any instrument is to measure the same thing with more basic instruments. In the end, all instruments must reduce to a measuring stick and a clock — though I wouldn't want to prove this in the case of the compass.

No-instrument skills are a vital asset to anyone's navigation. But in perspective, the best navigator is not the one who can do the most with the least, but the one who can do the most with what he has. The goal of navigation is knowing exactly where you are and how to choose the shortest safe course to where you want to go, under all conditions, using *all* navigation equipment available — whether this includes Sat-Nav, two radars, sonar, Loran, gyrocompass, weather facsimile, and a computer, or just a stick with a string tied to it.

1.2 Scope of this Book

This book is not a "survival manual" in any sense. The subject matter is restricted to navigation and things related to navigation. I can't offer advice on such basic decisions as whether to make for land or stay put after an accident at sea — the conditions of mishaps at sea are never the same. What is offered, instead, is the background in emergency techniques that should help you make this and other navigational decisions in the particular circumstances at hand.

The purpose of this book is to show the capabilities and limitations of makeshift navigation. The subject is limited, but it is covered thoroughly and practically. The methods described are not gimmicks; they are tested procedures. Errors and uncertainties are also analyzed. The methods of this book can be used on any vessel, anywhere in the world, at any time of year. Exceptions to this are clearly indicated. Some of the methods in this book are original, others are reformulated to show their utility and limitations, but most are basic celestial and coastal navigation procedures that you can carry out with makeshift instruments.

This book is intended for anyone familiar with the rudiments of marine navigation. Many of the methods rely on basic principles of celestial navigation, but you need not be an expert celestial navigator to use this book. All topics begin with the fundamentals. Experienced navigators will find things here that are already second-nature, but the more specialized no-instrument procedures are less well known and should be of interest to even seasoned navigators. Any navigator, after all, gains confidence and versatility as he becomes less dependent upon perishable aids.

The only conventional navigation aids used in some of the emergency methods are watches and sunrise-sunset tables (tables that list the times of sunrise and sunset at various latitudes throughout the year). Watches are included both because you are likely to have one and because they are such a tremendous help to navigation. Methods without watches are, of course, also covered. Methods that use sunrise-sunset tables are described because these tables are included at the back of the *U.S. Tide Tables*. Of all special publications for navigation, tide tables are the most likely to be found on a boat, so there is a reasonable chance these tables will be available. As we shall see, there is much to be learned from sunrise-sunset tables besides the times the sun goes up and down.

Naturally, if a sextant, chronometer, compass, or *Nautical Almanac* were available, it would be a bonus. Application of these aids to the emergency techniques will be obvious. For example, you can use the height of a star in some cases to judge its bearing for use in steering without a compass. With a sextant, you could measure its height accurately and not have to estimate it.

This book was not intended to be stowed for emergency use. It's far better to stow an extra compass than to stow a book on how to steer without a compass — it takes up less space. There are no special tables or fold-out diagrams that are intended to make the book itself an aid to navigation. The tables that are included can be used in an emergency, but their primary purpose is for practice. The techniques in this book are much better practiced and learned before they are needed.

Many of the techniques in this book can be practiced, even mastered, on land or on short cruises on inland or coastal waters. It's a good idea to practice as much as you can before departing on an ocean voyage — those vast amounts of spare time we anticipate on a long, slow ocean passage don't always materialize.

In a sense, this book offers you a hobby — a pastime that will exercise your ingenuity, measurement skills, and memory. A hobby that is bound to make you more familiar with the sea and the sky. And a hobby that could save your boat — so to speak.

1.3 Preparation for Navigational Emergencies

Again, in discussing emergency preparations, we limit ourselves to navigational matters. A full check list for emergency preparation includes such things as life rafts, food and water supplies, first-aid kits, seasickness aids, fishing gear, signaling gear, and other supplies. Books on seamanship and sea survival discuss these preparations. For navigational preparedness on an ocean voyage, the following items are the basics.

(1) The cardinal rule: Know where you are to the best of your ability at all times. In mid-ocean, small-boat skippers are tempted to be lax on navigation. This is a bad habit to get into. It could well be that when you do need an accurate position, the sun and stars are obscured. This leaves you to carry on for another day or so by dead reckoning. Close to your destination, this could be hazardous or at least inefficient. Also, if you should need to send a radio distress signal, the better you know your position, the better your chances are for rescue. Remember that if a ship is diverted to look for you, the range of visibility from the bridge of the ship may be only 10 miles or less.

(2) Wear a watch and keep track of the rate at which it gains or loses time. As we shall see, you can accurately navigate around the world with a watch alone. It is the most important piece of emergency gear you could have.

(3) Carry a Class-B EPIRB on board. EPIRB stands for Emergency Position Indicating Radio Beacon. These are relatively inexpensive, waterproof radio transmitters that emit a distress signal when activated that can be picked up by aircraft and satellites passing over the region. EPIRB batteries last from two to seven days, depending on the ocean temperature. An aircraft's reception range is some 200 miles in all directions. Near great-circle air routes between major cities, this provides a reasonable probability of aircraft detection, though it is difficult to predict air traffic routes precisely, as they vary with the weather and winds aloft.

Satellite detection is more probable. The COSPAS/SARSAT system of satellites provides global coverage, with a satellite passing in range of every point on earth several times a day. Passing satellites can locate the position of an activated EPIRB to within some 10 to 20 miles. They then relay the information to a ground station, which initiates the rescue. This satellite search-and-rescue program is a collaboration among the United States, the Soviet Union, Canada, and France. Since its inception in the fall of 1982, the program has established an impressive record of assists with marine search and rescue. With planned expansions and improvements, it promises to be even more effective in the future. But by no means should you feel confident of rescue simply because you have activated an EPIRB. Class-A EPIRBs are the same as Class-B, except that they activate automatically when submerged. Class-C units are for coastal use only; they broadcast short-range signals on VHF channels 15 and 16.

(4) Tell someone where you are going and when you expect to arrive, and of course let them know when you do arrive or if your itinerary changes. The Coast Guard calls this filing a "float plan." It is fundamental to safe boating on any waters.

(5) If you have radios on board, learn their full potential and the specific uses of various frequencies, especially the standard distress frequencies and other channels monitored by the Coast Guard. Teach others on board to use the radios. In an emergency, someone else may have to use the radio while the skipper stays at the wheel. Monitor weather broadcasts at least once a day. The schedule of times and frequencies of weather broadcasts is given in *Selected World-Wide Weather Broadcasts,* published by the National Oceanic and Atmospheric Administration (NOAA).

(6) Study the seasonal weather patterns, prevailing winds, and ocean currents along your intended route. For American coastal and connecting waters, this information is given in the *U.S. Coast Pilots* (NOAA). There are also equivalent publications for Canadian waters, called *Sailing Directions*. These books contain a wealth of navigational information beyond that shown on nautical charts; they also include wind, weather, and current data. For international waters, similar information is available in the *U.S. Sailing Directions*, published by the Defense Mapping Agency Hydrographic/Topographic Center (DMAHTC). Worldwide sailing directions, called *Pilots*, are also published by the British government.

Special charts called U.S. Pilot Charts are a convenient and reliable source of seasonal wind and current data. They are published by the DMAHTC according to month and ocean (see Figure 1-1). Magnetic variation, great-circle routes, and other useful data are also given on pilot charts. There are also British Pilot Charts.

(7) With your other emergency gear, stow a hiker's compass, a Davis Mark III plastic sextant, a waterproof quartz watch (with known rate), a pilot chart, pencils and notebook (preferably with waterproof paper), and a copy of the Davies *Concise Tables for Sight Reduction* (which includes a long-term almanac for sun and stars). All of this fits in a boot box and costs less than $100. See Figure 1-2. With this kit you can find your way to any port in the world.

(8) Keep track of where you are relative to shipping lanes (great-circle routes between major ports) shown on pilot charts. If you run across commercial traffic at sea, it will probably be near one of these lanes. If you are looking for help, shipping lanes are the place to be. Even if you aren't looking for help, when you sail across or along a shipping lane, keep on special alert for traffic. A freighter can come over the horizon and be on top of you in 15 minutes or so. It is fundamental to safe navigation, as well as to the International Rules of the Road, to have a watch on duty at all times.

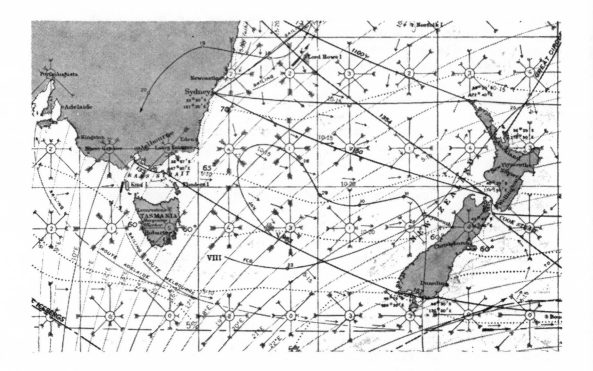

FIGURE 1-1. *Section of a U.S. Pilot Chart. This chart is for December, January, and February. Pilot charts show wind roses (arrows fly with the winds; number of feathers equals the average Beaufort force number), magnetic variation (which shifts from about 9° E to 24° E in this region), prevailing currents (small arrows labeled with daily drift in nautical miles), great-circle routes between major ports, traditional sailing routes (which, in some cases, not necessarily these, tend to be more downwind than required for modern yachts), and various ice limits of interest in these low latitudes. Other parts of the chart show sea and air temperatures, barometric pressures, gale frequencies, and other information of marine interest. Also see Figure 4-3.*

(9) And finally, study the principles and practice the methods of emergency navigation. All the safety precautions imaginable cannot guarantee that you won't end up with nothing to go by but your own knowledge and skills.

If you are crew or passenger on an oceangoing vessel, the main responsibility for emergency preparation and navigational safety lies with the vessel's captain and officers. But even in this case, for true self-reliance, the first and last points above remain basics for everyone on board: Keep track of your position as well as your duties allow and master the rudiments of emergency navigation. Remember, in any emergency the role of leader goes to the one who is best prepared.

Navigating a long ocean voyage without modern instruments is a full-time job. It takes continuous concentration. But if you are prepared, you can keep track of your

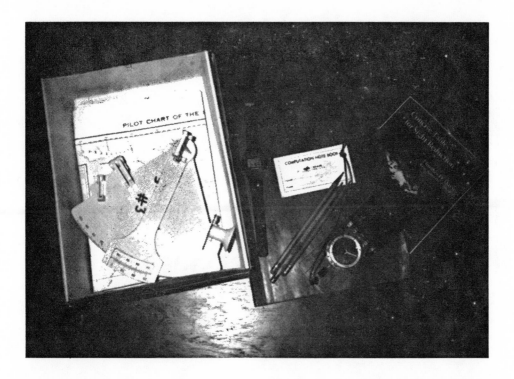

FIGURE 1-2. *Back-up navigational gear. Store this equipment in a waterproof bag, inside or near your regular emergency throw bag. Back-up navigational procedures are discussed in Chapter 14. Since 1989 the Nautical Almanac has included a copy of the Davies Concise Tables in a very slightly modified form, now called the NAO Sight Reduction Tables. These can be removed from any expired almanac and saved for a back-up kit. A long-term almanac can be copied from Bowditch, Volume 2. Both the back-up almanac and NAO tables can be made water resistant with coating solutions designed for chart protection. The author's Emergency Navigation Card (an 8½" x 11" waterproof card) is a valuable addition to a back-up kit. It includes sight reduction tables, sun almanac, ways to figure sun bearings, notes on steering by the stars, and reminders of several key procedures covered in this book.*

position across any ocean. Columbus did it five centuries ago with little more than a compass, and he didn't even know how that worked. We are far better prepared today for a similar voyage with similar "instruments."

2

Time and Place at Sea

In sight of land, the best way to keep track of position on the water is relative to charted landmarks. Calling for help in near-coastal waters, it's usually better to report your position as, say, "two miles north of Point Wilson" than it is to read off your latitude and longitude from a chart or electronic device. The latter method is more prone to error; it also assumes your rescuer has a chart of the area. I stress this point because more and more skippers are beginning to rely on the direct latitude and longitude readouts of their Loran units, even on inland waters. It appears more precise, but may well not be.

Though Loran was intended as a coastwise aid, it generally works well in other waters. With proper calibration, modern Loran units can be very accurate on inland waters, or far out to sea on the fringe of their prescribed coverage areas. Nevertheless, it is dangerous to rely on any one aid alone. The more we rely on electronics, the less practice we get at basic piloting and dead reckoning. In short, we get lazy. There are many documented accidents that have resulted from overconfidence in Loran latitude-longitude positions.

Out of sight of land, on the other hand, on a featureless sea, we have little choice but to rely on latitude and longitude for position. For record keeping on ocean passages, we could use a small-scale nautical chart of the entire ocean or a plotting sheet that shows only the latitude and longitude grid. In an emergency, we might use just a blank sheet of paper on which we sketch parallels of latitude. With this we might use a hybrid notation for position, giving our latitude and estimated distance run east or west from a specific longitude.

What we use will depend on what we've got. In the extreme case, we could estimate our latitude from the sky using only our fingers, hands, and arms, with very little special knowledge required. But unless that arm has a watch around it, we will never be able to figure our longitude from what we see in the sky. We will only be able to keep track of how far we sail east or west. Hence the potential usefulness of the hybrid notation.

2.1 Latitude Regions and Seasons Defined

In emergency navigation and meteorology, it is convenient to divide the globe into latitude bands according to the relationship of the sun to the earth. The three regions are the tropics, the temperate latitudes, and the polar regions.

The tropics are defined as the central belt of the earth extending from latitude 23° 27' S to 23° 27' N. The special latitude of 23° 27' derives from the earth's rotation axis, which is tilted 23° 27' relative to the plane of its orbit around the sun. Because of this tilt, the sun can be viewed overhead only from somewhere within the tropics. During the fall and winter (from the autumnal equinox on September 23 to the vernal equinox on March 21), the sun is directly overhead at some latitude in the southern tropics. During the spring and summer, the sun is directly overhead at some latitude of the northern tropics. We shall come back to this point when we discuss navigation by the sun.

Throughout this book, we refer to summer and winter as they are defined in the Northern Hemisphere. In the Southern Hemisphere, these seasons are reversed. July and August are called summer months in the United States; in Australia they are called winter months.

The latitudes of the tropics have special significance to emergency navigation for somewhat subtle reasons. Apparent motions of the sun and stars are governed by trigonometric equations involving the sine and cosine functions of the observer's latitude. Throughout the tropics, the latitude angle is small, and consequently the sine and cosine functions are approximately equal to their limiting values of 0.0 and 1.0. This greatly simplifies the trigonometric equations, and from these simpler equations, we can learn simple rules that apply in the tropics — we will use the rules, but we won't get involved in the trigonometry itself. For example, within the tropics it is easy to predict the bearing of any star on the horizon for use in steering without a compass. This is not so easy from other parts of the globe.

The two polar regions are defined as latitudes greater than 66° 33', north or south. These regions are unique as the only places on earth where the sun can remain above or below the horizon for more than one day. In a sense, the polar regions are the opposite of the tropics (the latitude 66° 33' comes from 90° minus 23° 27'), especially in emergency navigation. Navigation in general must be specialized for the polar regions, and many of the emergency celestial methods we cover do not apply in the polar regions. These restrictions are clearly pointed out when they arise.

Everywhere between the tropics and the polar regions, that is, between latitudes 23° 27' and 66° 33', is called the temperate latitudes, or just the latitudes. In this

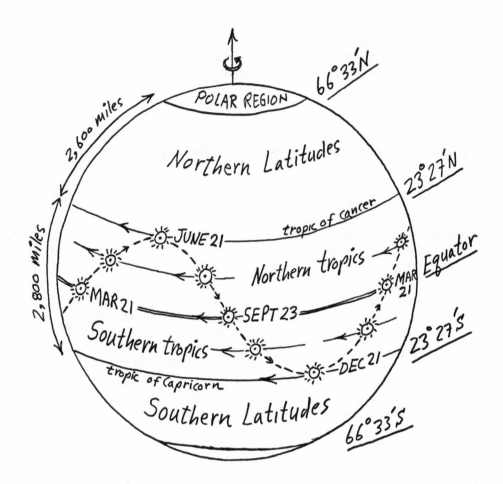

FIGURE 2-1. *Latitude regions in emergency navigation. The sun passes overhead in some latitude of the tropics, defined by the northern and southern limits of the sun's latitude. Some rules and procedures of emergency navigation work only in the tropics (40 percent of the earth's surface), and many of the methods we cover do not work in the polar regions (8 percent of the earth's surface). The temperate latitudes between these two regions comprise 52 percent of the earth's surface.*

book, the phrase "northern latitudes" refers to the general region in the Northern Hemisphere north of the tropics and south of the polar region.

These latitude regions defined by the sun are important for navigation because we can navigate by the position of the sun. They are important for meteorology because the average position of the sun determines the weather. (See Figure 2-1.) There are no similar divisions of the earth according to longitude. Because of the daily rotation of the earth, the earth is essentially symmetric in the east-west direction.

It is easy to think of latitude differences in terms of nautical miles, since the nautical mile was invented for just this purpose. For practical use, a nautical mile can be defined as the distance equal to a latitude change of one minute. Or in terms of degrees,

$$1° \text{ of latitude } = 60 \text{ nautical miles.}$$

This relationship is the key to the language of navigation. If my latitude is 20° S, I am 1,200 nautical miles south of the equator. If I am to sail from Cape Hatteras at latitude 35° N due south to Nassau at latitude 25° N, then I must sail south for 10°, or a distance of 600 nautical miles. For several purposes in navigation, it is convenient to remember that a nautical mile is just about 6,000 feet (some 15 percent longer than a statute mile). In this book, the words "mile" and "nautical mile" are used interchangeably; any reference to miles means nautical miles.

At the equator, 1° of longitude also equals 60 nautical miles, and, for the trigonometric reasons mentioned above, this is very nearly true throughout the tropics. But as you go still farther from the equator, this is no longer a valid approximation. The conversion of longitude increments to miles is not as simple as it is for latitude increments, since longitude meridians converge at the poles. At latitude 48°, for example, there are only 40 nautical miles to a degree of longitude. We shall return to this problem later on when we discuss longitude.

2.2 Time in Navigation

There are many kinds of time in navigation books. There is watch time, standard time, zone time, chronometer time, Greenwich mean time, and universal coordinated time. There is also mean time, apparent time, solar time, sidereal time, and probably others. We must start right off by simplifying this or get bogged down forever.

To navigate we need to know only one time, Greenwich mean time, GMT. Unfortunately, all clocks gain or lose time, so we can't have watches that always read GMT precisely. The time we actually read from our watches is called watch time. Our watches are set to some standard time, which is some whole number of hours different from GMT. Eastern standard time, for instance, is 5 hours behind GMT. If I am wearing a watch set to eastern standard time that gains 10 seconds a month, I will always know GMT, providing I remember the date I set it. If I set it on July 4, then two months later when the watch reads 13:20:45 I know that the correct eastern standard time is 13:20:25 and that GMT is 18:20:25 — I subtract 20 seconds to correct for the current watch error and add 5 hours to correct for the standard time of the watch. And please note, especially, that it does not matter at all where I happen to be when I read this watch; I will always know GMT. For telling time, it is the time zone of the watch that matters, not the time zone of the boat.

This is standard procedure in celestial navigation. The key points are to know the watch rate — how fast it gains or loses time — and to know that the "watch" is indeed a "chronometer." A chronometer is simply a watch that gains or loses time at a constant rate. It doesn't matter much what the rate is, so long as it's constant. A typical quartz watch these days has a constant rate of some 15 seconds a month, or less. You learn the rate and verify that it's constant by checking it daily for a few months using the National Bureau of Standards time signals broadcast on WWV — or similar broadcasts around the world. These broadcasts refer to GMT by its more official name of "universal coordinated time."

Another key point is this: Don't change your watch time at sea. You might be tempted to change it as you sail into new time zones, or perhaps reset it to remove the watch error once in a while, but this is dangerous procedure. It is far better to wait till you make your landfall and then reset it to the local time. The convenience at sea is not worth the risk, and you have more to remember if you keep changing it.

As for all the other types of time, we won't need to bother with them. The only other time of interest in emergency navigation is solar time, and we will come back to it when we discuss keeping track of the sun's direction throughout the day.

2.3 Finding Position versus Keeping Track of Position

In emergency navigation, we must distinguish between finding our position from an unknown spot versus keeping track of our position as we move away from a known spot. Keeping track of position using boat speed and course sailed is called dead reckoning. In emergency situations, we must rely heavily on dead reckoning, since it is not easy to find our position accurately from the sun and stars without proper instruments.

Our concern with the distinction between finding and keeping track of position rests entirely with the question of accuracy. With modern electronic aids, like Loran or SatNav, a navigator can simply read his latitude and longitude from a dial to an accuracy of a few hundred yards. But these aids are still far from commonplace on private vessels, primarily due to their cost and their ultimate vulnerability to the rigors of the sea. The more reliable and less expensive alternative for ocean navigation is traditional celestial navigation using sextant, chronometer, almanac, and sight reduction tables. With these, a small-boat navigator can find his position from an entirely unknown location to within 5 or 10 miles, or even routinely to as little as 1 or 2 miles with good procedure. Celestial accuracy can be pushed to about 0.5 miles, but this is not typical and requires special procedures and skills, especially if the boat is moving.

As soon as any one of the celestial tools (sextant, chronometer, or tables) is lost or broken, we must rely on some form of emergency navigation. And the form we choose depends on the accuracy it offers.

To illustrate this point, consider a plane crash that leaves you in a life raft somewhere in mid-ocean. You are wearing an accurate watch — meaning you can figure GMT from it to within a few seconds — but have no other navigational equipment. Using the methods of emergency navigation, you could, by doing little more than looking at the sky, discover where you are to within about 300 miles. You can obtain this level of accuracy no matter where you are, on any day of the year, using only the most elementary principles and very little special knowledge. If you have practiced these methods and have learned a few of the more specialized techniques presented here, you could improve on this accuracy significantly. Under favorable conditions, you might find your position from scratch to within about 100 miles, or maybe even 50 miles. Without a proper sextant, however, it is unlikely that you could obtain accuracy greater than 50 miles regardless of preparation or conditions. Furthermore, without accurate time you could not *find* your longitude at all, although with a watch on erroneous time, you could keep track of changes in longitude by means other than dead reckoning.

Though this by no means represents pinpoint accuracy, finding your position from scratch to within 100 miles, using only your wits, a watch, and makeshift gear, is an admirable achievement, considering the size of the earth's surface — some 200,000,000 square miles. And knowing your position to within 100 miles out of sight of land is sufficient to tell you which way to go to reach safety. This book does cover the best possible ways to find your position from scratch, but, realistically, this is not a challenge we are likely to face. Furthermore, this level of from-scratch accuracy wouldn't do you much good if you were lost in one of the Great Lakes, for example, though it could possibly be helpful in coastal waters. Approaching the coast of Central America or numerous other places around the world, one might well care to know what country lies ahead.

The more likely situation we should be prepared for is the loss of some *part* of our standard navigational equipment, such as the compass, sextant, or accurate time. We would then, presumably, be starting our emergency navigation from a known position. The point is this: You can sail a long way from a known position using emergency methods of dead reckoning before your position becomes uncertain by 100 miles.

There is still another aspect to the distinction between finding and keeping track of position. Later chapters explain several ways to keep track of *changes* in latitude and longitude by noting changes in the sun and stars. These are basically the same as the methods used to find position, but the difference is you only have to measure relative angles and know relative times in order to determine changes in position. To actually *find* latitude and longitude from scratch, you must measure exact angles and know exact times. It is much more difficult to measure exact values than it is to measure relative ones.

To show this more specifically, if the sun sets 5 minutes later today than it did yesterday, I can use this observation to figure out how much my longitude has changed. But I would need to know the exact GMT of sunset in order to say what my longitude actually is. Likewise, one way to find latitude is to measure the angular height of the *North Star* above the horizon. In higher latitudes, this is not easy to do accurately without a sextant. It is easier to determine how much this height has changed since the previous measurement — in short, to find a change in latitude. Again, it is a relative measurement versus an exact measurement. Relative measurements of the sun and stars provide information for navigation that is more accurate than trying to find actual position from the sun and stars. On a long voyage, this can be a significant improvement over pure dead reckoning.

But you can't take advantage of relative measurements if you don't know where you started from. The cardinal rule for navigational safety and emergency preparation is to know where you are at all times, to the very best of your ability. An equally important rule is to wear an accurate watch. The value of a watch emerges in nearly every aspect of emergency navigation. You can accurately sail around the world with nothing but a watch. Take it away, and you've got a lot of work to do just to go straight for a hundred miles.

3

Directions at Sea

Keeping track of directions is more challenging at sea than it is on land. Lost on land without a compass, you can use the sun or stars to find directions once, and then use these directions to note the bearing of a distant landmark. From then on, you can use the landmark to keep your bearings. At sea there are no permanent reference marks. The wind and swells serve this purpose for short periods of time, but ultimately we must orient ourselves using the changing positions of the sun and stars.

On a clear night in the Northern Hemisphere, we have the *North Star* for orientation — it's the one star that essentially doesn't move, always bearing due north. But this leaves cloudy nights, daytime, and all of the Southern Hemisphere. In short, we are not too well prepared for emergency orientation if all we know is that the *North Star* bears due north. Luckily, we need not rely on the *North Star* alone; we can find directions from many different stars, in northern or southern latitudes, and from the sun during the day.

A basic point to remember with regard to directions at sea is that finding our bearings and holding the proper heading does not guarantee that we will arrive at our desired destination. The problems are current and leeway. Current moves you off course in the direction of the current, and leeway moves you off course in the direction of the wind. In the ocean, most currents flow in the general direction of the wind, so the problems tend to add. A sailboat, for example, beating north in 15 knots of true wind from the northeast might slip to leeward some 10° depending on its draft. If the boat is making 6 knots through the water and the current flows west at just over 1 knot, the current would set the vessel downwind another 10° or so. In

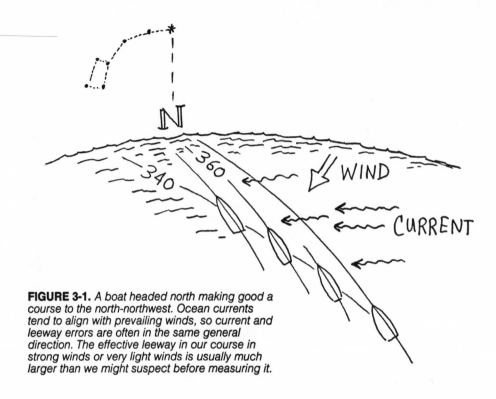

FIGURE 3-1. *A boat headed north making good a course to the north-northwest. Ocean currents tend to align with prevailing winds, so current and leeway errors are often in the same general direction. The effective leeway in our course in strong winds or very light winds is usually much larger than we might suspect before measuring it.*

these circumstances, we could sail with the *North Star* fixed on the bow, thinking we are headed due north, when in fact we were making good a course of some 20° to the west of north (see Figure 3-1).

Orientation and steering are vital parts of navigation, but a successful emergency voyage may equally well depend on your knowledge of the currents and the response of your craft to various wind and sea conditions. We will come back to these topics later, with helpful tricks for estimating the effects of current and leeway. For example, how did I know instantly, without plotting or elaborate calculations, that a current of 1 knot on the beam will set me 10° off course when I am making 6 knots?

3.1 Choosing a Route

If a long voyage must be made, there are several routes one might consider. The route between two points that is most commonly used in small-boat navigation is the rhumb-line route. This route is simply the straight line drawn between the two points as they appear on a nautical chart. All along a rhumb line, the true heading of the boat remains constant, although the magnetic heading will change if the magnetic variation does. Strictly speaking, the rhumb line is not the shortest distance between two points on the globe. The shortest distance is the great-circle route. But the difference in course distance between these two routes is insignificant except for voyages of over two thousand miles or so, and even then only when the departure point and destination are *both* at high latitudes.

In an emergency situation, it may not be possible to determine an accurate rhumb-line course. Even if it were possible, prevailing winds or currents might not permit the route. An alternative is a variation of what is called parallel, or latitude, sailing. In this case, you estimate the rhumb-line heading and then sail well to windward of your destination. Once you reach the latitude of your destination, you turn and sail at constant latitude until you get there. This is the best route for a long voyage with limited instruments, since you can find and keep track of your latitude from the stars without instruments, whereas you need an accurate watch and other information to keep track of your longitude.

This same philosophy should be applied when approaching a coastline. Do not head straight for your destination but well to windward of it (see Figure 3-2). Then

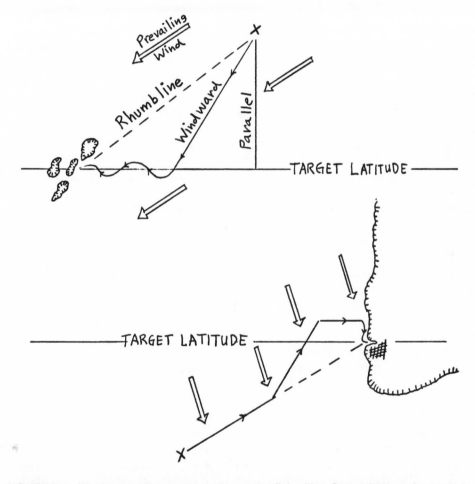

FIGURE 3-2. *Windward sailing as a variation on parallel sailing. Generally the safest route is well to windward of your destination. With practice in emergency navigation, however, one need not be so conservative as to sail a strictly "parallel" route. Prevailing currents and expected wind shifts along the route or near the shore must also be taken into account. On reaching an unidentified coast, remember that the general bearing of the coastline may help you determine where you have landed—but this can be tricky on irregular coastlines or in reduced visibility.*

when you reach the coast, you know which way to turn. If you head straight for a harbor or landmark and it's not in sight when you reach the coast, you may not know which way to turn. Under power in light winds, the choice of windward or leeward side of the destination is not so critical, so long as you are definitely to one side of it. In strong winds, however, it is better, even under power, to do your pounding to weather well offshore — if you can. In big seas you may have no safe choice but to go downwind.

3.2 Compass Checks

A large part of this book covers steering without a compass. An accident at sea, however, won't necessarily destroy your compass. The compass may suffer damage but remain apparently functional — meaning, when the boat turns, the compass turns. But is it working right? Another situation might be that your primary compass is destroyed, but you have a spare. The task then is to rig the spare and check its adjustment. A lightning strike could damage your compass at sea and wipe out all of your electronics as well. Be sure to check your compass if your boat is struck by lightning, even if it appears to be working properly.

If you suspect that your compass may be faulty for any reason, the first thing to do is check that the compass card rotates freely. This can be tested by magnetically disturbing the compass (with a magnetized screwdriver or magnet from a radio speaker) and carefully watching to see if it returns smoothly to the exact reading it had before you disturbed it. If it doesn't, or if its motion is jerky, the pivot point may be damaged or worn. In the middle of the ocean, there is not much to do about this but remember it and hope that the motion of the boat is enough to keep the card on the proper average orientation. If the pivot sticks at all, you must be especially careful when doing the deviation checks given below. Be sure the card is not stuck when you read the compass to check for error. Without a magnetized object to kick the needle around, you can try swinging the ship slowly and watching the needle for jerky motion.

Next check the lubber's line alignment. The line defined by the pivot point of the compass card and the index pin that you read your heading from is called the lubber's line. It should be parallel to the boat's centerline. A misalignment of more than a few degrees can usually be noticed by simply looking at it relative to structures on the boat. If the lubber's line is off, readjust it if possible. If this is not possible, establish a new index mark that makes the lubber's line parallel to the centerline, and read the compass card against this new index mark. Or equivalently, simply note that the compass reads too high by, say, 5° on all headings — the effect is just to offset the reading a constant amount for all headings. Normally, a careful compass check (deviation measurement) will reveal even a 1° offset in the lubber's line. But the trick method we must use at sea without special aids will not do this for us. We must do the best we can to establish this line, assume it is right, and go on.

Next we must check for deviation error, remembering that a compass with deviation error on any one heading has different errors on other headings. We obviously care most about the error in the general direction we want to go, so we check that one first, and remember to check the compass again if we change course.

The standard way to check a compass at sea is to use celestial navigation. To do it, you hold a steady compass heading, note the bearing of the sun according to the steering compass, and then do a standard sight reduction to determine the true bearing (azimuth) of the sun at that time, from that location. This true bearing is then corrected for local magnetic variation (read from a chart), and the resulting magnetic bearing is compared to the compass bearing of the sun. If they agree, the compass is right on the heading you steered as you did the comparison. If not, the difference is your compass deviation on that heading. Then repeat the process for other headings of interest. With a binnacle-mounted compass that has a shadow pin in the center, this can be done very accurately when the sun is low. Use the reciprocal of the sun's shadow to get its bearing.

This standard procedure requires correct GMT, sight reduction tables, an almanac, and a known location to begin with. If you have these aids and information, this is the obvious way to check the compass. If any one of these is missing, you can't use this procedure. Later on (Section 14.7) we cover a trick for replacing the almanac, but it's a trick that requires somewhat more than average memory work.

Without any of these aids, and without sun or stars visible, you can still check your compass out of sight of land, from an entirely unknown location. This procedure is fundamental to emergency preparation on all waters. To do the check, throw a life vest, jerry can, or some other floating object overboard and sail directly away from it, roughly opposite the direction you want to go. Note the compass heading as you sail well away from the object, keeping it dead astern. This takes some practice, but not much. Try aligning it with a boom tied to centerline or backsighting along the edge of the cabintop, a hand rail, or other structure parallel to the centerline. Two people can do this much more easily than one. Then once your "away" compass heading has been determined in this manner, turn (as sharply as possible) and sail back toward the object, and note your "toward" compass heading. If the toward heading is exactly 180° from the away heading, your compass has no deviation on either heading. You have verified that the compass works right on these two particular headings.

If the toward compass heading is not the exact reciprocal of the away heading (exactly 180° different), and you have verified this difference with several trials (turning back in alternate directions), then the compass has error on each of these headings. Figure the actual error this way: The correct magnetic course toward the object is "halfway between what you got and what you expected." For example, sailing away from an object, the compass heading is 040, and sailing back toward the object (the approximate way I want to go), the compass heading is 240. Since the reciprocal of 040 is 220, "halfway between what I got and what I expected" is halfway between 240 and 220, which is 230. So the correct magnetic course toward the object is 230. The compass reads 240 on this heading, so the compass reads 10° too high in the direction I want to go (see Figure 3-3).

With several tries, you can discover your compass error this way to within an accuracy of about 5°. Note that this procedure assumes that the leeway of the object in

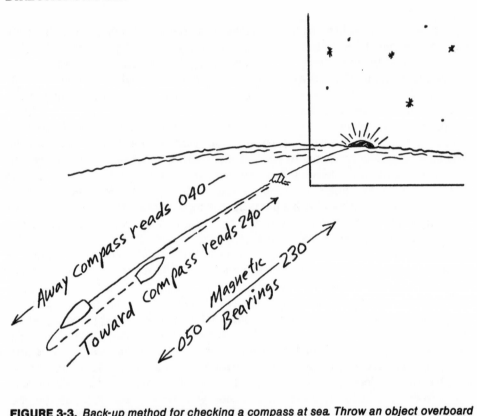

FIGURE 3-3. *Back-up method for checking a compass at sea. Throw an object overboard and sail away from your desired course, keeping the object astern. Then the correct magnetic bearing toward the object is "halfway between what you get (toward compass reading) and what you expected (reciprocal of away compass reading)." The procedure assumes that your turning radius is very small compared to the distance back to the object. This method can also prove useful on inland or coastal waters in reduced visibility. If available, it is best to use a celestial body or distant landmark for your reference point in place of a cast-off object.*

good conditions and the boat are the same. If the wind blows the boat sideways through the water more than it does the object, your conclusions about the compass will be wrong. In strong crosswinds, this method is unreliable. But in calm weather or straight into and out of the wind, it works. Currents have no effect, because they move both boat and object the same. On inland or coastal waters, you can do this much more easily using a distant landmark for the object. At sea, if the sun happens to lie near dead ahead or astern during the day, use it for the object. You can also use a star at night, but the back bearing is less accurate if the star is at all high, even with someone assisting with the steering. If you use sun or stars, though, you must do the toward and away bearings fairly rapidly since these bodies are moving across the sky. Toward and away bearings measured within some 10 minutes of each other will do the job with no problem.

The toward and away courses, as we have used them, are reciprocal magnetic headings. In using this method, we have assumed that compass deviation is equal and opposite on reciprocal *magnetic* headings. Strictly speaking, this is only an approximation to the more correct statement that deviations are equal and opposite on reciprocal *compass* headings.

To do this deviation check in the strictly proper way is a more difficult measurement. In principle, you should sail away from the object to get the away course, and then turn and sail on the reciprocal course according to the compass. Then sighting over the compass card, note the bearing to the object while holding the reciprocal course. The deviation error is then equal to one-half the angle of the object off the bow. The distinction between these two methods, however, is usually insignificant. The only time it might make a difference is when the maximum deviation on any heading is large, say, 20° or so. In this case, it would be worthwhile to try this method as a double check.

If you intend to compensate the compass by adjusting the internal magnets to remove the deviation you find, then you can stick with the first method, even if you start out with large deviations. Your first adjustment probably won't be exactly right, but it will be close enough that the resulting deviation is small. With only a small deviation left for the final adjustment, the first method is accurate enough.

An alternative compass check is to use the true direction of the sun or a star that you figure from one of the methods of Chapters 5 and 6. In this approach, you do not need to know the local magnetic variation. The most accurate of these methods uses the *North Star* at any time of night from the Northern Hemisphere, or the sun at noon from any latitude if you have a watch. Several of the other star methods are also reliably accurate to within 5° in special cases. Using any of these true directions and a makeshift "portable compass card" (described in Section 3.3), you can head the boat in the direction you want to go. Then read the compass. The difference between compass heading and true heading is the compass error, the sum of deviation on that heading and the variation at that location.

There is still another way to check the steering compass on a non-steel vessel that shouldn't be overlooked. That is simply using a hand-held bearing compass as a reference. This is standard equipment for inland and coastal navigation, so it's quite possible that one will be on board. The advantage of these compasses is that they have no internal adjustment magnets that can throw them off. Also, when you are standing up and holding one at eye level, you are usually sufficiently far from any disturbing magnetic materials so that it will read the earth's magnetic field correctly. To check the steering compass this way, read the magnetic heading of the boat from the bearing compass and compare it to the steering compass heading. Any difference you find is most likely due to an error in the steering compass.

This method — and bearing compasses in general — may not work on steel vessels because of the magnetic disturbance they cause. But on any vessel, it is best to first check the bearing compass with the *North Star* or noon sun to verify that it works as expected from your particular position on deck. Or better still, sight some celestial body (or distant landmark in coastal waters) and watch its bearing with the hand-held compass as you swing ship. If the object's bearing remains constant for all boat headings, you are assured that your hand-held compass is not being influenced by the boat. Beware of steel eyeglass frames, don't lean against iron rigging or hold a flashlight too close to the compass, and heed other standard precautions and procedures for bearing sights.

3.3 Steering without a Compass

Without a compass, we must get directions from the sun and stars. The directions we get this way are always true directions. The local magnetic variation and magnetic disturbances on the boat are completely irrelevant when we don't use a magnetic compass.

A makeshift "compass card," however, is still extremely valuable. This is simply a circle drawn on a flat surface and marked off in degrees. Draw a cross to represent the cardinal directions, then draw in the diagonals for the intercardinal points. Smaller divisions can be estimated from there. A piece of paper can be folded square and then on the diagonals, and the diagonals folded again, to set up reference angles. It will more than likely prove handy to have a compass card drawn right on the boat, in clear view of the helmsman. With this, the helmsman can orient the boat relative to the sun or a star more accurately than would be possible by just guessing the angle.

With a little practice, you should be able to divide a circle into accurate 5° intervals. There are many ways to improvise. You can always draw a circle with a shoestring and a nail. One trick is to draw a circle with a radius of 57 units. The circumference of this circle will then be 360 units, which makes each unit 1°. The units can be millimeters, tenths of an inch, or any convenient distance between two marks made on a piece of paper used as one unit. See Figure 3-4. The compass rose from any chart is a ready made compass card. It can be cut out, taped to a board, and the radials extended for better precision.

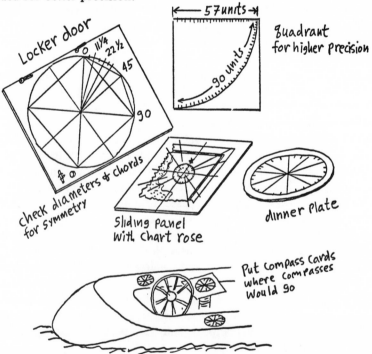

FIGURE 3-4. *Portable compass cards. There are numerous uses for these in emergency navigation. Find a direction from celestial bodies, orient the cards, and then use them as a compass (of sorts). Quadrants of compass cards (essentially a protractor) are useful for measuring relative angles in various applications.*

FIGURE 3-5. *A portable compass card in use. Here the morning wind is used as a reference to find the sunrise direction. The planet Venus is often a valuable common reference to both star directions and sunrise or sunset directions, since it can often be seen with the naked eye both at night and well into the brighter part of twilight. Also see Figure 7-6.*

There are numerous uses for a portable compass card, for which you might even use a dinner plate. Using the solar time method of Section 6.4, for example, you might find that the sun lies 30° to the east of due south, bearing 150°. You can then orient the plate with 150° pointing at the sun and read the boat's heading or bearing along the troughs of swells from the plate. Figure 3-5 shows how to measure wind direction with a portable compass card.

Another thing that helps with emergency direction finding and with many aspects of emergency navigation is the ability to estimate angles using your hands at arm's length (see Figure 3-6). Basically, this is no different from sighting over a compass card, but in some cases it can be even more accurate. Your arm's length corresponds to the compass-card radius, and the larger the reference circle, the more accurate the angular measurements can be.

In most situations, stars are the best source of direction. But with the exception of the *North Star* — the use of which we do not here consider as "steering by the stars" — star directions won't be accurate to the degree. There will, though, usually be several ways to find directions from the stars at any one time. The best approach is to use as many ways as possible and average the results. As an example, suppose you have a bright star near the horizon. One star method might tell you that this star bears 40° south of west. Another, completely independent method might imply that

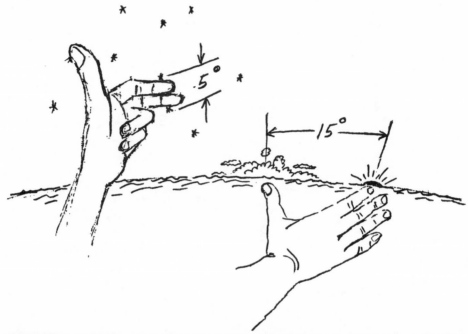

FIGURE 3-6. *Estimating angles with the hand and fingers at arm's length. The angle sizes shown are only rough averages. With a sextant available, "calibrate" your own hand, using angular distances between distant landmarks that you measured with the sextant. Skill at angle measurements with your hands is a big asset in emergency navigation. Similar calibrations can be made at sea using the distances between low stars, but check that the eye-to-hand length is the same when looking up and looking toward the horizon. If this length changes, the angle calibration changes.*

its bearing is 20° south of west. If this is all you have to go by, and you have no reason to favor one method over the other, then, at least for the time being, you must consider the bearing of the object to be 30° south of west, with an uncertainty of about plus or minus 10°.

You can steer toward a star or cloud formation on the horizon for short periods of time, but these directions soon change. Surface winds and ocean swells can often be used for reference directions over longer periods of time — especially the swells, which can in some cases persist from a well-defined direction for several days. Another possible reference in the temperate latitudes is the direction of winds aloft, which can be read from "wave patterns" in high and middle-high clouds. These jet-stream winds are much more stable than the surface winds, but it is only occasionally that we can determine their direction.

The general procedure is to steer by the surface wind and ocean swells, using the sun and stars to continuously monitor their directions. The more often you check their directions and the more varied your methods, the more accurate your course becomes.

In fact, the very motion of the sun and stars that makes direction finding difficult at any one time also tends to make the average directions you find more accurate. Generally speaking, a star method that errs in one direction when the stars are to the east of you will err in the opposite direction when they are to your west. Consider the sun as an example. From northern latitudes, the sun bears due south at noon. If my goal is to sail due south, I could simply follow the sun throughout the middle part of the day. I would err to the east all morning, but I would err to the west all afternoon by the same amount. The net effect is a fairly good course to the south, but not a very efficient one. We can do much better than this.

To get a feeling for just how well we can do, we must distinguish between our heading error at any one moment and our net error averaged over an extended run. What we want to know is how much we will be off course due to steering errors alone after traveling a certain distance. Currents and leeway also take us off course, but that's another matter.

If someone were to use all the methods of Chapters 5 and 6 to find directions, and used each method many times over a long period of time, each time comparing the result with the correct direction measured with a compass, then the *average* value of all of the errors would be about 12°, or maybe even a little more. The largest individual errors would be about 30° or so, if we exclude those methods that give only general directions, east or west, north or south.

Now if we had a way to steer a perfectly straight course and that course was 6° in error, we would go 1 mile off our intended track for each 10 miles we traveled — a "10 percent position error." This reasoning can be extended with improving accuracy up to a factor of 5 (see Figure 3-7). A constant 12° steering error causes a 20

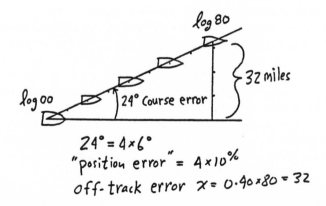

FIGURE 3-7. *Estimating distance off course from errors in course steered. This trick can also prove useful in constructing makeshift instruments for angle measurements.*

percent position error (2 x 10 percent), and a constant 18° steering error causes a 30 percent position error. With a constant 12° error in steering, we would be 200 miles off course after a 1,000-mile voyage. In other words, a *constant* error of some 12° causes a large course error after a long voyage. On closer inspection, though, the situation is not so bleak. The error is not going to be constant.

Errors in star steering come from two independent sources. First, some methods are not exact in principle, or they are accurate only under certain conditions. For example, in northern latitudes an imaginary line through *Procyon* that passes between *Castor* and *Pollux* intersects the horizon near due south, providing *Procyon* is at least halfway up the sky. When these stars are high in the sky (yet not overhead), this method is accurate. When the stars are rising, this rule errs to the east, and when they are setting, it errs to the west. The condition of "halfway up the sky" is included to restrict the size of this error in principle.

The second source of error comes from the navigator's application of the principle. In the Gemini-*Procyon* example, the navigator must somehow project the imaginary line down to the horizon. This could be done by sight or using a stick as a guide. But however we do it, we can't expect to do it accurately to the degree. The amount of error that enters at this stage depends on the individual and how much he has practiced these things. Even with practice, an error of 5° to one side or the other is hard to avoid.

For the most part, however, the errors in principle and the errors in practice are unrelated. They are just as likely to cancel each other out as they are to combine into a larger error. As mentioned before, the combined effect of these errors is about 12° on the average. To find your own average error, you can practice on land and check yourself with a compass or the orientation of streets.

Again, the quoted error of 12° is only the typical error one might expect on any single measurement. The saving feature is that the error of a second measurement, from a different set of stars, can be in the opposite direction. When you average the two, you have a roughly 50 percent chance that the average is more accurate than either one. Your chances that individual errors cancel each other out when you average them increases with the number of measurements and the number of different types of measurements.

On a clear night, many star methods are available at any one time, so an accurate average can be found on the spot. If you are restricted to one method, like the sun during the day or a few stars on a hazy night, then it is possible that your course will be off by 20° or more at any one time, but your average course throughout the day or night will be more accurate. Generally speaking, the longer you sail on a particular course, continually checking and crosschecking its direction with the stars, the more accurate the course becomes.

The steering accuracy required depends, of course, on the situation. A hundred miles off the coast of New York, you need to know only which way is west. If the nearest accessible land is an isolated island, visible only from 30 miles off, with 1,000 miles of ocean on either side, then steering is more critical. But we must still keep the importance of steering in perspective. Suppose we are 200 miles from this island and can travel at 3 knots. On a direct route, the island is about three days off. If we have a net steering error of 6°, after 200 miles we would be about 20 miles off course but still in sight of the island. However, if there were ocean currents in the area, a typical current might make the boat drift about 12 miles a day; although near a tropical island, the ocean current might easily be twice this large. If this current happened to be perpendicular to the course and we did not know about it, it would take us 36 miles or more off course in three days, enough that we might miss the island. In this example, knowing the currents would be just as important as being able to steer by the sun and stars.

An important practical point that deserves mentioning more than once is the effect of rain and low clouds on the visible range of islands. Our example island may have a theoretical visible range (see Section 13.2) of 30 miles in clear weather and calm seas, but in heavy low-cloud cover, it may be visible only from 10 miles or less. The longer we must wait for the weather to clear, the more important it is to know what the currents might be doing.

Fortunately, prevailing currents in most parts of the world follow the direction of prevailing winds. Since we are likely to be approaching a landfall downwind in an emergency situation, it is not so likely that we would be sailing directly across a current. If we aren't actually crossing a current, it won't set us off course so much if we don't know precisely how strong it is; it would just change our time of arrival. Nevertheless, we must always keep currents in mind if we have reason to believe they may be significant.

When sailing to windward, we must also remember to take into account the leeway of the boat — how much it slips to leeward on a windward course. For a typical keelboat, this will be (in practice, not theory) somewhere between 5° and 15°, depending on the boat and the wind strength — we'll come back to this point in Section 10.3. But the effect of leeway on steering differs in an important way from that of current. We can measure or make realistic estimates of our leeway and take it into account in all conditions, whereas we can only make educated guesses about the current.

4

Steering by Wind and Swells

Steering by wind and swells means holding a steady course using wind and swell directions as references. Without a compass, the actual bearing of the course we hold must be found from the sun or stars. Once on course, we look for a temporary reference mark on the horizon near dead ahead. Then holding course by it, we note the relative bearing of the wind and swells. From here on, the general procedure for steering without a compass is not much different from normal sailboat steering.

The first or most immediate goal is to keep the bow pointed toward your temporary reference mark dead ahead. At night this temporary reference is likely to be a star. During the day it can be a cloud formation on the horizon or even a slight change in the shading of the sky color.

Each time the bow swings off your mark, you bring it back. Then each time you bring the bow back (or every other time or so), check that the wind direction is right when the bow is on the mark. Eventually, the wind angle won't be right when the bow is aligned. If the wind is off, check the waves and swells. If they still agree with the wind, it's time to adjust your heading and find a new temporary mark. Very generally, it's the wind you might check first when sailing to windward and the seas you check first when sailing downwind. In normal sailing, it might only be at this point that you first look at the compass.

In adjusting your heading relative to the temporary mark, you might go, for example, from keeping it right on the bow to keeping it halfway back the bow pulpit, and so on. Or maybe pick a new mark altogether. Do whatever it takes to get the wind angle right again, and then pick the new mark. In this adjustment, we are assuming that it was the temporary mark that moved, not the wind and swells. But since we won't have a compass to answer this question, we won't be able to make many adjustments like this one before we must go back to the sun or stars to see if the wind or swells have changed.

You can also steer without a temporary mark, using only the wind or swell directions themselves, but in practice it is easier to use a mark when available. Except for the darkest cloudy night, there is usually something ahead that you can point to. It is a rare day that does not have a low rim of clouds on the horizon.

A temporary mark, such as a distant cloud formation, could remain at constant bearing for an hour or more. Sometimes it might change forms but remain at the same bearing. On the other hand, clouds in front of you could move across the horizon very rapidly and not be of much use at all. It all depends on how far away they are and how they are moving. The motion of stars or the sun, on the other hand, is much easier to predict (we cover this in detail later on). The fastest any of these can move across the horizon when low in the sky is some 15° per hour. In short, any chance reference mark near dead ahead is not going to remain fixed in direction for much more than an hour, at best. There are exceptions, of course, which we cover in Chapter 5 on steering by the stars. But these are not just chance stars that happen to be in front of us. The exception would be when, by happy chance, we were headed toward a star whose bearing changed very little for long periods of time.

Away from moving weather systems, the wind direction is generally stable over much longer periods of time. It could remain constant all day if we were lucky, or even longer. It depends on where we are and when. Regardless of where we are, though, we can never count on the wind and swells alone for directions. Steering by wind and swells is merely the procedure to use between the times we check the directions of sun or stars. With no sun or stars to go by for long periods of time, we may simply have to stop and wait for them.

Just how long we might steer by wind and swells alone depends on the area we are in and our knowledge of its weather and oceanography. It is not within the scope of this book to cover these topics in detail — they are more appropriate to the subject of routine preparation than to emergency preparation — but we will mention a few of the important points as we come to them.

4.1 Reading the Wind

Steering by the wind is quite a natural thing in a sailboat. Some sailboats on some points of sail will even do it themselves. Windvanes and other rigging can also be set to help with this. But a boat sailing strictly by the wind on a featureless ocean could sail in circles if the wind clocked around. And even the steadiest winds shift. Even the famous tradewinds can shift by 90° without upsetting the weatherman. We simply cannot sail long distances by wind alone. We must check its direction as often as possible, using sun and stars.

To watch the wind direction, it is extremely helpful to rig a telltale, a piece of

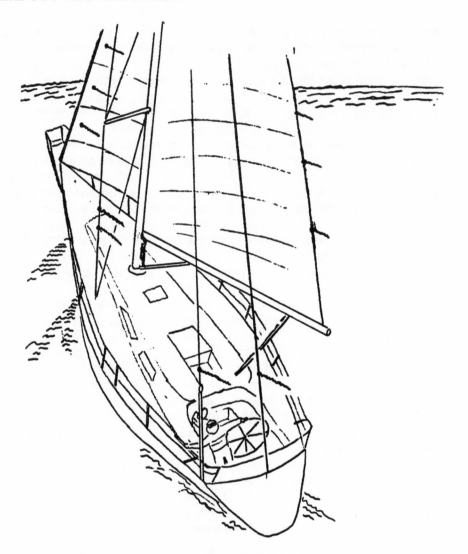

FIGURE 4-1. *Use of telltales to read apparent wind direction. Here they are shown flying from the luff of the headsail, leech of the main, windward shrouds, backstays, and running backstay. Long telltales streaming overhead from the backstays are often useful when sailing downwind.*

string or strip of light cloth tied high in the rigging, out of the way of other structures on the boat (see Figure 4-1). Strips of plastic bag or cassette tape also make good telltales. Telltales show the wind direction instantaneously. It is always better to use them than to guess the wind direction from the feel of it. Telltales are commonplace on sailboats, less so on powerboats. But on any boat, if you get stuck without a compass and must watch the wind direction carefully, the first thing to do is rig a telltale. It's an instrument you can rely on.

In reading a telltale, we need to keep in mind that it shows the direction of the

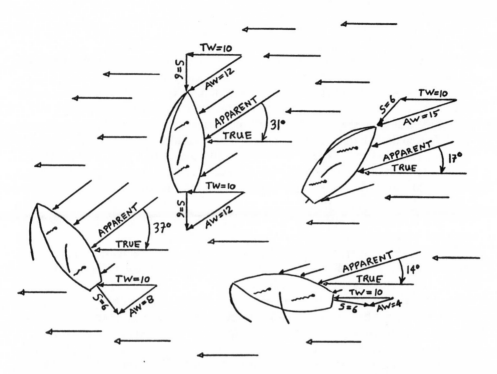

FIGURE 4-2. *True wind direction versus apparent wind direction. The true wind is always aft of the apparent wind. The difference between wind directions is largest when the wind is on the beam.*

"apparent wind" as distinguished from the "true wind." The apparent wind is the combination of the true wind over the water and the effective wind generated by the motion of the boat. The difference between the directions of the true wind and the apparent wind depends on how fast you are moving relative to the true wind speed. For boat speeds less than 10 or 20 percent of the true wind speed, the difference is negligible, and you can read the true wind direction directly from the telltale.

When you are moving, the direction of the true wind is always aft of the apparent wind. If the apparent wind is on the beam, you must face this apparent wind and turn aft to be looking in the direction the true wind comes from. This is true regardless of your point of sail. If the apparent wind is 45° on the bow, the true wind is closer to the beam. If the apparent wind is on the quarter, the true wind is closer to the stern as illustrated in Figure 4-2.

The exact number of degrees the true wind is aft of the apparent wind depends on your speed relative to the wind and on your point of sail. At any relative speed, the difference between the two is largest when you are sailing with the apparent wind on the beam. The difference is typically somewhere between 10° and 40°, where, generally speaking, the higher the performance of the sailboat, the bigger the shift can be.

When relying on the wind for directions, it is ultimately the true wind direction you care about. Apparent and true wind directions won't always be different enough to matter, but in order to steer by the direction of the wind, we should keep their potential differences in mind. The cases to remember are these:

(1) On a beam reach, the true wind can be well aft of the apparent wind. For example, in 5 to 10 knots of true wind, a typical sailboat travels at some 0.6 to 0.7 times the true wind speed. At speeds of 0.65 times the true wind, when the apparent wind is on the beam, the true wind is 41° aft of the apparent wind.

(2) If the true wind speed changes and your boat speed doesn't, the apparent wind will shift even though the true wind has not. For example, with the apparent wind on the beam, traveling at hull speed of 7 knots in 10 knots of true wind, if the true wind increases to 15 knots but the boat speed stays at 7 knots, the apparent wind will shift aft some 20°, even though the true wind did not shift at all.

(3) Sailing downwind with the true wind well aft, a small change in true wind can result in a large shift in apparent wind direction. For example, at a boat speed of 6 knots in 12 knots of true wind at 170°, if the true wind shifts forward 20° and drops to 10 knots, the boat speed would likely remain about the same, but the apparent wind would shift forward some 40°. With only the apparent wind shift to go by, we could easily misinterpret this wind shift.

An obvious way to read the true wind direction is to stop the boat. Typically, though, you don't have to go to this extreme; you can usually read the true wind direction from the wave direction or from ripples on the water. These cat's paws, as they are sometimes called, are the scalloped ripples that look like fish scales on the surface of the waves. The bigger waves do move in the direction of the wind if it is stable, but when the wind shifts, the wave direction does not follow immediately. Surface ripples, on the other hand, respond instantaneously to the wind, as if the wind were stroking the surface with a paint brush. Sometimes you have to stare at the water for a while to see them, but in any wind over a few knots they are there, and you can spot the wind direction from them.

To steer by the telltales, you keep the boat headed in such a way that the telltale flies in the same direction relative to some reference point on the boat. The trick is to rig the telltale in a convenient place, usually on the windward side of the boat, well off the deck. Sailing downwind on some boats, you might find that a long telltale on the backstay can be seen overhead, looking up from the helm. When this works, it works nicely. If you happen to be beating or on a close reach, you can steer by telltales in the "usual" way by sticking them on or through the luff of the headsail, one in the center of each panel (away from seams and hanks), about 18 inches back from the luff. Then with the sails trimmed properly, you steer the course that keeps them streaming back along the sail.

Steering without a compass during the daytime requires more concentration than it does on a clear, starry night. To keep an accurate orientation during the day, you must watch not only the telltales and distant clouds but also waves and swells, shadows on the boat, even moving clouds around the sky. In one sense, the main job of steering during the day is to hold as steady a course as possible till nighttime. This is especially true if the sun is obscured during the day, or if the sun is out but you don't have a watch. At night you can get accurate bearings from the stars almost continuously.

To make full use of the winds in your navigation, it pays to study the prevailing

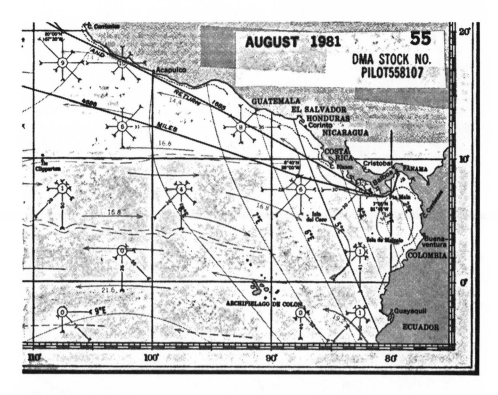

FIGURE 4-3. *Section of a U.S. Pilot Chart. August winds west of Guayaquil have a 50 percent probability of being from the south at Force 3 (on the Beaufort Scale, meaning winds of 7 to 10 knots) and a 36 percent probability of being from the southwest at Force 3. Where numerical probabilities are not given, values must be determined from the length of the arrows, using a scale provided elsewhere on the chart. Circled numbers in the centers of the wind roses are percent calms. The Beaufort Scale of wind and sea state is explained in* Bowditch, vol. 1. *Curved arrows represent prevailing current directions, labeled with their average drifts in nautical miles per day.*

winds of your route before you depart. This is standard procedure for a sailing cruise but probably less so on a vessel that does not depend on the wind for power. Pilot charts are the most convenient reference source for climatic ocean winds. They give directions and strengths of winds throughout the oceans for each month. The information is presented as wind roses that show the probabilities of various winds at each location (see Figure 4-3). A prevailing wind is simply one that shows a high probability. Similar wind predictions for coastal waters are in the weather appendices to the *U.S. Coast Pilots,* published by NOAA. Local winds are also discussed in the regional weather sections of the *Coast Pilot* text.

The extent to which a given wind prevails determines how much you can rely on the wind direction itself for an approximate true bearing. The tradewinds of the tropics are the most notable in this regard. They have a high probability (80 percent or so) of blowing from the northeast or east in the northern tropics and from the southeast or east in the southern tropics (strengths are 10 to 15 knots, but winds of 5 or 20 knots are not uncommon). Tradewind directions can remain stable for several days or longer.

Another example of prevailing winds on a global scale is the clockwise circulation around the Atlantic and Pacific highs and their counterparts in southern oceans with counterclockwise winds. The centers of these vast high-pressure areas, on the other hand, have little or no wind at all for many days. For the sake of emergency preparation, it helps to know what winds you might expect in order to plan your best course of action. Know that the doldrums separate the trades, and so on.

With experience, and in special circumstances, you might guess the wind direction from the weather in general. In several areas of the high temperate latitudes during summer, for example, you might well guess that moderate, steady winds with fair skies must be from somewhere in the northwest quadrant, and strong winds with foul weather must be from somewhere to the south. But this is nothing more than prudent familiarity with prevailing winds and weather patterns. It can't be accurate enough to help much with orientation over a long distance.

To steer by the wind, you don't always have to rely on surface winds alone. Sometimes you can read the direction of winds high in the atmosphere from the movement, shapes, and patterns of high clouds. The wind direction aloft is not the same as on the surface, but it usually remains constant for longer periods of time. Since this reference direction can be determined only from clouds, we postpone the topic till Section 7.3 on clouds.

4.2 Swells, Waves, and Ripples

It is usually possible to distinguish three types of wave motion on the surface of the sea: ripples, waves, and swells (see Figure 4-4). We discussed ripples in the previous section. They are the cat's paws, or wavelets, on the surface of waves that show us the instantaneous wind direction. Ripples are just tiny waves with very little inertia. Without inertia to keep them going, they disappear the instant the wind stops, or they change direction the instant the wind changes direction. The direction of ripples can change by the second in response to gusts or small wisps of wind. Ripples are usually riding on waves, and the waves are often riding on a gentle, rolling motion of the sea called swells.

The distinction between swells and waves is sometimes difficult to make, especially when the waves are bigger than the swells. But when the swells are at least as big as the waves, they are quite prominent. There can also be swells without waves. It is not uncommon to see a calm, waveless sea rolling like a giant corrugated-tin roof or washboard. In the more general case, though, the seas are a confused combination of waves and swells. For orientation from the seas, we must distinguish swells from waves because prominent swells can provide persistent reference directions despite changes in the wind and waves.

Waves are caused by local winds. They grow or subside with the wind, and they advance in the direction of the existing wind. The direction and size of swells, on the other hand, are not related to local winds. Swells may move with or against the local wind or at any angle relative to it. The origin of swells is usually a long distance from the local conditions.

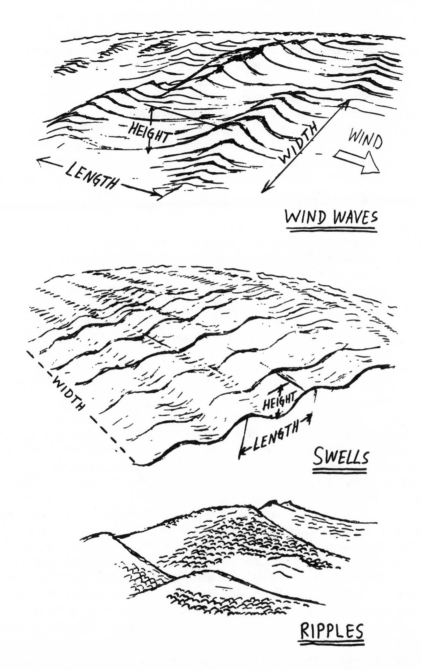

HEIGHT

WIDTH

WIND

LENGTH

WIND WAVES

WIDTH

HEIGHT

LENGTH

SWELLS

RIPPLES

FIGURE 4-4. *Swells, waves, and ripples. Swells may provide reference directions for many hours or even days. Though only one is shown here, there can be several swells running in different directions at the same time. The directions of swell propagation are unrelated to the local wind. Wind waves, on the other hand, flow in the direction of the existing (steady) wind. If the wind shifts permanently, the wind waves will develop in the new direction soon after. Ripples on the surfaces of waves and swells respond to the instantaneous wind. Persistent ripples across the waves may be the first sign of a wind shift.*

Swells are the remnants of waves that are no longer driven by the wind that created them. Either they outran a storm, or the winds died or changed direction. Swells persist purely from their own inertia, which is immense. When unopposed by counteracting winds, swells may run for a thousand miles or more and persist for several days or longer. In some areas and seasons, there are prevailing swells that reflect the prevailing storm patterns of some distant region.

To distinguish swells from waves, recall how waves are defined. Wave height is the vertical distance from trough to crest. Wave length is the horizontal distance between successive crests, measured in the direction of the wave's motion. And finally, wave width is the transverse extent of the wave in the direction perpendicular to the wave's motion.

The height of waves depends on the strength of the wind, the size of the wind pattern (fetch), and the duration of the wind. Wave-height tables in oceanography books show how wave height is determined by wind strength, fetch, and duration. A 20-knot wind might make waves of some 6 to 8 feet ("significant wave height," meaning the average height of the highest one-third of all the waves), if the wind blows for a day or so, over a distance of about 100 miles.

The height of swells we meet depends on the height of the waves they evolved from and on the distance they traveled from their source. As swells move away from their wind source, their height slowly decreases and their length increases. They become less steep. In general, the biggest swells are not as steep as even the smallest waves.

Though swells are not as steep as waves, their primary distinction is their shape. Swells have smooth, rounded crests, whereas wave crests are sharp and cusplike. Waves can break, swells do not. And swells are very much wider than waves. The width of swells can appear to be unlimited. The troughs of well-developed swells on calm water can look like highways extending out to the horizon — and they can be just as good a reference direction. The widths of waves, on the other hand, are typically only a few times their length, and they appear even narrower because their height is peaked near the center of the wave. Also, successive swells are remarkably uniform in height, like the ridges of a washboard, whereas wind-driven wave patterns are very irregular. If we have waves at all, we have waves of many heights.

Wave directions can sometimes be valuable for spotting the wind direction or occasionally even shifts in wind directions, but for a primary reference direction, it is the swells we care about, not the waves. Swell direction can persist for many hours, even days in some cases, regardless of wind and wave changes. On a starless night or during the day, prominent swells provide the best reference direction for steering.

The first task is to identify the swells. Sometimes this is very easy, at other times it takes concentration. There can be two or three swells running in different directions at the same time. When this happens, we must choose the most prominent one to use. Usually, the bigger the swell, the better it is, primarily because bigger swells are easier to see and last longer. But sometimes a weaker swell that approaches from ahead or astern, or directly on the beam, is easier to steer by than a stronger swell on a diagonal approach.

One trick that often helps to identify the swells is to close your eyes and feel the cadence of the seas. This is best done lying down in the cockpit or below decks, where you can relax without distraction. Once you have identified the rhythm of the seas (such as "LITTLE ONE, one two, LITTLE ONE, one, two, three, BIG ONE, one, two . . ."), you can then study the water as you keep track of the cadence to identify the swells that cause what you feel. It also helps to concentrate on the relative amounts of pitch and roll associated with the pattern. The swell pattern on the water can best be seen from a high vantage point (standing on the boom provides such a perspective).

To detect changes and repeated patterns in the swells, record the swell directions, their approximate heights, and the period of time between successive crests — usually somewhere between a few seconds on up to 15 seconds or so. Remember, the period you detect can depend on your speed and course heading relative to the swell direction. If you change course, you may have to take this into account to identify the pattern. You may find that the swells come from predominantly one direction. If so, and you get stuck without swells, sun, or stars, you will have some guideline for guessing the swell direction when they reappear.

When you do reach land, you may have to enter a harbor through a channel or over a river bar, or you may approach a beach in a life raft or dinghy. Remember that even a violent surf can appear meek and smooth when viewed from seaward. Be especially careful at the end of your voyage. Bar crossings are notoriously hazardous when an onshore swell meets an ebbing flow from the river entrance.

4.3 Wind Shifts

The biggest problem in steering without a compass is foul weather — no sun or stars, rapidly changing cloud patterns near the horizon, and many wind shifts. One option is to stop and wait it out, and you may have to do just that in some circumstances. But stopping, however much one might want to do it (by heaving to, lying a-hull, or whatever), is not always the safest thing to do. In big seas it may be dangerous. If you must run with a storm and still try to keep track of your position when your only reference is the wind and waves, it pays to have some experience in judging wind shifts. You can then make educated guesses about what is taking place and later put the pieces you remember back together to figure out how far off course you might be.

In light air and fair weather, sudden wind shifts are easy to spot relative to temporary reference marks on the horizon, especially if a prominent swell is present to verify it. In stronger winds, the waves might obscure the swell and make this observation more difficult. But with stronger winds, you have bigger waves, and you can usually tell if you've had a significant wind shift from the change in the ride. Though wind waves do move in the direction of the existing wind, it takes some time for them to respond to a shift in wind direction. During the transition, wind and waves are going in slightly different directions. If you follow the shifted wind around, you meet the waves (or they meet you) at a different angle than you were used to. And this is often quite easy to notice.

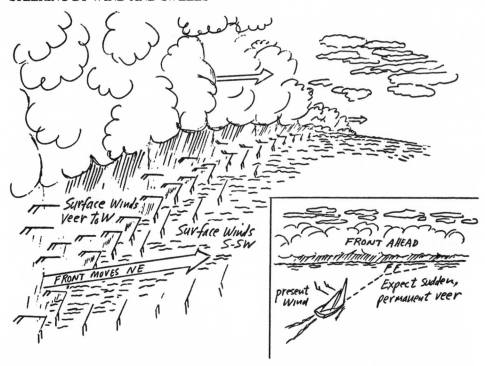

FIGURE 4-5. *Wind shift at a (cold) front. In the Northern Hemisphere, surface winds nearly always veer at any kind of front. Face the wind you have, and the new wind at the front will be from the right. Warm fronts are typically preceded by lowering clouds, long, steady rain, with the wind gradually backing around to the south. Cold fronts often follow close behind warm fronts, in a warm sector of fairly steady winds and broken cloud cover. They often appear as a notable line of tall cumulus clouds, with heavy rain at the front. Occluded fronts are not as easily characterized from their appearance, since they are a combination of warm and cold fronts, though they should also bring a veer to the surface wind.*

But one must be careful about calling such an observation a wind shift. Occasionally, you will get almost the same effect when a new swell pattern first meets your boat. A new diagonal swell can pass under big waves and change their apparent direction without the swell itself becoming prominent for some time. When this happens, one thing to check is the wind on the waves themselves. Check the cat's paws for wind direction relative to wave direction. Also when the wind does change, you can often see the spray blowing off the tops of the waves at an angle. Or there might be a noticeable bias to the curl of the breakers, which may signal a wind shift.

We have stressed the value of prominent swells for long-term reference directions, but this is not always the case. You can have prominent swell patterns pass you in a short time, almost as if someone had dropped a giant stone in the water somewhere. Generally, these more temporary swells tend to be steeper, implying a more local source — the more persistent swells tend to be long and low, from far away. It is these steeper, temporary swells that often appear as wind shifts on the waves. These are easily seen in routine sailing. You are holding a steady point of sail, and suddenly the waves are coming from a different direction, but your compass course hasn't changed. Then, after 20 minutes or so, you are back to normal.

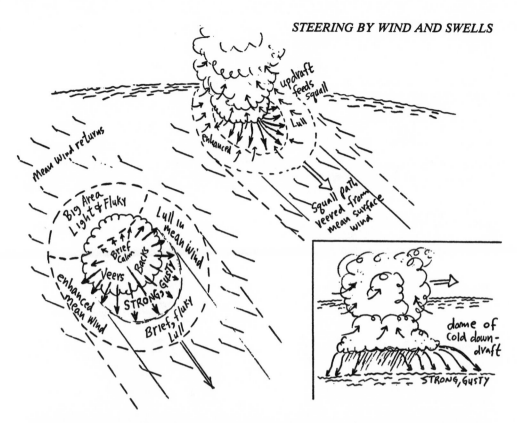

FIGURE 4-6. *Wind patterns around squalls. Just outside of the squall's strong wind regions, the updraft tends to enhance surface winds toward the squall and diminish surface winds away from the squall. The strong, gusty downburst of cold air comes with the heavy rains. If the squall has a dark ceiling and it is not yet raining, the worst is yet to come. If the squall approaches with light rain, the worst is past. Generally, there is a long period of light and fluky winds behind the squall.*

To anticipate wind shifts, you must be familiar with the weather patterns of the region. In the temperate latitudes of the Northern Hemisphere, for example, if you have spotted a frontal system approaching from the clouds, you can count on the wind veering when it crosses, regardless of what kind of front it is (see Figure 4-5). In other words, if you face the wind you've got now, the new wind will shift to the right. If you can tell from the clouds what type of front is approaching, you might be more ambitious with your predictions. Cold fronts bring stronger winds that typically veer more than those from warm fronts. Each frontal type has distinctive cloud formations and weather. (A wind shift to the left is called a backing shift).

Local thunderstorms or squalls have a different wind-shift behavior. Squalls are common in all waters, but they are easier to distinguish in warmer waters, where they often form during the evening and can be spotted as localized areas of tall cumulus clouds with low ceilings over heavy rains. Squalls are complex convective cells with complex wind shifts (see Figure 4-6). They pull warm, moist air up into them — which gradually alters the surface winds as they approach — and then blasts it suddenly back down in a strong cold dome of gusty winds at their leading edge. For emergency steering it is best to avoid them if possible but, since we often can't, it

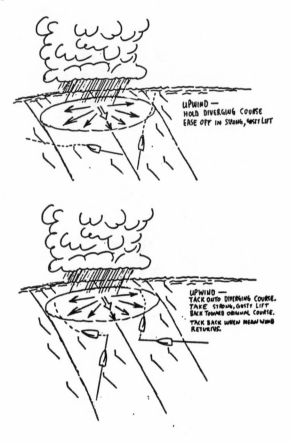

FIGURE 4-7. *Guidelines for minimum course loss in a squall. Expect a brief lull in the mean surface winds shown at the pictured boats, and then a sudden onset of the strong, steadily shifting winds that are shown under the approaching squalls. Note that it is essential to determine the path of the squall (and where you are relative to it) as carefully as possible. A first guess is that it comes from the right of the surface wind, but severe squalls are tall clouds, reaching up into, and being carried along with, the winds*

pays to have some guess at what is going to happen. Otherwise it is easy to lose orientation in a series of these things on an overcast night.

Guidelines for minimum course loss in a squall

Sailing upwind — tack away from the squall's path
Sailing downwind — jibe toward the squall's path

These rules are illustrated in Figure 4-7. They are, of course, based on an idealized wind pattern around a squall that won't always be the case. Nor can we always judge the squall's course properly, which can be critical to the choice (watch the *center* of the cloud or rain pattern as you would a ship, to judge your relative courses). Nevertheless, it helps to have some guidelines to negotiate these things.

The way to test the rules in routine sailing is to hold, tack, or jibe onto the recommended course as soon as it is apparent that the leading edge of the squall can't be

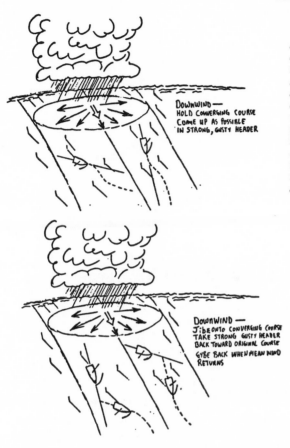

DOWNWIND —
HOLD CONVERGING COURSE
COME UP AS POSSIBLE
IN STRONG, GUSTY HEADER

DOWNWIND —
JIBE ONTO CONVERGING COURSE
TAKE STRONG GUSTY HEADER
BACK TOWARD ORIGINAL COURSE
GYBE BACK WHEN MEAN WIND
RETURNS

aloft. *These winds can come from a completely different direction than the surface winds. Watch the squall's motion (if you can see it) as carefully as you would a ship on a potential collision course. On a dark night, you won't see them coming, but these pictures might help you plan the rest of the night once one goes by. Though usually isolated individually, the existence of one usually means conditions are right for many, and they will all be moving in the same direction.*

avoided — but don't wait too long; the leading cold dome of bad news extends out several miles ahead of the clouds and rain. Later, try to remember what happened and make notes. If the rules work, you should not have to jibe, tack, or head off to China when the squall hits. In contrast, if we fail to do this, the squall might tack or jibe the boat for us; and without a compass in poor visibility we could flop around for some time in the trailing lull wondering which way to go.

Squalls typically come and go in twenty minutes to an hour, but occasionally if you're sailing fast downwind you might get in phase with the squall's motion and ride the leading edge of one for several hours. Generally though wind shifts from squalls are temporary, and eventually the mean wind you had prior to the squall fills back in. The veering wind shift at a frontal passage, on the other hand, is more permanent since the weather pattern is much larger.

To practice reading the wind, think of these rules on wind shifts for fronts and squalls during your routine sailing. If you prove to yourself that they work more often than they fail, you will be that much more prepared for them, and for steering by the wind without a compass.

5

Steering by the Stars

Stars are a part of our environment we can rely on, no matter where we are. In the Arctic or the desert or at sea a thousand miles from land, when you spot familiar stars it's like meeting dependable friends. It's comforting in any circumstance to recognize part of our environment, to at least have our bearings. With this attitude in mind, it helps to get to know our friends' names and occasionally look for them, even when we don't need them.

The methods of star navigation presented here work in all parts of the world since they make use of stars in all parts of the sky. The key to dependable star steering is knowing as much of the whole sky as possible. This is true for two reasons. First, not all methods of star steering have the same accuracy. Some, like the *North Star* methods, are always accurate to within 1°, while others may work well only when a particular constellation is high in the sky or low near the horizon — and this depends on the time of night and season of the year. Even if a method works well in principle, errors in judgment and measurement can't be avoided. But when you combine several independent ways to find directions, the errors in individual methods tend to cancel each other out and you end up with an accurate orientation.

On a clear night, you end up steering by the "shape" of the whole sky, rather than by any one rule. It is a lot like looking at a map in the sky. Most people can glance at a map of North America — in any orientation, even spinning — and tell which way is north. We do this by learning the shape and orientation of the continent. The same thing applies to star steering.

The second, perhaps more important, reason for knowing the whole sky is you may have only a limited part of the sky to go by in cloudy weather. The goal to strive for is the ability to find directions from an isolated patch of stars, anywhere in the sky — in the extreme case, from a single, unidentified star. This goal accounts for the many different ways we give to find the *North Star*. With clear skies, you need only one way to find the *North Star,* but when it's not clear, any one of six widely spaced constellations is almost as good as the *North Star* for finding true north.

Steering by the stars for short periods of time is common in routine navigation. Every sailor knows it's easier to steer toward a star than to follow a compass course. But you can't follow any one star indefinitely. Star directions change as the stars move across the sky. To steer by the stars over longer periods of time, it is important to know how stars move.

All stars rise to the east and set to the west. Halfway between rising and setting, a star reaches its peak height in the sky. At its peak height, a star always bears either due north or due south. Unfortunately, we can't often use this fact to find due north or south, since it is difficult at night without a horizon to tell when a star has reached its peak height.

A more useful direction is the bearing of a bright star when rising or setting. For any specific latitude, the place on the horizon where each star rises remains the same for that star throughout the year, and from year to year. In most parts of the world, if you change latitudes, the bearing to a rising star will change with your latitude. There are exceptions, though, and we shall take advantage of these for steering.

As the earth orbits the sun each year, the seasons progress and new stars become visible. The time of sunset changes with the seasons, but regardless of the time of sunset, all stars rise 4 minutes earlier each night because of the earth's orbit. This means that if you look at the eastern sky *at the same time* each night, you will find the stars slightly higher each successive night. Likewise, stars in the western sky are slightly lower each successive night at the same time. Stars near the western horizon at evening twilight will soon be gone for the season (see Figure 5-1).

The season of a star depends on where we are and where the star is. We see some stars all night long, every night of the year; others may be visible for only a few hours a night, a few months of the year. But whatever the season of a particular star, that season remains the same for that star from year to year. Each star in the sky — whether we can see it or not from our latitude — crosses our meridian at midnight local time on a specific day of the year, and that day does not depend on where we are. In this sense, each star in the sky has a "birthday," its own unique day when it will be at its peak height in the sky at midnight (here midnight means literally the middle of the night; not 2400, but halfway between sunset and sunrise).

In this sense, the stars make an excellent calendar, if only midnight were not such an inconvenient time to read a calendar (early evening would be better). Unfortunately, the time of "early evening" depends on the time of sunset, and the time of sunset depends on latitude, which in turn throws off the evening schedule of the stars as we sail north or south. From any latitude, though, we can always rely on the seasons of the stars determined by the midnight calendar. Orion, for example, will be on our meridian during the middle of the night in mid-December. Scorpio will be there in early June, regardless of whether we are in Australia or Canada, New York or Hong Kong.

As mentioned earlier, learning the stars is much like learning geography. To see

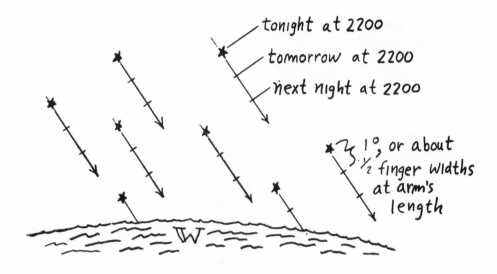

FIGURE 5-1. *Nightly progression of the stars. Because of the earth's annual motion around the sun, all stars appear 1° farther along their paths on each successive night, when viewed at the same time. Stars to the east are higher; stars to the west are lower.*

this, it might help to imagine the stars as painted dots on a glass globe that encloses the earth. Stars are grouped into constellations whose positions on the star globe are permanent, just as cities are grouped within countries whose positions are permanent on earth. In this model of the stars, the earth remains stationary, and the star globe rotates once a day about the earth's axis. This model shows how each star circles the earth directly above a specific latitude and that latitude remains constant for that star, essentially forever. The unique latitude of each star is called the star's "declination."

The bright star *Arcturus,* for example, has a declination of N 19° 17'. It circles the earth over latitude 19° 17' N, the latitude of Wake Island in the western Pacific, Hawaii in mid-Pacific, or Grand Cayman in the Caribbean. On Wake Island, Hawaii, Grand Cayman, or any other point on earth at this latitude, *Arcturus* passes directly overhead once a day, every day of the year. During late winter and spring, this happens at night, when we can see the star. But it's there once a day, even in other seasons when we can't see it because the sun is up (see Figure 5-2).

The prominent constellation Orion straddles the equator with his upper body over northern latitudes and his lower body over southern latitudes. The westernmost star of his belt has a declination very near 0°, which puts it right over the equator. Observers in northern latitudes watch Orion arc across their southern sky from left to right. At the same time, observers in southern latitudes watch Orion to the north, moving right to left. In each case the stars are moving east to west. Only at the equator, the "latitude of Orion's belt," will observers see Orion rise due east, pass overhead, and set due west.

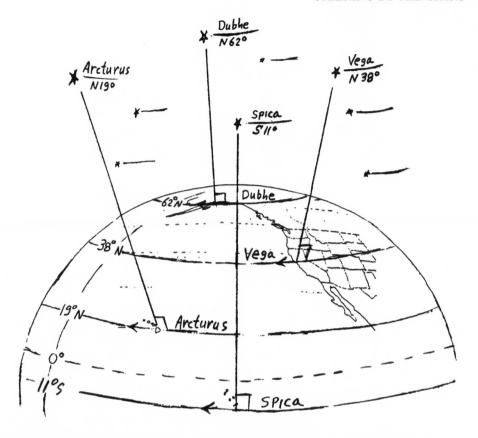

FIGURE 5-2. *"Pillars of light." Each star circles the earth daily over a specific latitude equal to the star's declination. Here we show* Dubhe *passing over Anchorage,* Vega *passing over San Francisco,* Arcturus *passing over Hawaii, and* Spica *passing over the Marquesas. The figure is especially schematic, since the fixed celestial longitudes of these stars would not place them over these locations at the same time.*

As we sail toward the equator from the north or south, we can watch Orion climb higher in the sky each night as we approach the equator. When we finally reach the equator, Orion's belt will pass overhead. Looking ahead to Chapter 11 on latitude, we can always tell what our latitude is from the stars that pass overhead. Our latitude must be the same as the declination of the stars overhead.

Stars with southern declinations, circling the earth over southern latitudes, are called "southern stars"; stars with northern declinations are called "northern stars." Now an important point that we shall come back to time and again: Southern stars always rise south of due east and set south of due west, and northern stars always rise north of due east and set north of due west. See Figure 5-3. This is true regardless of where you are on earth while watching the stars.

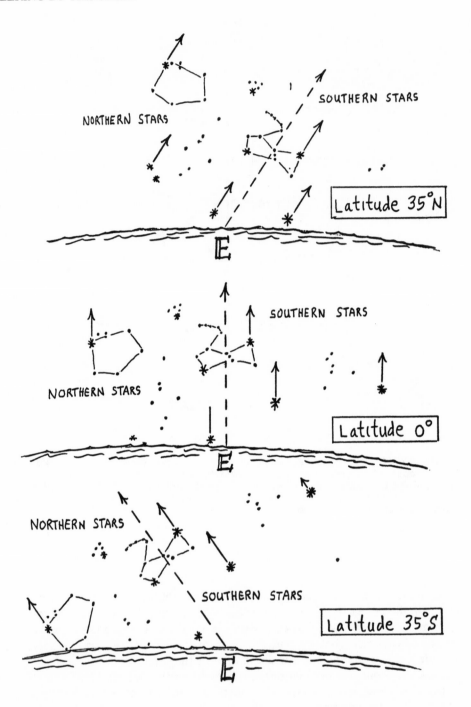

FIGURE 5-3. *Motion of eastern stars at various latitudes. Note how southern stars rise to the south, and northern stars to the north, of due east, regardless of the latitude you observe them from.*

5.1 The *North Star*

The northernmost star is the *North Star, Polaris. Polaris* is located above the North Pole, which coincides with the earth's axis. This puts *Polaris* at the hub of the sky. All stars rotate counterclockwise around *Polaris*.

To be strictly precise, however, we should point out that *Polaris* is not exactly at the pole, only very close to it. To be precisely over the North Pole, the declination of *Polaris* would have to be N 90° exactly, but its declination is only N 89° 12', which is 48' off the pole. Consequently, *Polaris* also circles the pole as all other stars do, but its circle (of radius 48') is so small that the star appears to remain stationary. In special cases, we can find our latitude from the height of *Polaris,* and when we do this, we will take this slight motion of *Polaris* into account, but for emergency steering it is of no significance.

Polaris always bears due north. With *Polaris* dead ahead, you are sailing due north. Sail any direction you choose by holding *Polaris* at a fixed point on the bow, beam, or stern. To sail west, hold *Polaris* on the starboard beam. When *Polaris* is visible, it will likely be your primary reference, but *Polaris* is visible only in the Northern Hemisphere. The star lies due north at a height above the horizon equal to your latitude. In high northern latitudes, *Polaris* is high in the sky. As you sail south, *Polaris* descends as your latitude decreases. Northern Oregon on the Pacific coast and central Maine on the Atlantic are at latitude 45° N, where *Polaris* is found about halfway up the sky. In the northern tropics, *Polaris* is low in the sky, and as you cross the equator, *Polaris* drops below the horizon. However, because of low clouds and haze on the horizon, in practice *Polaris* is rarely visible in latitudes much below about 5° N.

Steering by *Polaris* with the aid of a portable compass card is nearly as easy as steering with a compass. Finding *Polaris* among the other stars is fundamental to emergency navigation. *Polaris* is not a bright star. It's about as bright as the stars of the Big Dipper.

5.2 *North Star* from the Big Dipper

The two stars (*Dubhe* and *Merak*) on the cup end of the Big Dipper point to *Polaris*. These two stars are called the Pointers. The distance to *Polaris* is five times the distance between the pointing stars. If the distance from *Merak* (inside the cup) to *Dubhe* (on the tip of the cup) is 2 finger widths with your arm outstretched, then the distance from *Dubhe* to *Polaris* is about 10 finger widths, measured along the line extending from *Merak* through *Dubhe* (see Figure 5-4).

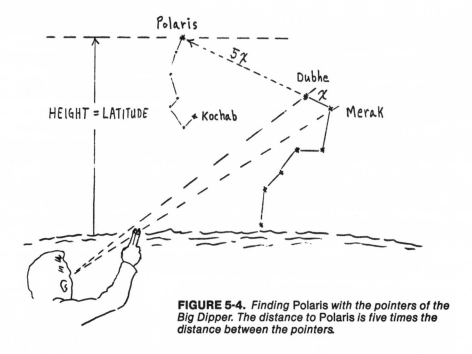

FIGURE 5-4. *Finding* Polaris *with the pointers of the Big Dipper. The distance to* Polaris *is five times the distance between the pointers.*

5.3 Leading Stars and Trailing Stars

The Pointers of the Big Dipper are also called the "leading stars" of the Big Dipper, since these stars are at the front of the constellation as it rotates around *Polaris*. All stars rotate counterclockwise around *Polaris* once every 24 hours. Leading stars are at the "bow" of a constellation as it sails around the *Pole Star*. Stars at the "stern" of a constellation are called trailing stars. In the Big Dipper, the cup leads and the handle trails.

It is very helpful for orientation to learn which stars of a constellation are its leading stars — it may even be the most important thing to know, because when you recognize the leading stars of a constellation, you can tell at a glance which way the constellation is moving. At night without a horizon, you cannot judge this very easily by simply watching them move. It takes too long and there is too much to remember. Once you know its leading stars, though, each constellation becomes an arrow in the sky. Steering by the stars is easy with a sky full of arrows pointing counterclockwise around the north celestial pole or clockwise around the south celestial pole.

Stars rise in the east and move toward the west. If we know where east is, we can say which way the stars are moving. The trick is to know which way the stars are moving in order to tell where east is.

5.4 Circumpolar Stars

Stars that never dip below the horizon as they circle *Polaris* are called circumpolar stars. If a star is circumpolar, it is visible all night long, every night of the year. In high northern latitudes, many stars are circumpolar because *Polaris* is high in the sky. Traveling south, stars that just skimmed the northern horizon farther north begin to dip below it. A specific latitude (equal to 90° minus the declination of the star) marks the circumpolar limit for each star. All Big Dipper stars are circumpolar above latitude 41° N. North of Cape Mendoceno on the Pacific or New York City on the Atlantic, the entire Big Dipper is visible all night throughout the year.

Circumpolar stars in the Northern Hemisphere travel counterclockwise around the north pole of the sky. In the Southern Hemisphere, stars move clockwise around the south pole of the sky. (See Figure 5-5.) This means that stars above either pole are headed westward and stars below either pole are headed eastward. Circumpolar stars are at their highest point in the sky when directly over their pole and at their lowest point in the sky when directly below their pole. In the Northern Hemisphere, there is a star at the pole, but in the Southern Hemisphere, there is none.

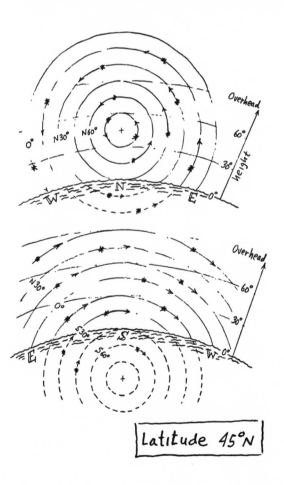

Latitude 45°N

FIGURE 5-5. *Polar stars viewed to the north and south from several latitudes. Circumpolar stars are those within the full circles over the horizon. Since they never set, circumpolar stars are visible all night long, every night of the year. Note that the range of stars we see along the meridian spans declinations of North (90° minus your latitude) to South (90° minus your latitude). Same-named stars with declinations*
continued

greater than 90° minus your latitude
are circumpolar, while contrary-
named stars with declinations greater than 90° minus your latitude are
never visible. At the equator we see
every star in the sky sometime during
the year.

Latitude 30°S

Latitude 0°

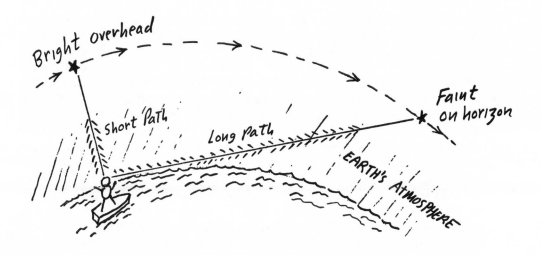

FIGURE 5-6. *All stars fade as they descend toward the horizon. Starlight is scattered and lost as it passes through the earth's atmosphere. Consequently, the longer the path through the atmosphere, the dimmer the star. It takes exceptionally clear nights to see stars low on the horizon, which is unfortunate, since low stars are very valuable to emergency navigation.*

5.5 The Brightness of Stars

In practice, circumpolar stars are not always visible at the lowest part of their circular path. It takes an unusually clear night to see stars near the horizon because of the thickness of atmospheric haze. Looking toward the horizon, you are looking through the thickest part of the earth's atmosphere; looking straight up, you are looking through the thinnest part. As a result, bright stars fade as they descend toward the horizon and fainter stars disappear (see Figure 5-6). If you see a single star low on the horizon, you can bet it's a bright one even if it appears faint. Since bright stars are well-known stars, this observation alone often identifies the star.

There are about 20 very bright stars, called magnitude-one stars. Approximately half of these are northern stars, which include *Vega, Capella,* and *Arcturus.* The two brightest stars of all are the southern stars *Sirius* and *Canopus.*

After the magnitude-one stars, the 70 or so next brightest stars are called magnitude-two. On the average, these stars are two or three times fainter than magnitude-one stars. Big Dipper stars are typical magnitude-two stars. Most magnitude-two stars have proper names, as opposed to the scientific labels that all stars have.

Magnitude-three stars are another two or three times fainter than the brightest stars. Stars of the Little Dipper are typical magnitude-three stars, except for *Kochab* (tip of the cup) and *Polaris* (tip of the handle), which are magnitude-two. There are some 200 magnitude-three stars, but only a few have proper names. On a clear night, many more stars than these are visible to the naked eye, but they are too faint to be relied on for navigation. Generally speaking, the 100 or so brightest stars, about half of which are visible during any one night, are more than sufficient for navigation. Although we need to know a few of the brighter stars, we luckily don't need to know the names of all these potentially useful stars. If you find a convenient star for your course but don't know its name, just make one up. The important thing is to know where the star lies relative to stars you do know.

Most stars have a color, or near-color, other than "white," but it takes a highly trained eye to recognize it in most stars. Exceptions to this are few, but prominent and beautiful. They are the "red giants." The red giants are red — or orange or yellow — even to the untrained eye. Once you recognize this, it is a big help in identifying these stars and the ones around them. The most prominent red giants are *Antares* in Scorpio, *Arcturus* in Bootes, *Aldebaran* in Taurus, and *Betelgeuse* in Orion. *Castor* and *Pollux* in Gemini provide a good test for spotting color in stars. They are close and bright, but only *Pollux* to the south, toward *Procyon,* is slightly reddish.

5.6 *North Star* from Cassiopeia

If the Big Dipper is not visible, the constellation of Cassiopeia shows the way to *Polaris* just as easily. Cassiopeia, the Queen of Ethiopia, is across from the Big Dipper, on the opposite side of *Polaris.* Cassiopeia looks like a big letter "M" or "W," depending on its position in the sky (see Figure 5-7). The constellation is almost symmetric, although its leading stars are slightly brighter than its trailing stars and the trailing side of the letter is lazy, or flattened out. But there is an easier way to tell which way this constellation moves. Viewed from *Polaris,* in the middle of its circular path, Cassiopeia always looks like an "M". *Polaris* is on the M-side of Cassiopeia — M for middle.

The distance from Cassiopeia to *Polaris* is twice the length of the M. To find *Polaris,* the distance should be measured off at right angles to the base of the M at the trailing star. Cassiopeia is circumpolar north of Cape Hatteras, North Carolina, or Point Conception, California.

5.7 *North Star* and the Little Dipper

Polaris is the last star on the handle of the Little Dipper. Stars of the Little Dipper are faint, except for *Polaris* and *Kochab* (Ko-kob). *Kochab* is on the opposite end of

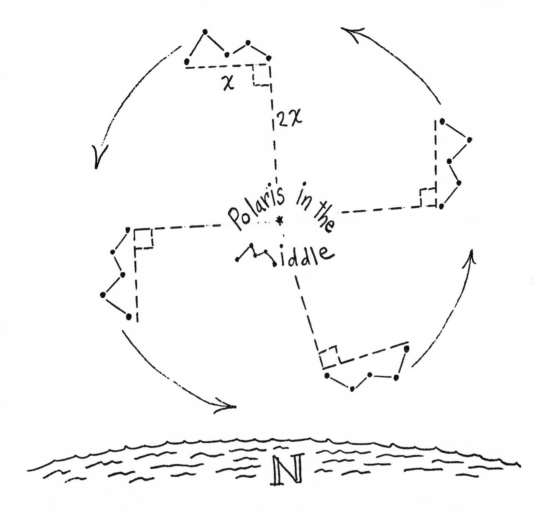

FIGURE 5-7. *Finding* Polaris *from Cassiopeia. Any view of Cassiopeia alone will tell where north is. Look at the constellation from the angle from which it appears as an M, and then move down from the bottom right leg twice the width of the base, measured at right angles from the trailing star. Due north is directly below the point you've found.*

the Little Dipper from *Polaris,* at the tip of the cup. Often when the sky is hazy, *Polaris* and *Kochab* are the only two stars to be seen in the entire region between Cassiopeia and the Big Dipper. The rules for finding *Polaris* from either Cassiopeia or the Big Dipper always tell which of these two is *Polaris*. On clear, dark nights, many stars may be visible near the pole. It's handy, then, to remember that *Polaris* is the one on the end of the handle of the Little Dipper.

The handles of the Big and Little Dippers bend in opposite directions. Both dippers have seven stars. Water pouring from one dipper always falls into the cup of the other dipper. The Little Dipper is circumpolar north of latitude 18° N, or, more practically, north of the tropics.

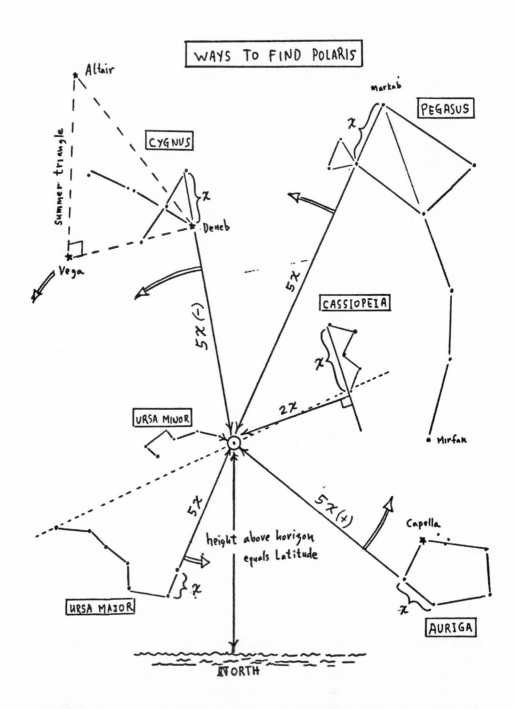

FIGURE 5-8. *Ways to find Polaris. Any one of these widely spaced constellations will locate north. The signs + or − indicate that the polar distances are somewhat larger or less than exactly five times the pointer spacings, but it is simpler and adequate to just remember the factor of five—"You point with your finger; each hand has five fingers.".*

5.8 *North Star* from Auriga

Auriga is a large, prominent pentagon of five stars. The pentagon is led across the sky by *Capella,* one of the brightest stars in northern skies. The lèading edge of the pentagon is marked by the Kids, a triangle of three faint stars next to *Capella.* The two stars (*Menkalinan* and *Theta Aurigae*) on the trailing edge of the pentagon are *North Star* pointers. The distance to *Polaris* from *Menkalinan* is about five times the distance between the pointing stars. The Auriga pointers, and several other ways to find *Polaris,* are shown in Figure 5-8.

Capella is bright enough to be seen near the horizon — setting northwest in early-summer evenings or rising northeast in late-summer evenings. *Capella* is circumpolar north of about latitude 45° N.

Auriga means charioteer. The constellation is usually pictured as a charioteer (without chariot) holding a mother goat, *Capella,* on one shoulder, with her kids at hand.

5.9 The Summer Triangle

Throughout the summer and fall, three of the first stars seen at twilight form a perfect right triangle, called the Summer Triangle (see Figure 5-8). The Summer Triangle is not a constellation; it is made up of the brightest stars of three different constellations. The brilliant *Vega* is at the right angle. It leads the triangle across the sky. *Deneb* trails from the east, and *Altair* to the south completes the triangle. The Summer Triangle is large; overhead, it covers the whole top of the sky.

Whenever the triangle is high in the sky (the lowest star at least halfway up the sky), the *Deneb-Vega* line points in the east-west direction, with the much brighter *Vega* to the west, since it leads. This is a valuable directional aid, since overcast skies often obscure all but these three stars. If the triangle is low in the sky, the east-west direction can't be found this way, but north is always on the side of the *Deneb-Vega* line that is opposite to the side that *Altair* is on.

5.10 *North Star* from the Northern Cross (Cygnus)

The Summer Triangle is the easiest way to find the constellation of Cygnus, the Swan — equally well known as the Northern Cross. *Deneb,* the northernmost star of the Summer Triangle, is at the head of the cross. *Deneb* and the trailing star of the cross (*Gienah*) are *North Star* pointers (see Figure 5-8). Again, the distance to *Polaris* is five times the distance between the pointing stars. The cross is symmetric, but it's easy to spot the trailing star since the cross is part of the Summer Triangle and *Vega* leads the triangle. *Vega* is the brightest star in the northern sky.

Except for *Deneb,* stars of the Northern Cross are faint, but the symmetry of the cross makes it stand out among background stars.

5.11 The Great Square of Pegasus

The Great Square of Pegasus, like the Summer Triangle, is huge. Nearly everyone in the United States could claim this giant square is overhead at the same time. The Great Square could also be called the cup of a Giant Dipper whose handle stretches across two constellations toward *Capella.* As with the Big Dipper, the cup of this Giant Dipper leads, and the two leading stars of the cup (*Scheat* and *Markab*) are *North Star* pointers, with the (now famous) distance to *Polaris* equal to five times the distance between the pointers (see Figure 5-8). If the handle of the dipper cannot be seen, a small equilateral triangle on the tip of the cup marks the leading edge. You can think of the little triangle pulling the Great Square across the sky.

The top and bottom edges of the cup (perpendicular to the pointers) make good east-west lines whenever the square is high in the sky. Stars of the Great Square are not bright, but the symmetry of the square makes it prominent when high in the sky.

The five equally-spaced stars stretching from the tip of the cup to the tip of the handle form an arc across the sky that is often prominent, even when the Great Square is not.

5.12 Finding North without the *North Star*

You don't have to see *Polaris* to find north. If you can point to the place where *Polaris* would be if it weren't for the clouds, that's good enough. And that's just what pointing stars do for you. Every prominent northern constellation has pointing stars, as we have shown: the Big Dipper, Cassiopeia, Auriga, the Northern Cross, and the Great Square. Learn the pointers, and any of these constellations is almost as good as *Polaris* for finding north. In Auriga, for example, *Capella* leads and the trailing edge of the pentagon points to *Polaris.* Point your finger straight in from these two stars, a distance of five times their separation, and (clouds or no clouds) you are pointing to the pole of the sky. Due north on the horizon is directly below your finger.

You need to remember only which stars are the pointers. The distance is always the same, five times the distance between the pointers. "You point with your finger, each hand has five fingers, five pointers — the distance is five times the pointers." That's not much of a jingle, but even if its silliness helps you remember the factor, it has served its purpose. Technically, the factor is not exactly five in every case, but

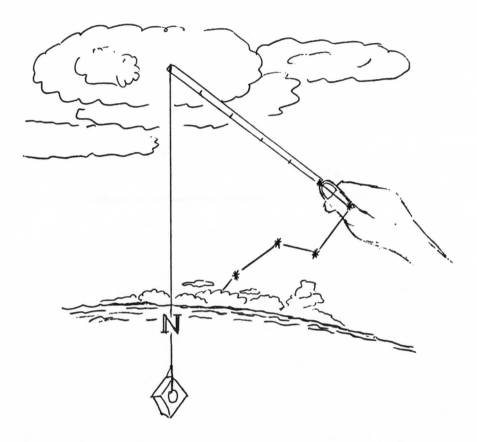

FIGURE 5-9. *Using pointers to find north when* Polaris *is obscured. Hold a stick in line with the pointers, mark the distance between them, and then mark five times this distance from the end of the stick. Hold the stick as shown, and you have found north. The weighted string is seldom required.*

it's close enough to justify this simple rule and spare the extra memory work. Since there are pointers in every part of the sky, chances are if just one patch of sky is clear, pointing stars will be in it.

Test yourself with a compass when the *North Star* is obscured (see Figure 5-9). It helps to use a stick at arm's length. Align the stick with the pointers and mark off the pointers' distance on the end of the stick. Take the stick down and put a mark at five times this distance from the end of the stick. Align the stick again with pointers, holding the mark on the innermost pointer. The tip of the stick will then be at the position of *Polaris*. If *Polaris* is high, you might tie a weighted string to the end of the stick. With the stick in place, the string intersects the horizon at due north. The simplicity and versatility of this way of finding north are reward enough for the time it takes to learn the pointers.

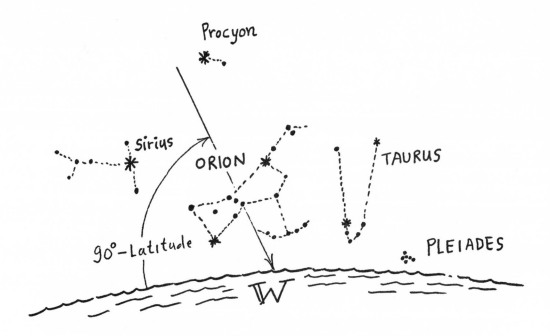

Procyon

Sirius

ORION

TAURUS

90°-Latitude

PLEIADES

W

Above: FIGURE 5-10. *Orion on the horizon. From any point on earth, at any time of night, Orion's belt always rises due east and sets due west. The Seven Sisters, Pleiades, lead the chase of nearby stars. Taurus the Bull follows, fighting off Orion whose faithful hunting dogs, Sirius and Procyon, trail close behind. Betelgeuse, at the base of Orion's raised arm, and Aldebaran, at the eye of the Bull, are brilliant red giant stars.* **Below: FIGURE 5-11.** *Pointing Mintaka (leading star of Orion's belt) backward to the horizon to find east. The rising angle to use is 90° minus latitude. The figure shows this being done from latitude 35° N (rising angle 55°) at 2.5 hours after Mintaka rose. The method works from most latitudes for 2 to 3 hours past the rising time. The figure is roughly to scale, showing that the same method applied 3.5 hours after rising would give an error of about 10°. Hourly positions of Mintaka, after rising, are marked with circled Xs.*

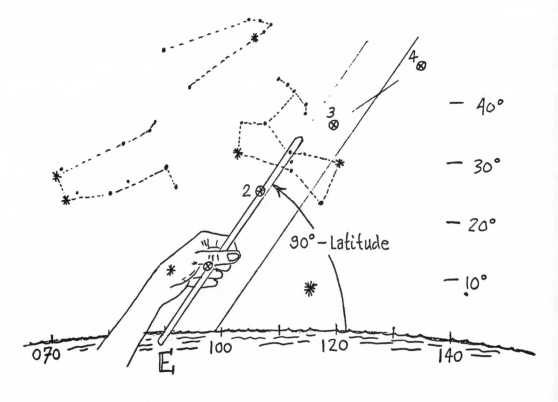

— 40°

— 30°

— 20°

— 10°

90°-Latitude

070   100   120   140

E

5.13 Orion

Orion the Hunter circles the earth above the equator. During winter, everyone on earth shares this majestic constellation of bright stars. Because of its unique location precisely over the equator, the leading star of Orion's belt, *Mintaka,* rises due east and sets due west. We should know this star well when it comes to steering by the stars. Orion's belt rising is as good as a big letter E for east, or W for west when setting (see Figure 5-10). This is true any time you see the belt on the horizon, regardless of your location on earth, the time of night, or the time of year. The belt is easy to spot. It is three close stars in a line at the center of the figure.

The bright stars of Orion form a roughly symmetric pattern, so it's hard to label leading and trailing stars. But the mythology of neighboring stars tells nicely who's going where. Orion is fighting Taurus, the Bull, placed in the sky by Atlas to protect his daughters, the Seven Sisters, known as the Pleiades — to protect them from Orion, as it turns out. The Sisters lead in flight, the Bull follows, pursued by Orion with his faithful hunting dogs, *Sirius* and *Procyon,* close behind. This story paints an arrow across the sky from the Pleiades to *Sirius,* showing at a glance the direction of many stars. Orion is led by the Bull, whose eye is the brilliant, red *Aldebaran.* Trailing Orion is the *Dog Star, Sirius,* brightest star in all the sky.

From northern latitudes, Orion rises on his side and stands up to the south-southwest. In the Southern Hemisphere, Orion crosses the sky standing on his head. But north or south, the Pleiades-Taurus-Orion-*Sirius* chase is on.

Even after Orion's belt rises above the horizon, we can still use it to find east. For a couple of hours after the belt rises, we can use our knowledge of star motions to retrace *Mintaka*'s invisible path back to the horizon. This path emerges from the horizon at due east.

The path of any star that bears east or west makes an angle with the horizon equal to 90° minus your latitude. At latitude 50°, eastern stars climb at an angle of 40°; at latitude 20°, eastern stars climb much more steeply, at an angle of 70°. At the equator, eastern stars rise straight up from the horizon. Western stars descent at the same angle at which they rise. This is the reason twilights are long in high latitudes and short near the equator. At the equator, the sun sets straight down over the western horizon. At high latitudes, the sun sets at a gentle angle, which keeps the sun just below the horizon for a much longer time.

To retrace the path of *Mintaka,* hold a stick up to the star and orient it with the horizon at an angle equal to 90° minus your latitude. The stick then intersects the horizon at due east (see Figure 5-11).

Rising and setting angles at bearings other than due east or west are discussed later in Section 6.2. You can do the same thing when *Mintaka* is setting. Align the stick with *Mintaka* and point it down toward the horizon at the proper angle to locate the place where the star will set, due west. Don't be too concerned about judging the rising and setting angle just right. Even if it is off some, you still get a good indication of due east or west this way. Practice this, checking yourself with a compass, and it should stick with you. We will use the same trick for keeping track of sunrise bearings after the sun leaves the horizon.

5.14 Gemini and *Procyon*

Castor and *Pollux* are the two bright stars of the constellation Gemini, the Twins. They lie north of *Procyon,* the lesser of the two *Dog Stars* trailing Orion. A line from *Procyon* that passes between *Castor* and *Pollux* is a valuable north-south line viewed from many locations. Within latitude of about 30° N to 50° N, this line often rises conveniently to give a north-south direction as Orion's belt moves away from the east (see Figure 5-12). This line gives a general indication of your meridian whenever visible, but it is an accurate way to find south only when the stars are high in the sky — that is, when the lowest is at least halfway up the sky. South of about 50° N, it is easier to locate north than south using this line. The line is useful down to about 15° S. The *Dog Stars, Procyon* and *Sirius,* form an equilateral triangle with *Betelgeuse,* the bright reddish star on Orion's trailing shoulder.

The Gemini-*Procyon* line is just one example of lines in the sky that might prove useful for orientation. Once you have established directions from known stars, look around the sky for pairs of prominent stars that indicate north or south from your latitude. Then check them occasionally throughout the night; such lines can be quite valuable but their value may be limited to certain times of night. Within 15° of the equator, for example, any two stars that rise together give a fairly good bearing to the elevated pole until the highest is about halfway up the sky.

5.15 Scorpio

Scorpio is on the opposite side of the sun from Orion. As the earth orbits the sun each year, we see Orion in the winter and Scorpio in the summer. Scorpio looks like a scorpion and moves like a scorpion — the head leads and the tail trails. At the neck of the figure is the bright red star *Antares.* Scorpio passes overhead in Australia, but most of the figure can be seen low in the southern sky as far north as the U.S.-Canadian border. From high northern latitudes, the view of Scorpio low in the sky is short and often obscured. But sailing south, Scorpio rises to become an impressive part of the summer sky (see Figure 5-13).

Any time you see the full scorpion from higher northern latitudes, it must be to the south. To find due south, note, if the horizon can be discerned, whether the head or tail stands straight up from the horizon. The head is south when the tail stands up, and the tail is south when the head stands up. From farther south, Scorpio is higher in the sky, and it's harder to tell when head or tail stands up (is perpendicular to the horizon). But even then, this trick often tells whether Scorpio is to the east, west, or near due south.

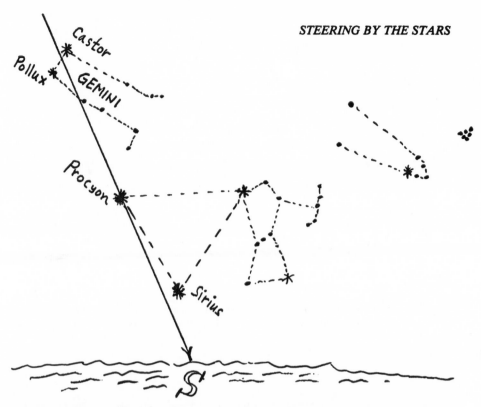

Above: FIGURE 5-12. *The Gemini—Procyon line. Within latitudes of roughly 50° N to 30° N and from 5° N to about 15° S the indicated line from Gemini through Procyon will intersect the horizon near the meridian when the lowest star is about halfway up the sky. Look for similar lines among the stars once your bearings are established from other stars. Numerous star pairs can be found that lead to the meridian this way, although they often don't work well when the line between them passes overhead—even though both are high in the sky at the time.*
Below: FIGURE 5-13. *Finding south from Scorpio. From higher northern latitudes the figure can only be seen near due south. From lower latitudes, check the relative orientation of head and tail. Try "head south, when tail stands up, and tail south when head stands up," as shown, or make up another such trick to locate south on the figure when bearings are known from other stars. This particular prescription takes some practice to apply since the head is not quite a straight line of stars.*

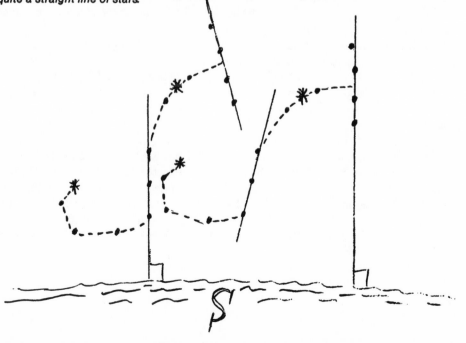

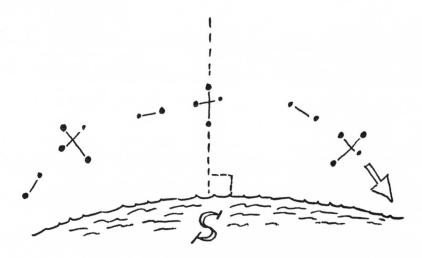

FIGURE 5-14. *The Southern Cross. When the Cross stands up, it bears due south. This rule is most convenient when the Cross is not too high in the sky. This rule is easier than similar ones for Scorpio, since the vertical stars of the Cross are pointers but the star lines on Scorpio's head and tail are not.*

5.16 The Southern Cross and the South Pole

The Southern Cross is a small cross of four bright stars, easily spotted because of the two very bright stars that trail right behind it. As the name implies, these are southern stars; the full cross cannot be seen north of the tropics. Viewed from the tropics, the cross rises on its side to the south-southeast and stands up as it passes over due south. It lies down on its side again as it sets to the south-southwest. Any time you see the cross standing up, it bears due south (see Figure 5-14). The two bright stars pushing the cross through the sky tell at a glance the direction in which the Southern Cross is moving.

The Southern Cross can also be used when it's not standing up, since the upright member of the cross points to the south celestial pole. South of the equator, the south pole of the sky is above the horizon, but there is no *"South Star"* at this pole — there are no bright stars anywhere near the south pole. Nevertheless, the south pole can be used to find directions just as the north pole is used when *Polaris* is obscured.

The south pole is the mirror image of the north pole. When you cross the equator headed south, the north pole of the sky (where *Polaris* is) drops below the horizon and the south pole rises above it, but no star marks the spot. As you sail farther south, the south pole continues to rise, 1° for each degree of latitude you make to the south. Consequently, throughout the Southern Hemisphere, the height of the south pole above the horizon is always equal to your southern latitude, just as the height of the north pole equals your northern latitude in the Northern Hemisphere.

The only difference between the two poles is the apparent motion of the stars around them. Facing north, we see stars moving counterclockwise around the north pole, but facing south, the same east-to-west rotation of the sky results in a clockwise circulation of stars around the south pole of the sky. Viewed from right at the equator, the north pole is on the northern horizon and the south pole is on the southern horizon. But at any other latitude, only one pole can be above the horizon. Nevertheless, the motion of stars counterclockwise around the north pole and clockwise around the south pole remains the same viewed from any latitude in either hemisphere, even though one of the poles must be below the horizon.

The south-pole pointers are the two stars that form the upright member, or long axis, of the Southern Cross. The distance to the pole is (again) five times the distance between the pointers. Knowing the pointers and how they work, it's easy to see why the cross stands up when it bears due south. This, and other ways to find the south pole of the sky are shown in Figure 5-15.

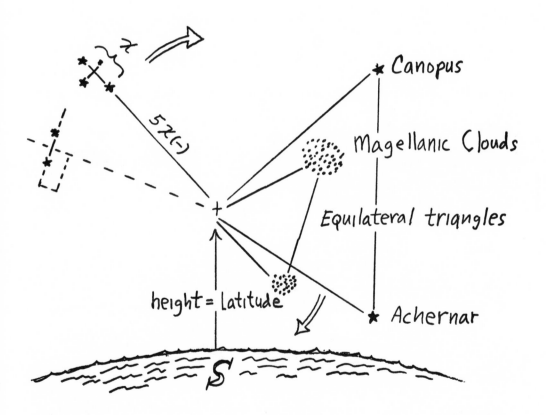

FIGURE 5-15. *Ways to find the South Pole of the sky. Use of the Southern Cross and of the star triangles are illustrated further in Figures 5-14 and 5-16.*

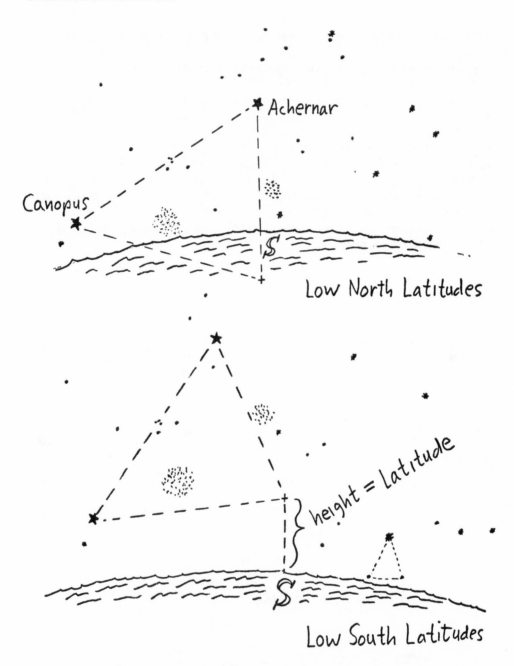

FIGURE 5-16. *Finding south from* Achernar and Canopus. *Note that the equilateral triangle these stars make with the South Pole can also be used to find south from low northern latitudes, even though the pole corner of the triangle is below the horizon.*

5.17 South Pole from *Achernar* and *Canopus*

When the Southern Cross is below the horizon, two other very bright stars cross the sky on about the same path as the Southern Cross. The two are *Achernar,* leading to the west, followed by the brilliant *Canopus.* These stars are not close together, but they are so bright that they stand out clearly among neighboring stars. The south pole makes up the third corner of an equilateral triangle with *Achernar* and *Canopus.* Due south is directly below the invisible corner of this triangle. If you remember that the height of the pole is equal to your latitude, you should have no trouble picturing where the third corner of the triangle should be. North of the equator, the south pole is below the horizon, but even then you can still use this method to estimate the direction of due south. (see Figure 5-16).

Canopus, the second brightest star in the sky, lies halfway between the south pole and *Sirius,* the brightest star in the sky. When *Sirius* is high in the sky, the *Sirius-Canopus* line intersects the horizon near due south. *Sirius* passes overhead in Tahiti. *Canopus* passes overhead in the Falkland Islands.

5.18 South Pole from the Magellanic Clouds

The equilateral-triangle method of finding the south pole from *Achernar* and *Canopus* can also be applied to the Magellanic clouds (see Figures 5-15 and 5-16). These are two fuzzy objects in the southern sky that look like small chunks of the Milky Way, though they are actually independent galaxies a long way from our own. These two galaxies also form an equilateral triangle with the position of the south pole.

The Magellanic clouds lie about halfway between the *Achernar-Canopus* line and the south pole. Since they are closer to the pole, it is easier to picture the triangle with them. Unfortunately, these two objects are faint, whereas the two stars are very bright. Since they lie in the same general region of the sky, they won't necessarily be an improvement over the two stars. On clear nights, though, they offer one more means of orientation, and every piece of reliable information is helpful.

5.19 Overhead Stars

When the sky is hazy, the only stars visible may be one or two unidentified stars overhead. You can find directions from these stars, since any star overhead moves due west, no matter where you are. You know due west as soon as you know which way overhead stars are moving.

Tied up at dock, it's easy to spot the direction of overhead stars by looking up at the stars along the edge of a mast. Stars that line up with the masthead of a 50-foot mast move away from the masthead at an apparent rate of 1 foot per 5 minutes. Still and comfortable, you can find west this way in 5 or 10 minutes.

At sea, this is not quite so easy and it takes longer. First you must hold a steady course while watching the stars move — a problem that you don't have at dock or on land. You can do this steering by the apparent wind or sea swells. The main difficulty, however, is the motion of the masthead as the boat rocks with the seas. Even in calm water, the masthead moves, tracing out a regular pattern in the sky. The task is to note the star's position relative to the average position of the masthead as it sways back and forth, tracing out a roughly elliptical path. Since the reference point is less accurate when it's moving, the star must move farther to show the west direction. If the sea is rough, you might do just as well by simply looking up at the stars, but it could take an hour or more to spot the star's direction this way (see Figure 5-17).

Another method is to use a weighted string tied to the end of a stick. Hold the stick overhead and sight up the string, using the tip of the stick as the reference point. The weight will still swing with the boat, but you can stop it and look again. Unless it is very calm, it generally takes about an hour or more for a star to move far enough away from the zenith to be able to tell its direction, regardless of how you measure it.

If a star is not directly overhead but only very high in the sky, either of these methods still works fairly well. Remember, though, it is always the direction of motion that is west, not the direction of the star. Unless the star passed exactly overhead, its actual bearing could be well to the south or north of west, even though its motion is due west.

5.20 Half-Latitude Rule

The overhead-star method of the last section would be used only when these were the only stars visible, since it takes some time to find directions this way. But even on clear nights, stars that pass directly overhead are extremely valuable for steering by another method.

The point in the sky directly overhead is called the zenith, and stars that cross over your zenith are called zenith stars. Any star overhead moves due west. If the overhead star passed right across your zenith, or very near to it, then the star itself must bear due west for some period of time after crossing your zenith. When you are near the equator, any celestial body that passes through your zenith bears due west all night long until it sets. Once you recognize it the following night, you will know it bears due east all night until it passes overhead.

Recall the principles. Northern stars (or any celestial bodies with northern declination) always set north of due west and southern stars always set south of due west. Consequently, any celestial body with declination 0° must set, not north or south, but exactly due west. Examples are the star *Mintaka,* the sun on the equinoxes, and

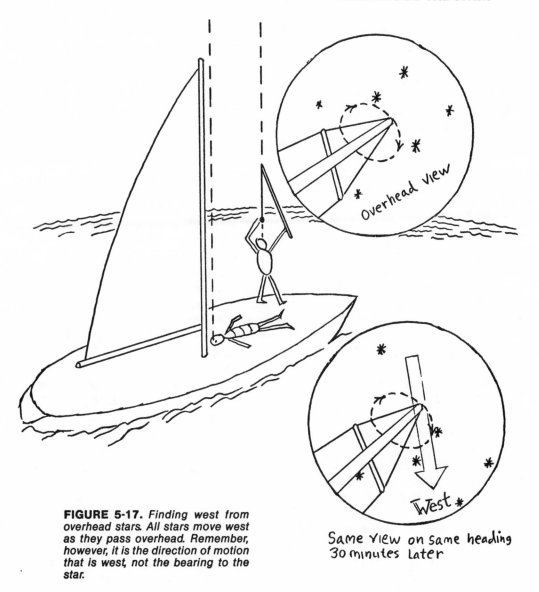

FIGURE 5-17. *Finding west from overhead stars. All stars move west as they pass overhead. Remember, however, it is the direction of motion that is west, not the bearing to the star.*

Same view on same heading 30 minutes later

the moon or planets as they happen to cross the equator. Viewed from the equator, anything that passes overhead must have a declination near 0°. It bears due west as it leaves your zenith, it is headed toward due west to set, therefore it must bear due west all night long.

At latitudes away from the equator, however, life is not so simple. Away from the equator, star bearings change as they move away from your zenith. North of the equator, zenith stars set north of due west, so as they descend to the horizon, they must move toward the north. In southern latitudes, overhead stars move from the west to the south as they descend.

Luckily, a simple rule tells how long we can follow any overhead star. When any zenith star descends to a height above the horizon equal to your latitude, its bearing has moved away from due west by an amount equal to one half of your latitude. We call this the half-latitude rule for zenith stars.

For example, suppose you are at latitude 40° N and you watch a star pass overhead. As soon as it moves away from the zenith, you can assume it bears due west. As it descends in the sky, its bearing moves slowly to the north, and when its height is about 40° above the horizon, it bears 20° north of west. See Figure 5-18. The job of the navigator is to use this information to estimate the star's bearing as it descends. When the star is about halfway down to 40° (at a height of about 65°), an estimate of its bearing would be 10° north of west. The procedure works the same way from any latitude, north or south, but from southern latitudes the star would move the same amount south of west.

In practice, it is not difficult to estimate a height approximately equal to your latitude — especially in the Northern Hemisphere, since this is the height of *Polaris*. You will probably be watching the height of *Polaris* to keep track of your latitude, and whatever method you use for that can also be used for this job. Obviously, if *Polaris* is visible, it will be your primary source of directions. One trick is to note the height of *Polaris* in hand widths when it is visible; then, when *Polaris* is obscured, you have a convenient measurement for this application. In the Southern Hemisphere, use either of the two triangle methods or the Southern Cross pointers to locate the position of the south pole. Its height equals your southern latitude.

On clear nights you need not rely on just one zenith star till it drops too low for this application — though lower stars are usually easier to use when available. Other stars are continuously passing overhead, so you can pick the ones that are most convenient. Watch the stars as they pass overhead. One after the other, they keep an east-west line drawn across the sky. The lower your latitude, the longer you can watch any one star.

The main value of this method is that you don't have to know the stars you follow — you can even use a vacant point between two or three stars. Just make up a name for each star or point to remember it by. It may help to make up your own constellations from overhead stars. If you don't change latitude much, you can use the same stars each night. After the first night you can also use zenith stars as they approach from the east. These begin to be useful when they reach a height equal to your latitude, then bearing half your latitude to the north (or south) of east, and from there they move toward due east as they climb to the zenith.

As you change latitudes, the stars overhead will also change, since each star is restricted to a specific latitude. But this is no problem. When you note a star has moved away from the zenith, pick new zenith stars to follow. You may begin to see from this how we can keep track of our latitude from zenith stars if we recognize them and know their declinations.

Sailing east or west, you can literally follow unknown zenith stars using the half-latitude rule. If the sun, moon, or a planet happens to pass overhead, you can follow it just as you would a zenith star. To use the sun or planets this way, you would have

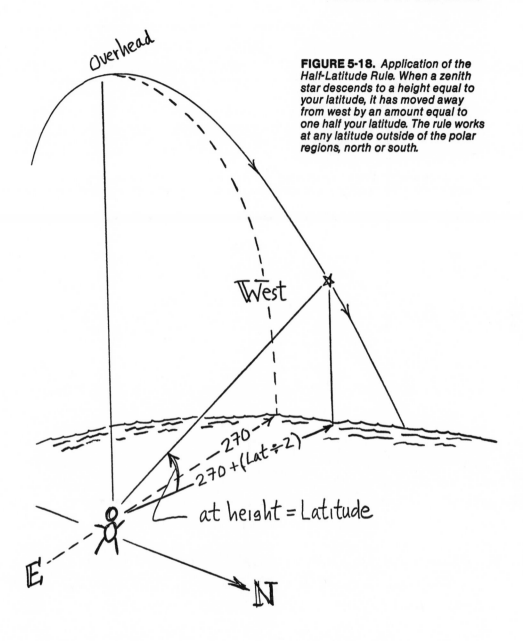

FIGURE 5-18. *Application of the Half-Latitude Rule. When a zenith star descends to a height equal to your latitude, it has moved away from west by an amount equal to one half your latitude. The rule works at any latitude outside of the polar regions, north or south.*

Overhead

West

270

270+(Lat÷2)

at height = Latitude

E

N

to be in the tropics. The moon might pass overhead at latitudes as high as 29°, but it could be used only once — from zenith to setting — since its position in the sky changes rapidly each day. The half-latitude rule is accurate to within 5° from any latitude outside of the polar regions as shown in Figure 5-19.

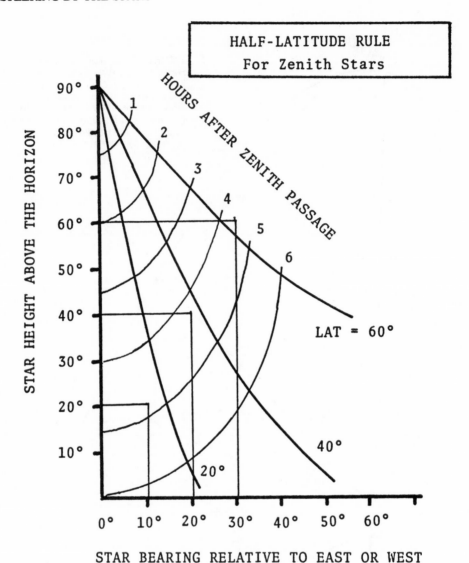

FIGURE 5-19. *Accuracy of the Half-Latitude Rule. The heavier curved lines are actual zenith-star bearings as the stars descend. Corners of the rectangles mark predictions of the Half-Latitude Rule. At latitude 40° (N or S), for example, a zenith star descends to a height of 40° in just under 4.5 hours. At that time, its bearing is 23° off of due west—to the north in north latitudes, or to the south in south latitudes. The rule error at this latitude is only 3°. Remember, however, that even though the rule is fairly accurate in principle, we can't apply it to this precision in practice. If we achieve a consistent accuracy of some 10° to 20° this way, we are doing well.*

5.21 The Tropics Rule

The half-latitude rule works anywhere in the world, any time of year. But sailing in the tropics, you can use an expanded version of the rule that lets you keep track of zenith-star bearings all the way to the horizon. It works only in the tropics, but when you are there, it is very convenient. Anywhere in the tropics (latitudes 23° 27' N to 23° 27' S), your zenith stars will set at a bearing that is different from due west by the number of degrees equal to your latitude. At latitude 20° N, zenith stars set 20° north of west and rise 20° north of east. At latitude 10° S, your zenith stars rise 10° south of east and set 10° south of west.

The rule is simple and accurate. And again, you don't need to know the names of the zenith stars to use the rule. In the tropics, with the aid of this rule, you can follow any star that passes overhead for as long as it is visible, providing you know your approximate latitude. When the star descends to a height equal to your latitude, its bearing is half your latitude off of west; when it reaches the horizon, its bearing is your whole latitude off of west.

This expanded version of the half-latitude rule is a special case of a much more powerful rule that also works throughout the tropics. In the tropics, you can use a rule to tell where any star (not just zenith stars) rises and sets, providing you know the declination of the star. In other words, viewed from anywhere within the tropics, the place where each star rises and sets depends only on that star's declination, not on your latitude.

We call this the tropics rule. In the tropics, a star rises and sets off of due east and west by an amount equal to the star's declination. The declination of *Sirius,* for example, is about S 17°; it passes overhead in Tahiti in French Polynesia and at Lake Titicaca in southern Peru. Whenever you see *Sirius* setting in the tropics, its bearing is 17° south of west. The bright northern star, *Capella,* has a declination of N 46°. It passes over the mouth of the Columbia River on the Washington-Oregon border and over Cape Breton Island in the northern part of Nova Scotia. In the tropics, north or south, when you see *Capella* rising, its bearing is 46° north of east, which is due northeast. Likewise, in the tropics, *Capella* always sets due northwest.

This rule is restricted to the tropics because generally the direction of a rising star depends on the latitude of the observer as well as the declination of the star — a point discussed further at the end of this section. But within 20° or so of the equator, the change due to the observer's latitude is so slight it can be neglected. At latitudes greater than 24°, however, star bearings on the horizon begin to change more rapidly with latitude. Consequently, this rule is not reliable for latitudes greater than about 24°. The rule, as we applied it to unknown zenith stars at the start of this section, works even though we don't know the names of stars, because we know their declination must be the same as our latitude since they did pass overhead.

The tropics rule shows the value of knowing the geography of the stars. If we are to use horizon bearings of stars for directions, we need to know the declinations of a few stars — most stars in the sky, of course, do not pass overhead. The tropics rule for all these other stars becomes more valuable as you learn more stars. There is a

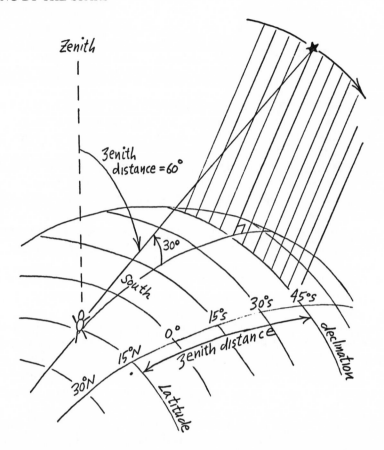

FIGURE 5-20. *Finding the declination of an unknown star from its peak height on the meridian. A star that crosses your meridian at a height of 30°, must be 60° down from your zenith. This means its declination is 60° south of your latitude, since the distance between you and the point directly under a star is always equal to the zenith distance of the star. This is true even when the star is not on the meridian, but we can use this fact to find declination only as it crosses the meridian. The peak height of a star can be determined most accurately with makeshift instruments when it is either very low (less than 10° or so), or very high (within 10° or so of the zenith). Measurement methods for finding latitude are covered in Chapter 11. To figure star bearings, however, we do not need to determine declinations very precisely.*

way around this limitation, however, if you don't mind tuning up your measuring skills. If you have a convenient star, but it's not a zenith star and you don't know its declination, you can figure out the star's declination relative to your latitude.

But this is not something you can do from scratch. You must first know your directions before you can find the declination of a star. It is a circular process, an example of reading and steering by the whole sky. You use some stars to find directions; then, knowing directions, you can find the declination of an unknown star. Then you can use the unknown star for directions.

To find the declination of a star, you must note how far the star is off your zenith when it bears due north or south at its highest point in the sky. If a star passes north of you, 10° below your zenith, the declination of that star is 10° north of your latitude. Or suppose you see a star due south at twilight at a height of about 30° above the horizon. Since the full range of heights in the sky is 90°, a star 30° up from the horizon must be 60° down from your zenith. The declination of this star must be 60° south of your latitude (see Figure 5-20). If you are at latitude 15°N, the declination of the star must be S 45°. This star rises 45° south of east and sets 45° south of west, throughout the tropics. You can use this trick to find the declination of a star no matter where you are, but the tropics rule gives its direction on the horizon only when you are in the tropics.

This procedure for determining declination from known latitude and (at least temporary) bearings can prove very valuable for finding the declinations of the bright planets, Venus and Jupiter. Because of their brightness they are convenient steering guides, but their declinations cannot be memorized because they change throughout the year in irregular ways. Makeshift methods of measuring heights above the horizon and off the zenith are covered in Chapter 11 on latitude.

Once you know the declination of a star or planet, you can then determine where it will rise and set when viewed from any latitude by using a plotting trick. To explain this best, we need a new term. The bearing of a rising star relative to east, or a setting star relative to west, is called the star's "amplitude." A star with north declination rises north of east and sets north of west, so it is said to have a north amplitude. Amplitudes are thus labeled north or south depending on the declination of the body — later we will use the sun's amplitude to keep track of its bearings. With this new term, we can restate the tropics rule in a neater form: *From any latitude within the tropics, a star's amplitude equals its declination.*

Outside of the tropics, a star's amplitude is bigger than its declination, and you can figure out how much bigger using the plotting procedure illustrated in Figure 5-21. With this technique, the sky begins to open up even further for star steering. From any known latitude you can figure the declinations of prominent stars, and from these determine where the stars will rise and set.

5.22 Polynesian Star Paths

The concept of a star path comes from island navigators of the tropical Pacific. The "path" implied is a sequence of stars with nearly the same declination, which means they rise at nearly the same place on the horizon throughout the tropics (tropics rule). By learning the sequence for the bearing from one island to another, Polynesian navigators have, in essence, established sets of celestial sailing directions. They follow one star as it rises above the horizon until the next in the sequence appears, at which time they shift to the new star for orientation. In this way, they keep track of a particular bearing on the horizon throughout the night. The same technique can be used with setting stars. It is easy to see how indigenous star paths could evolve into finely tuned routes that account for both prevailing currents and the leeway of traditional craft. Poor choices would be removed from the lore by natural selection.

To figure a star's amplitude from its declination and your latitude.

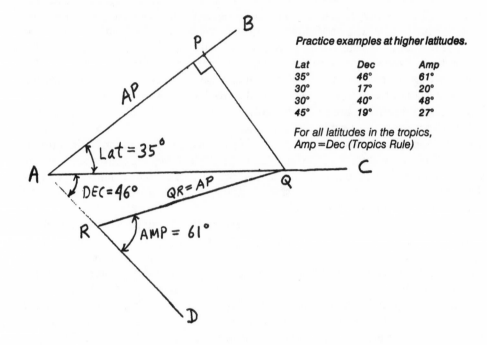

Practice examples at higher latitudes.

Lat	Dec	Amp
35°	46°	61°
30°	17°	20°
30°	40°	48°
45°	19°	27°

For all latitudes in the tropics,
Amp =Dec (Tropics Rule)

Procedure:

1 *Draw angle BAC = Latitude and, below it, angle CAD = Declination*

2 *At any point P on line AB, draw line PQ perpendicular to line AB*

3 *Find point R on line AD that is a distance AP from Q*

4 *Then the angle QRD = Amplitude of the star*

FIGURE 5-21. *Graphical solution for amplitude. With this procedure we can figure the amplitude of any star whose declination we know or determine. Note that as latitude de-creases, point P approaches point Q, and point R approaches point A, so amplitude ap-proaches declination—the Tropics Rule. With a calculator, solve for amplitude from: Sin(Amp) = Sin(Dec)/Cos(Lat).*

This approach to star steering, unfortunately, is not as versatile outside of the tropics. At higher latitudes, stars do not rise as steeply from the horizon as they do in the tropics (rising angle equals 90° minus your latitude), so their bearings change much faster as they rise. As a result, we can't follow any one star very long. Another problem at higher latitudes is that the horizon bearing of a star changes with latitude, which further restricts this method at higher latitudes to east-west voyages.

Left to steer by the stars in the tropics, however, we can borrow the method of Polynesian star paths directly (see Figure 5-22). Unlike our Polynesian counterparts, however, we won't know ahead of time which stars make up the path we need —

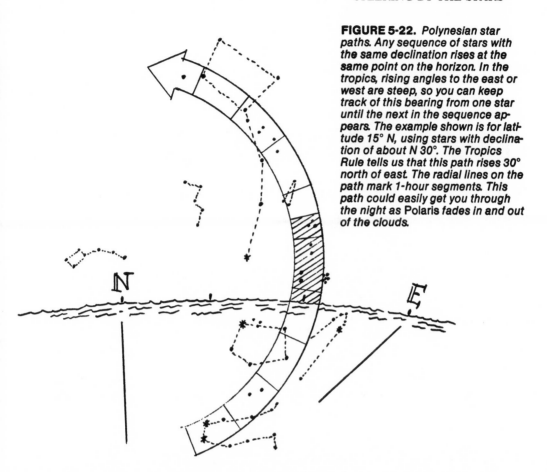

FIGURE 5-22. *Polynesian star paths. Any sequence of stars with the same declination rises at the same point on the horizon. In the tropics, rising angles to the east or west are steep, so you can keep track of this bearing from one star until the next in the sequence appears. The example shown is for latitude 15° N, using stars with declination of about N 30°. The Tropics Rule tells us that this path rises 30° north of east. The radial lines on the path mark 1-hour segments. This path could easily get you through the night as Polaris fades in and out of the clouds.*

unless we happen to have a table of star declinations. But we can discover a convenient path using the various other methods of star steering to keep ourselves oriented as we note the sequence of stars on the horizon dead ahead. If we are steering without a compass, this process happens almost automatically, since we continuously look to the stars ahead for short-term references. All that remains is to picture patterns or figures in the constellations and make up names for the stars we intend to follow each night.

In its broadest sense, a star path is nothing more than using the same steering stars on successive nights. In this sense, the concept of star path can be useful at any latitude, especially if your voyage is primarily to the east or west. One example, already mentioned, was the use of the half-latitude rule for overhead stars as they approach the zenith from the east or descend toward the west. Once we have identified the zenith stars for our latitude, we can use their trail across the sky as a star path to the east or west, even though we may not be headed that way. With a southern component to our course, for example, we can watch the stars just south of our zenith each night to anticipate which new stars will become zenith stars as we proceed.

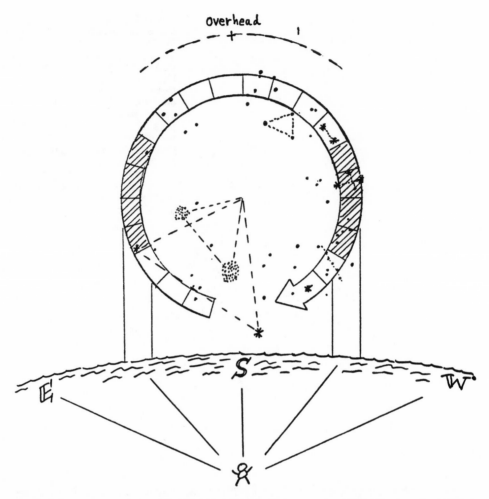

FIGURE 5-23. *Circumpolar star paths. At higher latitudes, circumpolar stars form an elevated "star path"—keeping constant bearings for several hours—as they pass to the right and left of the pole. This example is for latitude 45° S, using stars with declinations of about 60° S. The radial lines on the path mark 1-hour segments. When no timepiece is available, you could use the heights of prominent stars along such a path for watch changes.*

5.23 Circumpolar Star Paths

At high latitudes, we can borrow the Polynesian concept of star paths by looking in a different place for stars that hold their bearings for long periods. In the tropics, we look to the east or west near the horizon to find stars that move nearly vertically with little change in bearing. At high latitudes, we can find similar stars by looking to the middle of the sky toward the intercardinal directions. Here we see circumpolar stars moving nearly vertically along the east or west sides of their circular paths around the poles.

At higher latitudes, we can take advantage of the larger numbers of circumpolar stars. Circumpolar stars with the same declination (which puts them on the same circle around the pole) also form a star path of sorts, as they pass to the left or right of their pole. At this position, they are traveling nearly vertically and therefore remain at the same bearing for long periods. We can pick out a path of these stars by noting which stars are equidistant from the pole position — a relative measurement that is fairly easy to make. These stars would then be "on their path" when they are at roughly the same height as the pole, just below or above a height equal to our latitude (see Figure 5-23).

From latitude 45° N, for example, the star *Dubhe,* at the tip of the cup of the Big Dipper, will remain within 5° of bearing 320° for over 5 hours as its height drops from about 65° to 30°, coming down around the west side of the pole. Rising through the same arc on the eastern side, it stays at 040° for the same period. *Dubhe* is far enough from *Polaris* that it could easily be visible with *Polaris* obscured; but this technique is potentially much more valuable in high southern latitudes.

In the southern sky, there is an almost continuous ring of prominent stars with declinations near S 60°. These are circumpolar for all latitudes south of 30° S. The illustration shows how these stars form a convenient star path viewed from latitude 45° S. Remember, though, that the bearing to this type of star path changes as your latitude changes. But the change is gradual and can be monitored. The primary virtue of this approach is that it gives you a bearing at a glance, without having to draw imaginary lines across the sky.

5.24 Timing Low Stars

If you have a watch, any star, known or unknown, in about one quarter of the sky can be used for directions conveniently at any time of night. The method is the same as what we call in Section 6.4 the solar time method for steering by the sun, but it applies even more readily to stars. The principles are explained in Section 6.4, so here we only state the method.

First, find directions accurately using any, preferably many, of the previous methods. Then, use a portable compass card to note the directions of a few prominent stars low in the sky, bearing roughly opposite to the elevated pole. That is, use stars to the north in the Southern Hemisphere and stars to the south in the Northern Hemisphere. And note the time according to your watch. The time could be wrong; we don't need accurate time here, only relative time. These low stars will then move west along the horizon at a rate of 15° per hour. If we know their direction at one time, we can quickly figure out what it must be at some later time.

Example: At latitude 35° N, at watch time 2230, I see *Antares* to the southeast at a bearing of 140°, which I determined by other methods. At watch time 0230, the next morning, 4 hours later, the bearing to *Antares* will be 140° + (4 x 15°) = 200°.

The trick here is to use several different methods to determine accurate bearings to several of these low stars and then simply use these stars from then on. As they ap-

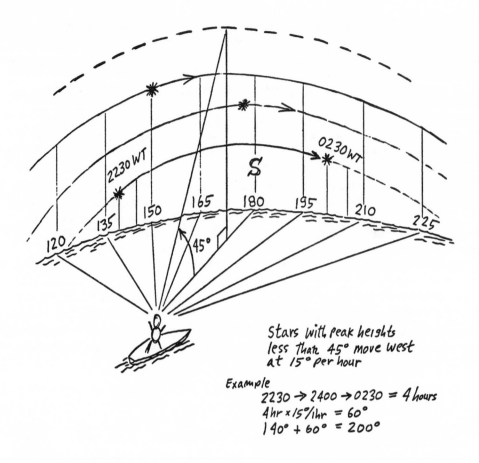

Stars with peak heights
less than 45° move west
at 15° per hour

Example
2230 → 2400 → 0230 = 4 hours
4 hr × 15°/1hr = 60°
140° + 60° = 200°

FIGURE 5-24. *Keeping track of star bearings by timing low stars. Any star with a peak height less than halfway up the sky moves west as 15° per hour. When a watch is available—once you find bearings from other means—you can use this method the rest of the night. This is the stellar equivalent of the solar-time method covered in Section 6.4, Figures 6-9 and 6-10.*

proach the western horizon, use their positions to find bearings to subsequent stars to the east that follow along their general path. This is the easiest way of all to keep track of bearings by the stars. In essence, you only have to use the various other methods once or twice a night to check your calibration of these low stars. But you need a watch. See Figure 5-24.

And the stars don't even need to be so very low. As explained in Section 6.4, so long as the stars you choose remain less than 45° above the horizon at their highest point, your error from this method will rarely be more than about 5°, and the errors are equal and opposite on either side of your meridian. If you follow a star this way from one side of the meridian to the other, the errors will cancel. The lower the star, the more accurate the method, but the lower stars are above the horizon for shorter periods. Generally, you won't know how high some random star to the east is destined to rise, so it is best to start with stars near your meridian. Just look toward the meridian, and any bright star less than halfway up the sky is a candidate. The next night when you see them coming, you know they are good guys.

That's all there is to it. The method takes little explanation, but don't let that distract from its extreme utility and versatility. With a watch at hand, this is a powerful aid to orientation. The rotation rate of 15° per hour is easy to remember. The earth rotates 360° in 24 hours, which is 15° per hour.

6

Steering by the Sun

Steering without a compass during the day is quite different from steering by the stars at night. On a clear night you can glance at the stars and pretty much point to any direction you choose. You can't do this very often with the sun, and you essentially can't do it at all without a watch. To tell the direction of the sun, you have to do some figuring or watch a shadow move. You can always get directions from the sun; it's just not as convenient as using the stars.

The big advantage of daytime steering is that you can see waves, swells, and various other signs of the wind on the water and boat — not to mention a good horizon throughout the day for sun-height measurements. During the day, you will typically steer by the wind and swells and only occasionally figure out the sun's direction to check your course. But when the swells are weak and the winds vary, we have no choice but to steer by the sun throughout the day.

6.1 Sunrise and Sunset

To get bearings from the sun in the morning, you need to know the direction of sunrise. The sun always rises to the east, but rarely due east. For most of the year, for most of the world, sunrise lies within 30° of due east, so sunrise always provides a rough determination of east. But you can't steer a boat very far with this much uncertainty.

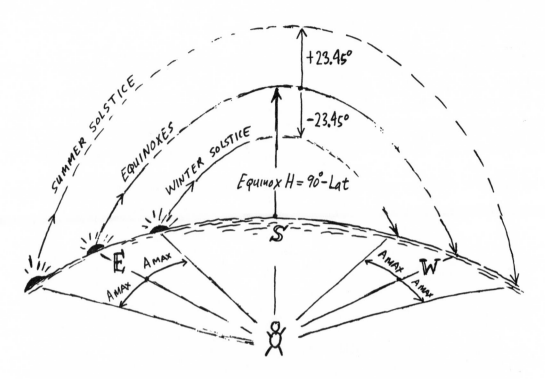

FIGURE 6-1. *Path of the sun observed from northern latitudes showing peak heights and sunrise-sunset bearings throughout the year. The sun's path is symmetric about the meridian—when the sun rises 20° south of east, it sets 20° south of west. Maximum amplitudes (A$_{max}$) are tabulated for various latitudes in Figure 6-2.*

The precise direction of sunrise depends on your latitude and the time of year. During fall and winter (between the two equinoxes, from September 23 to March 21), the declination of the sun is south, so the sun rises south of east. During spring and summer, when its declination is north, it rises north of east. See Figure 6-1. The sunrise is farthest from due east for about one month on either side of the two solstices, December 21 and June 21. Only for about one week on either side of each equinox can you safely assume that the sunrise lies within 5° of due east.

A procedure for figuring the direction of sunrise from your latitude and the date is given at the end of this section, but apart from this approach (which requires some memory work), the easiest way to find the direction of sunrise is to use the stars. Just before morning twilight, use the stars to carefully note your heading and the direction of the wind and swells. Then hold a steady course until sunrise and note the sunrise direction relative to your heading. In the Northern Hemisphere with *Polaris* visible, it is best, if possible, to alter course to due north for this — or alternatively from any location, to head parallel or perpendicular to the swells.

In practice, it is best to assign numerical bearings to your heading and the swells (rather than approximate labels like "northwest"), even though these values won't

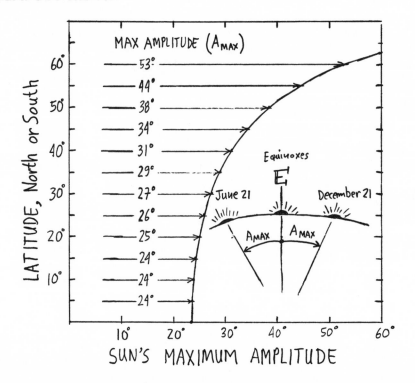

Above: FIGURE 6-2. *Maximum amplitude of the sun at different latitudes. These maximum values occur on the solstices, but throughout the year the amplitude is south when the sun's declination is south (fall and winter) and north when the sun's declination is north (spring and summer).* **Below: FIGURE 6-3.** *How the sun's amplitude varies with the date. Draw a circle and label the circumference with 1° per day with the solstices on the baseline as shown. Then scale the baseline with the maximum amplitude that applies to your latitude. The example shown is for latitude 48° N, where the maximum amplitude is 37° N. At this latitude, the amplitude on April 15th or August 25th is 15° north. This figure shows how the amplitude stays much longer near the maximum values at the solstices than it does near 0° at the equinoxes.*

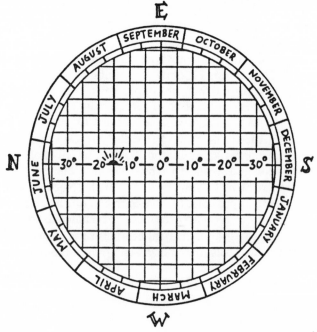

be very accurate unless you have *Polaris* to go by. For example, preparing for this measurement, you might turn to head straight up the trough of the swells, which you figure from the stars is toward direction 050° — and this puts the wind on your port beam. You then trim to this point of sail and hold course till sunrise. If the sun comes up 30° to the right of the bow, according to your makeshift compass card, then the sunrise bearing is 080°. Once you learn the direction of sunrise, it is most convenient to remember it relative to due east — in this example, it would be 10° north of east (see also Figure 3-5 for another method).

The bearing difference between sunrise and due east (or sunset and due west) is the amplitude of the sun. In the example, the sun's amplitude was 10°N. The amplitude label (north or south) is always the same as that of the sun's declination, since the sun rises and sets north when its declination is north. The amplitude is the thing to remember since it varies systematically throughout the year and applies to sunrise and sunset alike; it is more confusing to remember bearing changes. On the equinoxes the sun's amplitude is 0°, and from there it gradually increases from day to day to its maximum value at the solstices. How the amplitude changes with date and the maximum value it reaches depend on your latitude, as illustrated in Figures 6-2 and 6-3.

The sun's amplitude won't change much over a week or so, unless your latitude changes by more than several hundred miles. Nevertheless, it is good practice to check it daily. After several checks, you will know the value accurately. You can also find the sun's amplitude from the direction of sunset, using early evening stars. Establish the sunset bearing relative to your heading, or alter course straight toward the sunset. Hold course until stars appear, then figure your heading from the stars, and you have the bearing of sunset. From this, figure the amplitude and you can use it the next morning for orientation. Remember the sun's path is symmetric. Knowing the sunset direction is the same as knowing the sunrise direction. If the sun's amplitude is 20° N, it sets 20° north of west and will rise the next morning 20° north of east.

In Section 5.21 (Figure 5-17) we showed how to figure a star's amplitude from its declination and your latitude. This method can also be applied to the sun. A procedure for figuring the sun's declination from the date is given later, in Section 11.7.

6.2 Morning Sun and Afternoon Sun

Once you know the direction of sunrise, you can keep track of the sun's bearing for two or three hours after sunrise by tracing the sun's path back to the horizon. The procedure is to locate the point on the horizon where the sun came up (a bearing we know) and then estimate how far off this bearing the sun lies at the present time. There are two ways to do this; one requires a watch, the other doesn't.

Without a watch, the method of pointing the sun back to its rising position is the same as the one used to point Orion's belt (*Mintaka*) back to the horizon (see Figure 6-4). Imagine a line passing through the sun that makes an angle with the horizon

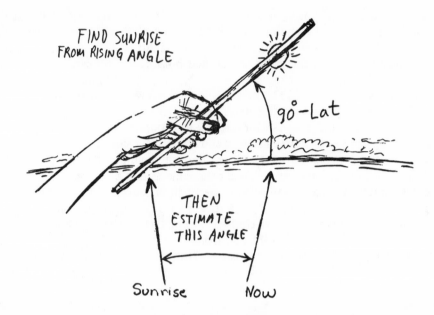

FIGURE 6-4. *Finding the sunrise location from the rising angle, which in turn can be used to find the present bearing of the sun from the known sunrise direction. The same angle pointed down toward the horizon can be used before sunset. Rising and setting angles are illustrated further in Figure 6-5 and Table 6-1.*

equal to 90° minus your latitude. This line intersects the horizon at the location of the sunrise. At latitude 30° N or S, for example, the eastern sun climbs at an angle of 60°. The angle is the same from north or south latitudes, the only difference being the direction in which the sun's path tilts. In northern latitudes the sun's path rises up and toward the south; in southern latitudes the path is tilted toward the north as shown in Figure 6-5. At latitude 10°, the angle of the rising (or setting) sun is about 80°. A stick and makeshift protractor (portable compass card) help in judging the angle, but to find the direction of sunrise you don't have to do this exactly. Just remember that the lower your latitude, the steeper the angle.

Likewise, for an hour or two before sunset you can use the same procedure to project the sun forward and down toward the horizon to locate the place where the sun will set.

Strictly speaking, this method is approximate, since the rising angle we use here is exact only if the sun bears due east or west at the time we point it toward the horizon. The worst case would be, for example, in high northern latitudes near the winter solstice, when the sun comes up well south of east and moves even farther from east as it rises. But for most of the year, in most parts of the world, the approximation is a good one — in part because the summer sun in northern latitudes and the winter sun in southern latitudes will likely lie near east or west at the time we do this estimate, even when the amplitude is large. Table 6-1 shows how rising angles vary with amplitude.

When you have a watch, the morning sun can be pointed back to the horizon in

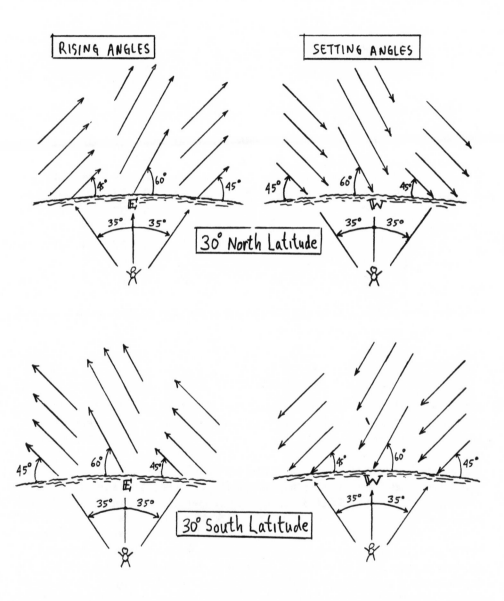

FIGURE 6-5. *Rising and setting angles at different amplitudes. Everything in the sky at a particular bearing climbs or sets at the same angle, which is always the steepest at due east or west where it equals 90° - latitude. Numerical values are given in Table 6-1.*

TABLE 6-1. RISING ANGLES*

		Amplitude (North or South)												
		0	5	10	15	20	25	30	35	40	45	50	55	60
Latitude (North or South)	0	90	85	80	75	70	65	60	55	50	45	40	35	30
	5	85	83	79	74	69	65	60	55	50	45	40	35	30
	10	80	79	76	72	68	63	59	54	49	44	39	34	29
	15	75	74	72	69	65	61	57	52	48	43	38	34	29
	20	70	69	68	65	62	58	54	50	46	42	37	33	28
	25	65	65	63	61	58	55	52	48	44	40	36	31	27
	30	60	60	59	57	54	52	49	45	42	38	34	30	26
	35	55	55	54	52	50	48	45	42	39	35	32	28	24
	40	50	50	49	48	46	44	42	39	36	33	29	26	23
	45	45	45	44	43	42	40	38	35	33	30	27	24	21
	50	40	40	39	38	37	36	34	32	29	27	24	22	19
	55	35	35	34	34	33	31	30	28	26	24	22	19	17
	60	30	30	29	29	28	27	26	24	23	21	19	17	14

* *Rising angles and amplitudes are illustrated in Figure 6-5.*

another way, which can be more accurate than the simple rising-angle method. To use this method, you must know the length of time that has passed since sunrise. You then convert this time to a length along a makeshift measuring stick, using a conversion factor for time passed to length along the stick.

The conversion factor we need is "1 inch per 10 minutes at arm's length." To see where this comes from, imagine that you could somehow see the sun's path drawn across the sky. If you held a stick at arm's length and lined it up with this path, you would find that the sun moves along the stick at a rate of about 1 inch per 10 minutes. The exact conversion factor depends on the length of your arm. This one assumes that the distance from your eye to the stick is about 2 feet, which is close to the average arm length. This conversion factor is the same one used in Section 5.19 to predict the apparent motion of overhead stars — everything in the sky moves at this rate, since "1 inch per 10 minutes at 2 feet" is equivalent to 15° per hour.

Naturally, we can't see the sun's path in the sky — that, after all, is what we want to find. But if we know the time of sunrise and the time of day, we do know how far the sun has traveled since rising. The trick is to put a mark on the stick at a distance from its end equal to the number of inches the sun has traveled since sunrise — a distance we figure from the time passed since sunrise and the conversion factor.

Then hold the stick with your thumb at the mark, put your thumb on the sun, and rotate the stick around the sun until the end of the stick touches the horizon. The sun came up where the end of the stick touches the horizon. What you have found is the only place on the horizon where the sun could have started its climb, in order to get to where it is, after traveling the distance it did. See Figure 6-6.

In the afternoon you can use the same method to point the sun ahead to find the sunset direction. If you don't have a stick, you can use your hand at arm's length. According to the conversion factor, an outstretched hand width is some 80 to 100 minutes, depending on the size of your hand.

But whatever method you use to point the sun to the horizon, don't forget the basics: In northern latitudes, whenever you face the sun, it is moving to your right — in the morning you point it back, to the left, and in the afternoon you point it forward, to the right. In southern latitudes, the westward motion of the sun is to your left as you face it. Pointing the sun back or ahead to its horizon position by this method can be used any time of year, from any latitude. Unlike the simple rising-angle approximation, this method is accurate (for an hour or two after sunrise and before sunset) regardless of the sun's bearing. This trick is just one example of the value of being able to estimate angles with your hands and fingers.

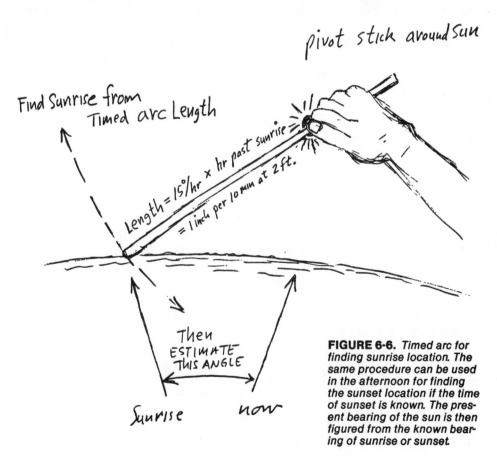

FIGURE 6-6. *Timed arc for finding sunrise location. The same procedure can be used in the afternoon for finding the sunset location if the time of sunset is known. The present bearing of the sun is then figured from the known bearing of sunrise or sunset.*

6.3 Local Apparent Noon

The keys to steering by the sun in the middle of the day are having a watch and knowing solar time. Solar time is figured relative to midday, local apparent noon, or LAN, as it is known to navigators. LAN is the time of meridian passage of the sun. At LAN the sun has reached its highest point in the sky, bearing due south from northern latitudes or due north from southern latitudes. Knowing solar time assures you of a precise direction of the sun each day at noon, and it helps throughout the day in many cases. Besides its value for sun directions, though, we also need solar time for keeping track of longitude, so we interrupt our direction finding briefly to clarify this concept.

Local apparent noon should not be confused with 1200 according to your watch. It is highly unlikely that your watch will read exactly 1200 at LAN. Your watch could be set on any time zone, but even if it is set on the proper local time zone, the time the sun crosses your meridian depends on where you are within that time zone.

If you have a watch but know it reads the wrong time (perhaps it stopped, but you don't know how long ago) and you don't know where you are, then the best thing to do is figure out the time of LAN and set your watch to 1200 at that time. Your watch is then at least running on a known time system, even though that system depends on longitude and date.

It is easy to set a watch on solar time; but if your watch is accurately set on another time zone, no matter what it is, you definitely should not change it. Accurate time is essential to finding longitude, and for long-distance navigation this is much more important than solar orientation. You don't want to do anything to your watch that may cause you to lose track of the correct time, regardless of the time zone of the watch. If your watch is accurate, don't change it. When we need the time of LAN we can find it, and it won't matter at all if it happens to be a number way off 1200.

From a stationary position, LAN always occurs exactly halfway between sunrise and sunset. And for emergency purposes, we are essentially stationary unless we change position during the day by more than 200 miles or so. To find the time of LAN, note the time of sunrise and sunset, add the two times, and divide by two. That's all there is to it.

It doesn't matter how you define sunrise and sunset, as long as you are consistent in the morning and evening. The usual definition of sunrise is the moment the top edge of the sun's disk first appears on the horizon — the full sun will only be visible another 2 or 3 minutes later, depending on your latitude and the date. The corresponding definition of sunset would be when the top edge of the sun's disk finally disappears below the horizon. In both cases, you must time the sun crossing the true sea horizon, not just a low layer of clouds near the horizon. When the horizon is obscured by only a small amount, say, less than half the sun's diameter, you can still estimate the time difference between the apparent and true setting times.

As an example, suppose the time of sunrise is 0915 by my watch and the time of sunset is 1933. Then the time of LAN is

$$\frac{(19\text{hr } 33\text{m } + \text{ } 9\text{hr } 15\text{m})}{2} \text{ } = \text{ } \frac{(28\text{hr } 48\text{m})}{2} \text{ } = \text{ } 14\text{hr } 24\text{m}.$$

LAN by this watch occurred at 1424. If I want to set this watch on solar time, I would set it back (from whatever it reads at the present time) by 2 hours and 24 minutes. Or I can leave it alone, knowing that according to this watch the sun will lie due south at 1424 tomorrow. This will be true even if my watch is not set correctly on any particular time zone.

It is not necessary to catch the sunrise and sunset on the same day. You could use the sunset one night and the sunrise the next morning. The sights can even be several days apart if you have not moved very far — say, 200 miles, as a rule of thumb. Within these limits, the time of LAN won't change by more than 5 or 10 minutes over a period of several days, and we don't need a more accurate LAN time if all we want is directions from the sun. We do, though, need a more accurate time for finding longitude.

Finding LAN from the sunrise and sunset is convenient, but unfortunately it is rarely possible to see the sun right on the sea horizon. Even on clear days, the rim of the horizon at sea is often obscured by distant clouds or haze. One way around this problem is to improvise a crude "sextant" — meaning here just some device for measuring angles. You can then measure the time it takes the sun to go from one fixed height in the morning to this same height in the afternoon. Since the path of the sun is symmetric, LAN still lies halfway between these two times.

The best type of makeshift sextant for measuring small angles is called a "kamal." It is an ancient Arabic device used for dhow navigation along the Persian Gulf and east coast of Africa. A kamal is nothing more than a flat stick or plate (a credit card!) with a knotted string attached. To use the kamal, you hold the knot in your teeth, and hold the plate forward with one hand so that the string is kept tight — the other hand is free for steadying yourself on the boat. The string keeps the plate at a fixed distance from your eye, and if you attach the string to the plate with a bridle, the tilt of the plate also remains constant. The kamal is a very reliable way to make reproducible measurements of small angles.

To do the sight, you align the bottom edge of the plate with the horizon, and note the time (in the early morning) when the upper edge of the sun first appears over the top of the plate. In the afternoon, you do just the reverse; note the time the sun's upper edge just drops below the top of the plate, again with the bottom edge aligned with the horizon. (See Figure 6-7.) The actual sun height you measure this way doesn't matter, as long as morning and afternoon heights are the same.

By placing several knots in the string, you can time several heights. Each knot gives a set of times, and the midpoint of each set gives a LAN time. Due to judgment errors, the LAN times you get from different knots won't all be exactly the same, but the average of several sets will be more accurate than any one set (see Figure 6-8). Again, high accuracy is not required for direction finding alone, but this measurement is accurate and we can use it for keeping track of longitude, as explained later.

If you don't have the materials to make a kamal, you can use your fingers held at

WHEN TRUE SUNRISE IS OBSCURED

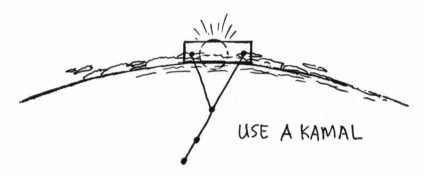

USE A KAMAL

FIGURE 6-7. *A kamal can be used to mark the time when the sun reaches a fixed height above the horizon. Halfway between morning and afternoon, at these heights, is the time of LAN. A kamal is just a card or plate held at arm's length. A knotted string attached to the card and held in the teeth keeps the card a fixed distance from the eye.*

a comfortable arm's length from the eye. With practice, your fingers may be just as good as a kamal. At the other extreme, if you have a proper sextant, you should, of course, use it.

Without a sextant, the main problem with sun-height measurements is the sun's brightness. We are usually restricted to measuring very low heights while the sun is not yet too bright to look at. Fortunately, the sun often has to rise only a finger width or so to clear the horizon clouds. And in any event, small angles (less than 10° or so) are much preferable to large angles because we can measure small angles more accurately. If you must attempt to measure higher angles when the sun is bright, be sure to use some form of sun shade. This may not be an easy problem to solve, though good sunglasses work sometimes for lower angles. Exposed camera film is one candidate for a sun shade; colored cellophane wrapping paper is another. Or smoke a clear sheet of glass or plastic by burning oil-soaked paper or cloth. Remember, an exposed sun can damage your eyes very quickly if you look directly at it.

So far we have discussed how to measure the time of LAN with a watch. To do this, we don't have to know where we are, and we don't even have to know if the watch is running correctly on any particular time zone. We also don't need any special aids. Now we will show that if you have a set of sunrise-sunset tables, and you know where you are, and you know the correct time — in any time zone, not necessarily the one corresponding to your present position — then you can figure out the time of LAN without doing any measurements. If all these conditions are met, you can usually figure out the time of LAN more accurately than you can measure it.

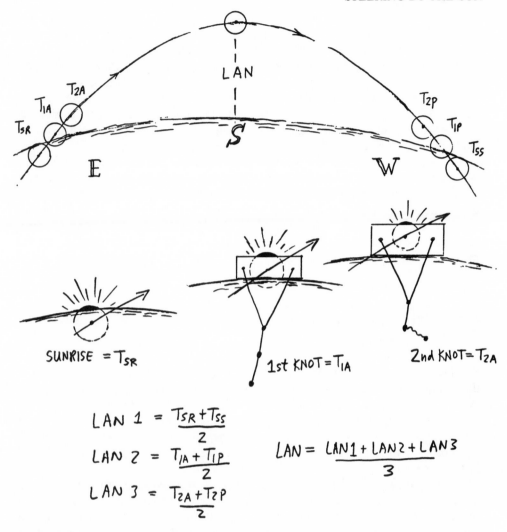

FIGURE 6-8. *Finding the time of LAN. The average of several sights is more accurate than one alone.*

Sunrise-sunset tables are included at the back of *U.S. Tide Tables,* so there is some chance that you might have a set of these on board. Look up the times of sunrise and sunset for your date and latitude, and then find the time halfway between these two, as in the earlier example. This midday time will be the GMT of LAN on the Greenwich meridian. Next convert your longitude (assumed known) to time using these conversion factors: $15° = 1$ hour and $15' = 1$ minute (which is the same factor expressed in smaller units). A table that helps with this conversion is also included in the *U.S. Tide Tables.* Then, if your longitude is west, add these two times to get the GMT of LAN at your longitude. In east longitudes, you subtract your longitude to find the time of LAN. This procedure is explained further in Section 12.2, on finding longitude.

Note that you can get the sunrise and sunset times from tables for any year; these times (to the accuracy we care about) depend only on latitude and day, not on the year. In fact, the midday (LAN) time that we want for this application does not even depend on latitude, even though the sunrise and sunset times themselves do. You will find that you get the same midday time for any latitude, as long as you use the correct day. You might also get these times from a commercial radio station, or from a recent newspaper that happens to be on board. Newspaper times usually include the longitude correction for the city the newspaper comes from.

The time of LAN (meridian passage) is listed directly in the *Nautical Almanac;* you have to make only the longitude correction to get the time you want. We include the tide-table method for those who find themselves offshore in need of sun directions when they didn't plan to be offshore and therefore didn't have a *Nautical Almanac* on board. In this situation, you are likely to have a watch, know the time, and also know where you are, at least to the level of accuracy needed for this measurement, which is not very high.

6.4 Solar Time Method

Finding directions from a watch and the sun is especially easy whenever the height of the midday sun is less than 45° above the horizon — that is, less than halfway up the sky. In this case, you need to know only the time of LAN and the time of day to get accurate directions from the sun throughout the day, sunrise to sunset. Your watch time does not have to be right on any time zone, you just need to know the time of LAN on your watch. So the first step is to find the watch time of LAN as explained in the last section.

To test the height of the sun at noon, check the shadow length of any stick near midday. Whenever the noon sun is anywhere near low enough to be considered for this test, its height does not change significantly for an hour or so either side of LAN, so the precise time you make the test is not critical. If the shadow length is longer than the stick casting the shadow, the height of the sun is less than 45°, and you can use solar time to find directions all day long.

This is an easy test, and it definitely should be made if the maximum height of the sun is in question. The solar time method explained below can produce serious errors if the sun is too high. When you do the test, the stick should be perpendicular to the horizon, and the surface that the shadow falls on should be parallel to the horizon. A nail in a board held aligned with the horizon is one way to do this, but it is easy to improvise.

We care about the height of the noon sun because this height, in effect, determines how fast the direction of the sun changes during the day. The sun always moves along its invisible arc across the sky at a rate of 15° per hour, but only when the noon sun is less than 45° high does the sun's bearing move *along the horizon* at a near-constant rate of 15° per hour. In these conditions, it does so to a good approximation throughout the day, sunrise to sunset as illustrated in Figure 6-9. And since

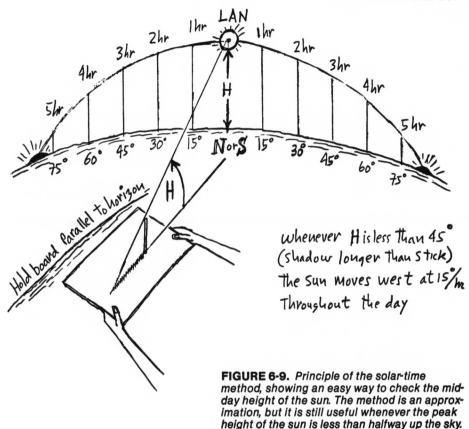

whenever H is less than 45°
(shadow longer than stick)
the sun moves west at 15°/hr
Throughout the day

FIGURE 6-9. *Principle of the solar-time method, showing an easy way to check the midday height of the sun. The method is an approximation, but it is still useful whenever the peak height of the sun is less than halfway up the sky.*

the sun is on our meridian at LAN, if we know the time of LAN and the time of day, we can easily figure out the direction of the sun. From northern latitudes, at LAN the bearing of the sun is due south at 180°. One hour after LAN the sun lies 15° to the west of due south, bearing 195°.

As a further example, suppose the time by your watch is 1120, and you know that LAN will be at 1340 according to your watch. Since it is 2 hours and 20 minutes (or 2.33 hours) before LAN, you know that the sun has to travel 2.33 x 15°, or 35°, before reaching due south. In other words, at 1120 the bearing of the sun is 180° − 35°, or 145°, as shown in Figure 6-10.

Strictly speaking, the solar time method yields only an approximation of the sun's direction. But whenever the noon sun is less than 45° high, this approximation is a good one. As explained in the last section, it is easy to find the time of LAN to within 10 minutes or so, even when moving. Once you've found the time of LAN by your watch, the solar time method always gives the direction of the sun to within about 10°, and it is often even more accurate than that.

In northern latitudes, the midday sun is lower in the winter than it is in the summer. So unless you are fairly far north, this method may work only during the winter half of the year. But regardless of your location or the date, if a midday shadow is

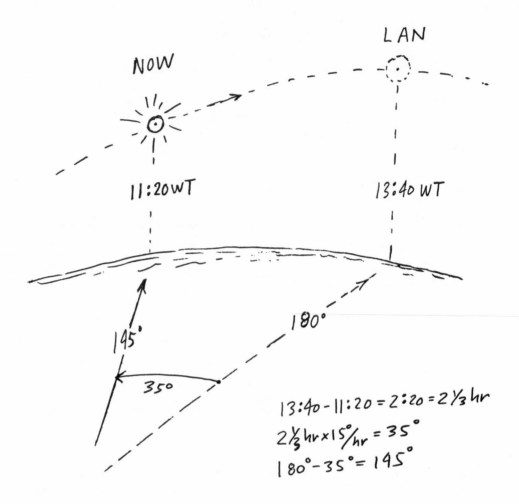

NOW

LAN

11:20 WT

13:40 WT

145°

180°

35°

$$13:40 - 11:20 = 2:20 = 2\tfrac{1}{3}\,hr$$
$$2\tfrac{1}{3}\,hr \times 15^{\circ}/hr = 35^{\circ}$$
$$180^{\circ} - 35^{\circ} = 145^{\circ}$$

FIGURE 6-10. *Using the solar-time method. Once you measure or figure the time of LAN, you can figure sun bearings throughout the day from the time alone. Again, the noon sun must be less than 45° high for this method to work.*

longer than the stick casting it, you can use the solar time method all day. If not, don't use this method, but instead use some form of a sun compass, as discussed in Section 6.8. The solar time method can never be used in the tropics.

The method that we have called the solar time method is a refinement of what is sometimes called the "Boy Scout watch method" — in which you point the hour hand of a watch to the sun and then locate the meridian at 1200 on the watch face. How this is intended to work and its severe limitations should be clear from the previous discussions. The method, in this form, is not reliable.

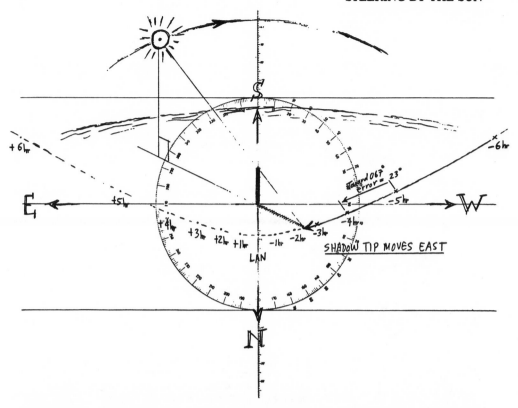

FIGURE 6-11. *Shadow tips move eastward throughout the day. The difference between due east and the direction they move depends on latitude, date, and time of year, but this error is always to the sunrise side of east in the morning and to the other side of east in the afternoon. Error values are given in Table 6-2. The example shows a summer sun (July 14th) viewed in the morning from latitude 45° north.*

6.5 The Shadow-Tip Method

As the sun moves westward, shadows move eastward as illustrated in Figure 6-11. We can find an east-west line from shadow motion just as we do from overhead star motion, but since we have shadows to watch, the sun doesn't have to be overhead for us to be able to do it. Near midday all shadow tips move due east, regardless of your location or the time of year. When the sun is high in the sky and you don't have a watch, the shadow-tip method is the best way to get directions from the sun.

Keeping track of shadow-tip motion at sea is not as easy as it is on land, but it's far from being impossible. In any event, you must improvise. The necessary conditions are that the heading of the boat remain constant as you watch the shadow move, and that the surface on which the shadow falls be level and parallel to the horizon. The stick or rigging catching the shadow does not have to be perpendicular to the horizon, although that may be the most convenient arrangement, but its

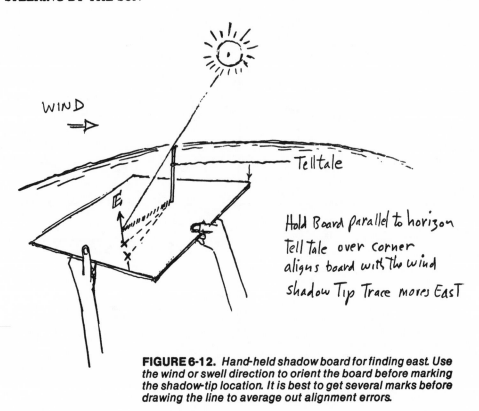

FIGURE 6-12. *Hand-held shadow board for finding east. Use the wind or swell direction to orient the board before marking the shadow-tip location. It is best to get several marks before drawing the line to average out alignment errors.*

orientation relative to the horizon must be the same each time you look at the shadow.

The shadow tip from an inclined stick moves in the same direction as the shadow tip of a vertical stick. Some manuals on direction finding on land suggest orienting the stick toward the sun, so you start out with no shadow at all. The shadow tip then moves eastward as it emerges from the base of the stick. There is no advantage to this method. The only effect this has is to shorten the effective length of your stick, so your measurements take longer. This is not a good way to do it even on land. At sea, this approach is entirely impractical.

Strictly speaking, the heading of the boat can change during your measurement, but when you are actually marking the location of the shadow tip to get its direction, the heading must be the same. You may want to alter course to align the boat with or against the seas when marking the shadow-tip positions. Or, it could be that you have a large plate or board available. If so, you could mark shadow-tip positions on it by orienting it each time, without worrying about your boat heading. Figure 6-12 shows one way to do this, using a telltale and the apparent wind.

In the absence of such a convenient shadow surface, the overall procedure is to orient the boat on a course you can hold or repeat, then mark the position of a shadow tip when the boat is not heeled over. After the shadow tip moves enough for

TABLE 6-2. SHADOW-TIP ERRORS*

hours from LAN	Same Name Declination					Contrary Name Declination				
	23.45	18	12	6	0	6	12	18	23.45	
0-1	3	2	2	1	0	1	2	2	3	
0-2	10	7	5	2	0	2	5	7	10	
2-3	15	11	7	4	0	4	7	11	15	Latitude
3-4	19	15	10	5	0	5	10	15	19	0°
4-5	22	17	11	6	0	6	11	17	22	
5-6	23	18	12	6	0	6	12	18	23	
0-1	3	2	2	1	0	1	2	3	4	
1-2	9	7	5	2	0	3	5	9	12	
2-3	14	11	7	4	0	4	8	13	18	Latitude
3-4	19	15	10	5	0	5	11	17	22	20°
4-5	22	17	12	6	0	6	12	19	25	
5-6	24	19	13	6	0	6	13	—	—	
0-1	3	2	2	1	0	1	2	4	5	
1-2	9	7	5	3	0	3	6	10	14	
2-3	14	11	8	4	0	4	10	15	21	
3-4	19	15	10	5	0	6	12	19	25	Latitude
4-5	23	18	12	6	0	7	14	21	27	30°
5-6	26	20	14	7	0	—	—	—	—	
6-7	27	21	—	—	—	—	—	—	—	
0-1	3	3	2	1	0	1	3	4	7	
1-2	9	7	5	3	0	3	7	12	18	
2-3	15	12	9	5	0	5	11	18	26	
3-4	20	16	11	6	0	7	14	22	30	Latitude
4-5	25	20	14	7	0	8	16	24	—	40°
5-6	28	22	15	8	0	8	—	—	—	
6-7	31	24	16	—	—	—	—	—	—	
0-1	3	3	2	1	0	1	3	6	11	
1-2	10	8	6	3	0	4	10	17	27	
2-3	16	13	10	5	0	6	14	24	35	
3-4	22	18	13	7	0	8	17	28	38	Latitude
4-5	28	22	16	8	0	9	19	29	—	50°
5-6	32	26	18	9	0	—	—	—	—	
6-7	36	28	19	—	—	—	—	—	—	
0-1	4	3	2	1	0	2	5	11	25	
1-2	11	9	7	4	0	6	14	28	48	
2-3	18	15	11	6	0	9	20	36	53	
3-4	25	21	16	9	0	11	24	38	—	Latitude
4-5	32	26	19	10	0	12	25	—	—	60°
5-6	38	31	22	12	0	—	—	—	—	
6-7	44	35	24	12	—	—	—	—	—	
		81 days	40 days	32 days	59 days	32 days	40 days	81 days		

*Shadow tips move these number of degrees away from due east. The error depends on latitude, declination, and time relative to LAN, but the error is always toward the sunrise side of east in the morning and toward the other side of east in the afternoon. At latitude 30° N, for example, with the sun's declination at N 18°, shadow tips more than 11° north of east in the morning from 2 to 3 hours before LAN and 7° south of east from 1 to 2 hours after LAN. The number of days that the sun's declination lies within the tabulated ranges is shown at the bottom of the table.

a new position to be clearly seen, mark a second point, then repeat this once or twice more. These marks should form a line, and this line points from west to east.

If you use the deck or cabintop, you can rig a stick perpendicular to the deck and check that the boat is upright by watching the stick relative to the horizon. In a life raft, you have little choice but to hold the stick upright and judge the shadow-tip motion as best you can.

The amount of time it takes to accurately determine the shadow-tip direction depends on the sea conditions and the length of the stick. The longer the stick, the faster the shadow tip moves. On land, using a 3-foot stick, you can easily find east this way in 10 minutes. Bouncing around at sea, it takes longer, sometimes as much as an hour or more. And sometimes the sea is just too rough to use this method at all.

You can rely on the shadow-tip method to be accurate to within 10° or so (at least in principle, if your heading remains constant) for about 2 or 3 hours either side of LAN. This is true regardless of your location or the date. The shadow-tip method works best for about one week on either side of each equinox. At these times, it works exactly all day long, everywhere in the world. But away from the equinoxes — which is most of the time — this method is not reliable in the early morning and late afternoon. In some conditions, it still works fairly well away from midday, but at other times the errors could be as large as 30° or so.

Table 6-2 lists shadow-tip errors for various latitudes, declinations, and time. These values can be used to practice this method.

6.6 The Tropics Rule for the Sun

Steering by the sun within the tropics has distinct advantages and disadvantages. One disadvantage is that the solar time method cannot be used. An advantage is that the tropics rule tells us the direction of sunrise and sunset if we know the sun's declination. Also, within the tropics the sun rises and sets at a steep angle, so horizon bearings are useful for a large part of the day.

Section 5.21 describes what we call the tropics rule for finding the bearings of stars when they are rising or setting. This method works only when you are in the tropics, latitudes 23° 27' N to 23° 27' S. Within the tropics, you can also apply this rule to the sun. The rule may even be more useful for the sun, because we can see the sun low on the horizon more often than we can see stars there.

To use the rule, you need to know the sun's declination, which changes slowly from N 23° 27' on June 21 to S 23° 27' on December 21. The sun's declination changes at most about half a degree per day, but the typical daily change is less than half that much, so if you only knew the sun's declination a week ago, you wouldn't be far off using that. Section 11.7 explains how to figure out the sun's declination from the date.

The tropics rule for the sun is simple. From anywhere within the tropics, the sun's amplitude equals the sun's declination. On July 23, for example, the declination of the sun is N 20°. Viewed from anywhere in the tropics, on July 23 the sun rises 20° north of east and sets 20° north of west.

When the sun passes overhead, your latitude equals the declination of the sun. In this case, you can apply the rule without figuring out the declination. You have, in effect, measured the declination by sailing under the sun.

6.7 Sun Crossing Due East or West

For half the year, the sun is never due east or west. Viewed from northern latitudes in the winter, the sun rises south of east and stays south throughout the day, setting to the south of west. But during the summer half of the year, the sun rises north of east and crosses over due east on its way to the southern sky, where it spends the middle part of the day. In the afternoons, it crosses back over due west on its way toward setting north of due west.

There is a trick for finding the time of day when the summer sun bears due east or west from northern latitudes; it applies equally well in the winter, viewing the sun from southern latitudes. To do this, you need a watch and sunrise-sunset tables, and you need to know your latitude to within one or two degrees.

The trick in northern latitudes is to look up the time of sunrise for your latitude and date, and then look up the sunrise time for your date but for a latitude that is 90° south of you. The difference in these two times is the length of time it takes the sun to reach due east after rising. In southern latitudes, use the time for a latitude 90° north of you. For example, at latitude 40° N on June 10, the sunrise time according to the tables is 0431. At latitude 50° S (which is 90° south of 40° N), the sunrise time is 0754. The difference is 3 hours and 23 minutes. In this case, the sun will bear due east 3 hours and 23 minutes after it rises. Likewise, the sun will bear due west 3 hours and 23 minutes before it sets. Note that you do not need to know your latitude to use this trick, and you do not need to know the correct time, since the times are relative.

This method is rather specialized, but it may come in handy someday. *U.S. Tide Tables* list sunrise times for latitudes of 60° S to 76° N. This means that this trick works in the north only when you are above latitude 30° N, or in the south only below latitude 14° S. But since sunrise times are symmetric in date and latitude, you can extend this in northern latitudes down to 14° N. Just assume you are at a southern latitude and use the date that is six months later than your present date.

6.8 Sun Compasses

If the noon sun is less than halfway up the sky and you have a watch, the solar time method of Section 6.4 is nearly as good as a compass. Using this method, you know

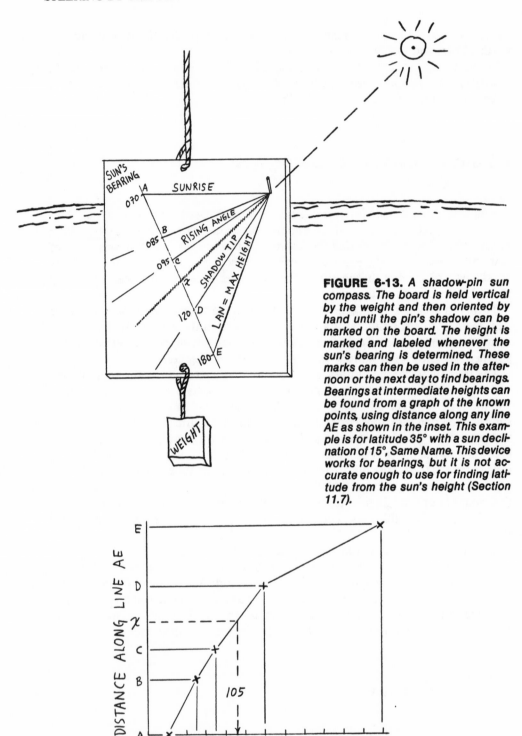

FIGURE 6-13. *A shadow-pin sun compass. The board is held vertical by the weight and then oriented by hand until the pin's shadow can be marked on the board. The height is marked and labeled whenever the sun's bearing is determined. These marks can then be used in the afternoon or the next day to find bearings. Bearings at intermediate heights can be found from a graph of the known points, using distance along any line AE as shown in the inset. This example is for latitude 35° with a sun declination of 15°, Same Name. This device works for bearings, but it is not accurate enough to use for finding latitude from the sun's height (Section 11.7).*

the sun's direction all day, and from the sun's direction you can find any direction you choose. To steer a boat this way, it helps to make a portable compass card, as explained in Section 3.3. With the makeshift compass card oriented toward the sun, you can read your heading directly from the card. To simplify things even more, you can mark the compass card with the times the sun is due at different bearings. This saves doing the arithmetic at each course check, since once you've labeled due south with the watch time you found for LAN, all other directions follow at 15° per hour.

If you have a watch, but the noon sun is too high to use the solar time method, you can still label your compass card with the sun's direction at various times of the day. One label would be due south at LAN, and a second would be the direction of sunrise at the time of sunrise. At one or two hours after sunrise, you could find and label the sun's direction by pointing the sun back to the horizon (Section 6.2). Next you could use the shadow-tip method to get a sun direction at about two hours before LAN. This covers the day; the intermediate times can be estimated. You then have a sun compass even though the solar time method itself cannot be used.

You can also make a sun compass without a watch. With this compass, you keep track of the sun's direction from its height. To do this, you need some improvised way to measure the relative height of the sun above the horizon. You don't have to know the actual height of the sun in degrees, you just need to know when the sun has reached the height you've marked, regardless of what it is. A kamal or a shadow-pin sextant (see Figure 6-13) can do this job, or even your outstretched hands at arm's length will do if nothing else is available.

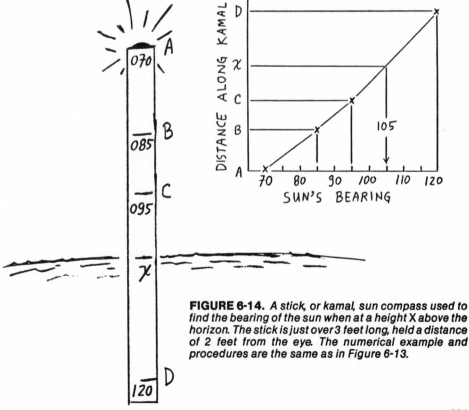

FIGURE 6-14. *A stick, or kamal, sun compass used to find the bearing of the sun when at a height X above the horizon. The stick is just over 3 feet long, held a distance of 2 feet from the eye. The numerical example and procedures are the same as in Figure 6-13.*

One convenient tool for keeping track of the sun's height, in this application, is a rod or flat stick about 3 feet long — two sail battens tied together will work well. To mark the sun's height, hold the stick at arm's length. Adjust the stick perpendicular to the horizon, with the sun just covered by the top of the stick when your thumb is aligned with the horizon. Then put a mark where your thumb is (see Figure 6-14). You now have the height of the sun in terms of a length on the stick. If you make the stick (or board, or book) into a large kamal by attaching a bridle and string to hold in your teeth, the results will be more reproducible. If you don't have string and are having trouble reproducing the measurements, try pressing your head against your shoulder as you make the sight. This may keep the eye-to-stick distance more constant.

The trick is to mark the sun's height and its direction just after finding its direction from the rising-angle method. Do this two or three times, each hour or so after sunrise. Then start a shadow-tip measurement, which might take another hour or so. And when you find east, and from this the sun's direction, again mark the sun's height and bearing on your stick. You now have a stick that shows how the sun's direction changes with its height — and it did not require a watch. You then know that when the sun falls to these heights in the afternoon, its bearing to the west will be the same as it was to the east in the morning. With several marks on the stick labeled with sun directions, you can estimate the intermediate directions.

You will be marking heights when the sun is bright, so you must be careful. If possible attach a makeshift shade to the side or top of the stick. Or using a wide stick or plate, cover the sun completely, and gradually let it slip in your grip until the sun's glare just appears over the top. Regardless of how you do it, though, you must be careful about looking into the sun.

In favorable conditions, you may have a nighttime swell pattern or steady wind that lasts all morning. Knowing their direction from the stars and sunrise, you can use this reference to calibrate a sun compass from sunrise till noon. Then if the swells or winds change, you still have your sun compass to steer by.

When the sun is high, it is nearly impossible to estimate its height with makeshift tools. Because of the sun's height, you won't be able to use a stick compass in the tropics near midday, but even then it will help in the mornings and afternoons.

It is important to remember that even the crudest measurement of the sun's height is more accurate than a guess. The height of the sun is deceiving near the horizon. When low in the sky, the sun always looks much bigger and higher than it is. The apparent size of the setting sun compared with the midday sun is only one example of the optical illusion that leads to overestimating angular heights near the horizon. With a sextant, you can measure the width of the sun to show that it is indeed the same throughout the day. The apparent change in size is only an illusion. The same illusion applies to the moon's size and height near the horizon.

If you must make a long voyage — long in time or distance — you must occasionally remake the sun compass. As a rough rule of thumb, it should be checked every 200 miles or so, or at least once a week even when moving very little. Besides, it won't be accurate the first time you make it. It will take some practice and repeated measurements before you are confident that it's doing the job for you. Accurate navigation without instruments is a full-time job — there's no way around it.

If a 2102-D Star Finder is available, don't forget its value for sun steering — you don't need an almanac to set it up. Just figure the sun's bearing at sunrise, and then plot the sun's position anywhere on the Star Finder that will reproduce this bearing at 0° height using the appropriate latitude template. It won't matter that the sun's celestial longitude that you marked is wrong; its latitude (declination) will be right if the sunrise is right, and that is all we need. With the sun plotted to match the sunrise, you have a sun compass that will work all day.

If a watch is available, note the time of sunrise and label the rim scale with time — each 15° rotation of the blue template corresponds to a 1 hour time interval. Then just rotate the blue template throughout the day and read off the sun's bearings. This timed sun compass will work regardless of the noon height of the sun. Without a watch, you can still read the sun's bearing as a function of its height and then label a shadow-pin sun compass directly or derive the calibration curve from a stick compass.

7

Steering by Other Things in the Sky

The heights and bearings of all celestial bodies are predictable from laws of nature. The only uncertainty comes from our ability to learn, interpret, and apply the laws. The moon and planets form a separate group in emergency navigation because their own orbital circulations complicate their apparent motions through our sky. Their value to emergency steering lies more in their prominence than in their predictability. They are bright and therefore serve as valuable references, once we have established how they move as seen from where we happen to be. On overcast nights, they may be the only source of directions.

If we happen to sail under the moon or planets, any of the overhead-star methods of Chapter 5 can be applied. And if a planet happens to fit into a star path for our route, so much the better for the length of time we can use it.

Other things in the sky like clouds, birds, and planes might also aid our navigation in special circumstances, but their value to orientation on the high seas must be carefully qualified. Once we do get close to our destination, clouds might get us closer, and birds could save the day. They have done so many times before for wayworn mariners.

7.1 The Moon

The moon is the most evasive of all celestial bodies. It moves westward with the stars each day because of the earth's rotation, but it also slips eastward relative to stars

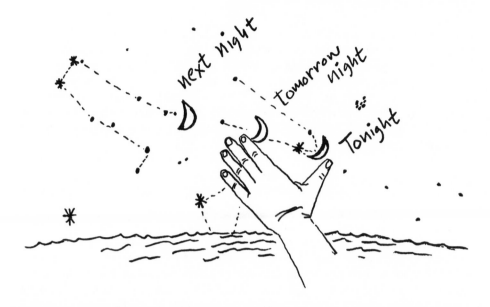

FIGURE 7-1. *The moon's eastward motion through the stars. The moon moves about 12° eastward through the zodiac each successive night. Here we see the moon moving from Taurus into Gemini.*

because of its own orbital motion around the earth. Since the moon circles the earth once a month, it progresses through the stars at a rate of 360° per (roughly) 30 days, or about 12° per day. If the moon is next to the star *Aldebaran* on one night, on the next night it will be about 12° to the east of *Aldebaran* (which is about half an outstretched hand's width at arm's length). See Figure 7.1.

The sun also slips eastward through the stars each day due to the earth's orbital motion around the sun, but this motion of 360° per 365 days represents only about 1° per day. For present purposes, we can overlook this detail and assume that the moon also moves relative to the sun at 12° per day. Nevertheless, the moon's motion through the sky is complicated. We simply can't predict its bearing from day to day as we can with the sun and stars. But we need not give up on the moon as a guide to steering. And we should not — in overcast skies it may be all we've got.

If you have a watch and know solar time, the moon can be helpful on special occasions. When the moon is full, it behaves just like the sun, with solar noon (LAN) changed to "solar midnight," meaning LAN plus 12 hours. A full moon crosses your meridian at solar midnight. For example, if I know the sun lies due south at 1330 according to my watch, then a full moon that night will lie due south at 0130. Furthermore, when the moon is full, you can figure its direction at other times of night using the solar time method of Section 6.4. But the same restrictions apply: The height of the moon at midnight must be less than halfway up the sky. When the midnight moon is low enough, the solar time method can be used for the moon all night long. In the previous example, at 0430, 3 hours past solar midnight, the bearings of the moon would be 180 + − (3 x 15°), or 225°.

When the midnight moon is just somewhat higher than 45°, you should not use this method more than an hour or so either side of midnight. When the midnight moon is notably higher than halfway up the sky, you can't use the solar time method at all. If the full moon is bright enough to cast shadows, you can test its height by the length of a shadow, as you do with the sun. Otherwise, just estimate its height using any square; you don't even need a clear horizon. Hold the square roughly parallel to the water and sight along the diagonal to see where the moon is relative to the 45° angle made by the diagonal.

The solar time method applied to the moon is less accurate than it is for the sun, since we must know the precise phase of the moon to use it. The moon is exactly full on only one night of the month, and it takes practice to spot this day by just looking at the moon. On a clear night, you can usually guess it right to within one day — unfortunately, though, we need the moon the most when the sky is not clear. A one-day uncertainty in phase creates a bearing uncertainty of 12°, since the moon moves 12° per day relative to the sun. But that's not the end of the problem. The precise time of full moon technically occurs for only a moment, and that time of day is not the same each month. In short, this method includes a basic uncertainty of plus or minus 12° at best, even if you did judge the correct day of the full moon.

Considering both these uncertainties (which are not independent), generally speaking we must assume that moon directions, no matter how or when we figure them, are uncertain by about 20°. The uncertainty is large, but it's much better than nothing at all. With a calendar or tables that tell us the precise phase, the uncertainty drops back to about 12°.

When the midnight moon height is below 45°, the solar time method can also be used two or three days before and after the full moon, without much loss in accuracy. When the moon is exactly full, the moon and sun are on opposite sides of the earth, which is why they pass us exactly 12 hours apart and why, to a good approximation, the full moon rises when the sun sets and the full moon sets when the sun rises. Each day following full moon, the moon moves 12° to the east of the sun. Since sun and moon move by us to the west, if the moon is now farther east of the sun, the time between the sun's passage and the moon's passage will be longer. The meridian passage of the moon is later than midnight on days following the full moon; at midnight, the moon has not yet reached the meridian. If you conclude from looking at the moon (or from other sources) that it is one day after full moon, then at midnight the moon would be 12° to the east of your meridian. Two days after full moon, the moon would be 24° east at midnight.

The same reasoning shows that on days before the full moon the time difference between sun and moon is less than 12 hours, so meridian passage of the moon occurs before midnight. If you conclude that it is two days before full moon, you can expect the bearing of the moon at midnight to be 24° to the west of your meridian — it passed you earlier than midnight.

With the inherent uncertainties involved, we do not lose much accuracy by considering the 12° daily motion of the moon to be about the same as the 15° hourly rotation of the earth. And with this approximation, we can expand the last example to conclude that since the moon is 2 x 12° farther along its orbit, it is about 2 x 15°, or 2 hours, ahead of schedule on the meridian. So we expect the moon two days

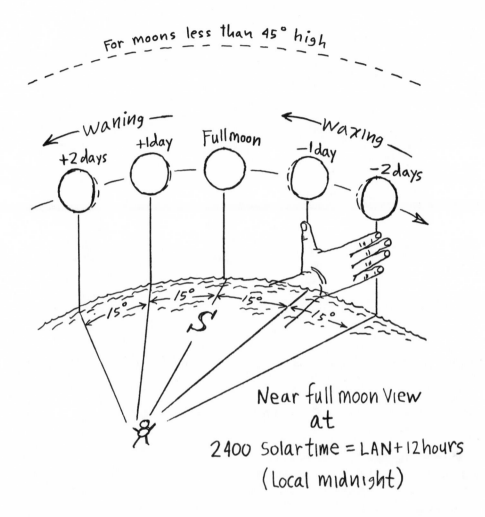

For moons less than 45° high

Waning —
+2 days +1day Full moon
Waxing —
–1 day –2 days

15° 15° 15° 15°
S

Near full moon view
at
2400 solar time = LAN + 12 hours
(Local midnight)

FIGURE 7-2. *Near full-moon view at local midnight. The full moon crosses the meridian at 2400 solar time. One day before full moon, the moon crosses the meridian 1 hour before 2400 (at 2300) and 1 day after full moon, the moon crosses 1 hour after 2400 (at 0100). Likewise, 2 days before means 2 hours before; 2 days after means 2 hours after. For moons less than 45° high, you can use this reference time on the meridian for moon directions several hours either side of meridian passage.*

before full moon to be on the meridian 2 hours before midnight, at 2200 solar time.

With this explanation behind us, we can restate the moon's behavior in a way that makes it easier to remember: The full moon is on the meridian at solar midnight. One day before full moon, the moon gets there one hour before midnight; one day after full moon, the moon is on the meridian one hour after midnight. Two days before, two hours before; two days after, two hours after (see Figure 7-2).

FIGURE 7-3. *The lighted side of the moon points in the direction of the sun. At night, the arrows shown at the moons point in the direction of the zodiac band of constellations (the path of the moon through the stars). In the Northern Hemisphere—or more specifically, when your latitude is north of the moon's declination—the moon is waxing when its right side is lit, and waning otherwise. Reverse the rule when you are south of the moon.*

When we conclude from looking at the moon that it is one or two days away from full moon, we must then decide whether it is before or after full moon. In other words, is the moon waxing or waning? The lighted side of the moon always faces the sun (see Figure 7-3), and the moon's daily motion relative to the sun is to the east. In the Northern Hemisphere, if the right side of the moon is lit, the moon is waxing, getting fuller each night. If the left side is lit, it is waning. In the Southern Hemisphere, the opposite is true. The key is to remember that the moon moves to the east. If it is moving closer to the sun (leading it across the sky), it is getting smaller; if moving away from the sun (following it across the sky), it is getting bigger. Practice making this call several times with a daylight moon when it's easier to reason through, since sun and moon are visible. Then it should be easy to do for a nighttime moon.

We can also use a half-moon to find directions, as shown in Figures 7-4 and 7-5. A waning half-moon crosses the meridian at 0600 solar time (6 hours before LAN), and a waxing half-moon crosses the meridian at 1800 solar time (6 hours after LAN).

Again, it must be the exact day of the half-moon. And as with the full moon, this is not always easy to determine exactly by just looking at the moon. But it is no more difficult, and others, like myself, may even find it easier to judge the phase of a

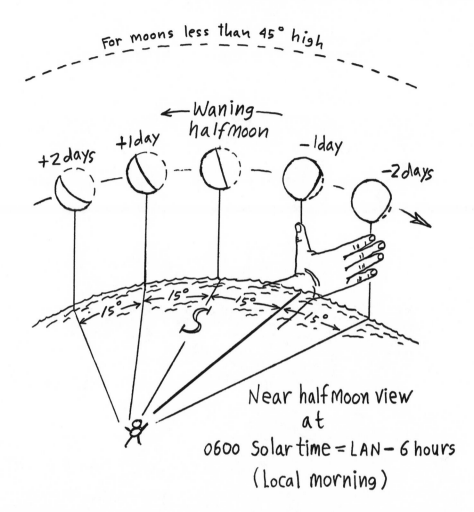

For moons less than 45° high

+2 days   +1day   —Waning—
                   half moon   - I day   -2 days

Near half moon view
at
0600 Solar time = LAN - 6 hours
(local morning)

FIGURE 7-4. *Local morning view of a waning half moon. The waning half moon crosses the meridian at 0600 solar time. One day before half moon, the moon crosses the meridian 1 hour before 0600 (at 0500) and 1 day after half moon, the moon crosses 1 hour after 0600 (at 0700). Likewise, 2 days before means 2 hours before; 2 days after means 2 hours after. For moons less than 45° high, you can use this reference time on the meridian for moon directions several hours either side of meridian passage.*

near-half moon than a near-full moon. With practice, you can judge it to within a day. And as with the full moon, the same procedures and basic uncertainties apply. If you decide it is two days before half-moon, expect the moon on the meridian 2 hours before six o'clock solar time. The rule is the same: Before half-moon, before six o'clock; after half-moon, after six o'clock. Whether the moon is on the meridian in the morning or evening depends on whether it is waxing or waning — on which side is lit. At least for practice, the half-moon is more convenient for directions than the full moon since the times we can use it are more convenient.

Most tide tables include the phase of the moon, and some calendars do also. On

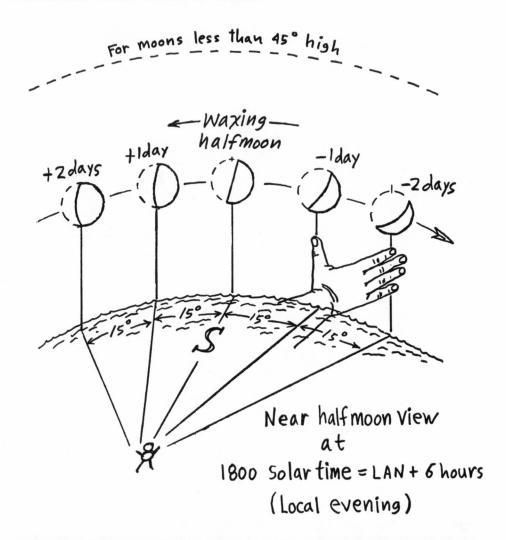

FIGURE 7-5. *Local evening view of a waxing half moon. The waxing half moon crosses the meridian at 1800 solar time. One day before half moon, the moon crosses the meridian 1 hour before 1800 (at 1700) and 1 day after half moon, the moon crosses 1 hour after 1800 (at 1900). Likewise, 2 days before means 2 hours before; 2 days after means 2 hours after. For moons less than 45° high, you can use this reference time on the meridian for moon directions several hours either side of meridian passage.*

calendars, the phase of the half-moon when waxing is called "first quarter"; a waning half-moon is at "third quarter." If you happen to have a calendar or tide tables, you can remove the uncertainty of judging the phase.

If you happen to have current *U.S. Tide Tables,* accurate time, and approximate longitude, you can expand and simplify your use of the moon for steering considerably, since these tables include moonrise-moonset tables. You can assume the moon crosses the meridian halfway between the tabulated times of moonrise and moonset. This will be accurate to within about an hour, but what is more important, you can figure this time for any day of the month (though of course the moon is of no value when it's in front of the sun or close to it). Note that the tables must be for the correct year as well as day to get moonrise and moonset times; expired tables work only for the sun. You must also make the longitude correction, as explained in Section 6.3 (and in the tables themselves), but you don't need your latitude. Just use some approximate latitude.

If you don't have correct time or don't know your position, you can still take advantage of these tables for moon steering by figuring the meridian passage time of the moon relative to LAN. Using the proper date and an approximate latitude, figure the time halfway between moonrise and moonset and halfway between sunrise and sunset. You then have the predicted times of meridian passage of the sun and the moon. If halfway between sunrise and sunset is 1210 and halfway between moonrise and moonset is 2030, you can expect the moon 8 hours and 20 minutes after the sun, regardless of its phase and without knowing it. Then when you measure the time of LAN, as explained in Section 6.3, you get both sun and moon directions from it. The sun will be on the meridian at LAN; the moon will be there 8 hours and 20 minutes later — and you have figured this without knowing your latitude or longitude. Then, if applicable, use solar time for sun and moon directions at other times of day.

The behavior of the moon is summarized in Table 7-1.

TABLE 7-1. SUMMARY OF MOON BEHAVIOR

Phase	Age	Rises	Meridian Passage	Sets
Waxing New Moon	0-3	Just After Sunrise	Midday	Just After Sunset
Waxing Half Moon	7-8	Midday	About Sunset	Midnight
Full Moon	14-15	About Sunset	Midnight	About Sunrise
Waning Half Moon	22-23	Midnight	About Sunrise	Midday
Waning New Moon	26-29	Just Before Sunrise	Midday	Just Before Sunset

7.2 The Planets

There are five planets visible to the naked eye: Mercury, Mars, Saturn, Jupiter, and Venus. The first three of these are not particularly useful for emergency steering, or

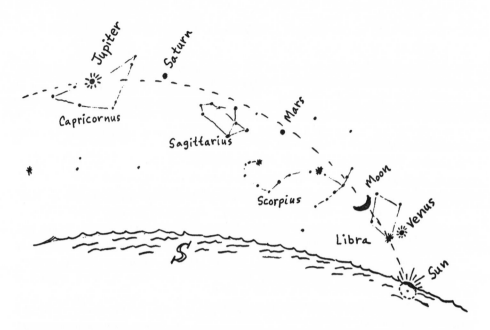

FIGURE 7-6. *Planet identification. Planets: (1) do not twinkle as stars do, (2) appear as tiny disks through steadied 10-power binoculars, (3) change positions (and brightness) among the stars, (4) are always found in line (a giant arc) with the sun and moon, and (5) are always within some zodiac constellation. Venus and Jupiter are always much brighter than the stars. A bright object seen for brief periods at sunrise or sunset very near the sun is likely to be the planet Mercury.*

celestial navigation in general. When visible, they appear similar to bright stars. Mars is the only one with color, being distinctly reddish. Mercury (the closest planet to the sun) is only rarely visible, either just before sunrise or just after sunset, very near the sun — it changes from a morning star to an evening star about every two months. The main effect these three planets have on celestial navigation is the confusion they can cause in star identification (see Figure 7-6). They, like all the planets and the moon, wander through the band of zodiac constellations in a way that is difficult to predict.

Jupiter and Venus, on the other hand, can be extremely valuable steering references because of their exceptional brightness. Though they also look the same as stars to the naked eye, Venus and Jupiter are always much brighter than any stars around them. When they are in the sky at sunset, they will be the first "stars" you see. On hazy nights, they may be all that you see. Venus is especially brilliant, sometimes shining like a spotlight in the sky.

Although Venus and Jupiter always remain brighter than any star, the brightness of each planet varies as it moves through the stars. And the planets move through the stars at different rates, even in different directions, though they all follow roughly the same eastward path through the 12 zodiac constellations that mark the sun's monthly position among the stars.

The orbit of Venus (like Mercury's) is inside our own, closer to the sun, so its apparent motion throughout the year is back and forth like Mercury's, from one side of the sun to the other (see Figure 7-7). Venus spends about seven months as a morning star, then takes about four months to sneak behind the sun to reappear as an evening star. It remains an evening star for another seven months, and then rushes back behind the sun in about one month to start the cycle again as a morning star.

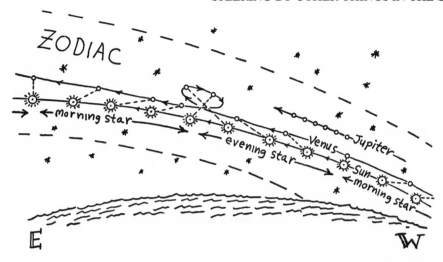

FIGURE 7-7. *Schematic view of the apparent eastward motions of Venus and Jupiter through the stars. To picture the times we see Venus, imagine each sun-Venus pair shown to be its position on successive weeks, and then imagine this sky rotating westward each day, bringing sun, stars, and Venus up over the eastern horizon and down over the western horizon. When Venus is west of the sun, it rises before the sun as a morning star that we see until the sky is too bright to see stars. When east of the sun, it follows the sun over the western horizon and we see it as an evening star, setting not long after the sun. Jupiter moves through the stars more slowly, progressing eastward through the zodiac at about one constellation per year.*

The cycle is regular, but without an almanac it is difficult to predict where the planet will be on some future date.

Jupiter, on the other hand, is a distant planet that creeps eastward through the zodiac constellations at a rate of about one constellation per year. In 1985, Jupiter was in the constellation of Capricorn. The season of Jupiter is the season of its neighboring stars.

Venus moves through the stars much faster than Jupiter, but the size of its orbit never lets it get farther than about 45° from the sun. When the sun goes down, Venus can't be more than about halfway up the western sky, although, for most observations, Venus is closer to the sun than that. For the half-year or so that Venus is an evening star, it follows the sun over the western horizon, never setting later than 3 or 4 hours after the sun. When Venus is a morning star it rises at most 3 or 4 hours before the sun.

When they are near the horizon, Venus and Jupiter always give a rough estimate of east or west, in the same sense that the sun does. Because the sun and planets follow the same path through the stars, the planets always rise and set some place where the sun does (on some date) at that latitude. For example, in mid-May 1985 Jupiter happens to be in Capricorn (at declination S 16° 30′), where the sun is in early February. So in May 1985 Jupiter rises and sets where the sun does in early February. It is not practical to reason through this in some arbitrary circumstance, but you might remember that the amplitude of any planet is always less than the maximum amplitude of the sun at your latitude.

For more specific directions from Venus or Jupiter, you need to identify their bearings relative to the stars. Because of their brightness, they are excellent guides, and it's well worth the trouble. Venus or Jupiter is especially valuable if its declination happens to be near 0° at the time of your voyage. It then behaves like the star *Mintaka* of Orion's belt, rising due east and setting due west — Sections 5.21 and 11.3 explain ways to estimate the declination of a planet viewed from a known latitude. Unfortunately, Jupiter is near the equator for only a month or two every six years, but Venus is near there for much longer periods each year.

In any event, it pays to note where these planets are and how they move when you have other stars for references. Then, if only these bright objects show through the haze, you have something to go by. You could, for example, use the *North Star* and a portable compass card to note the bearing of Jupiter at each hour throughout the night. Then if you happen to be sailing east or west at near-constant latitude, once you have checked often enough to get a good set of bearings, they will remain valid for a month or longer — since Jupiter moves so slowly, it behaves much like a fixed star. Venus, however, moves fast through the stars, so its bearings should be checked every few days. If you change latitudes, you have to recheck any of the planets, just as you do the sun.

7.3 Clouds, Birds, and Planes

In this section, we distinguish between steering aids and signs of land. Clouds and birds (and, to some extent, planes) are often strong evidence of nearby land. And if we turn to follow them, they are certainly steering aids in a sense, but this application is best postponed to Section 13.1 on the signs of land. Here we consider their value and limitations for orientation well away from land. When the task at hand is to maintain bearings, we should use all possible means, and when the task at hand is to decide whether land is near, we should also use all possible means. But it is equally important not to confuse the values of nature's various signs.

Moving clouds often help with orientation. In the vast tradewind belts, for example, the small puffs of cumulus clouds that fly by with the nighttime trades provide a quick visual check on the true wind direction. These are low clouds flowing with the surface winds, so they don't give directions we don't already know from the wind. Nevertheless, they are convenient references. Generally speaking, low clouds of any type move in the direction of the surface winds.

We might refine this slightly. In northern latitudes, if you face the true surface wind direction (as opposed to the apparent wind direction, discussed in Section 4.1), you should notice that low clouds come slightly from the right. In other words, winds just above the surface are veered. The amount varies from some 10° to 30°, depending on several factors but mostly the sea state — the rougher the seas, the larger the veer. In southern latitudes, winds just above the surface are backed, so look for clouds coming slightly from the left.

High and middle-high clouds, however, are potentially more valuable than low clouds for orientation, since we can sometimes use them to gauge the direction of the "winds aloft." We have now referred to three different winds: surface winds; veered, or backed, winds just above the surface that carry low clouds; and now the

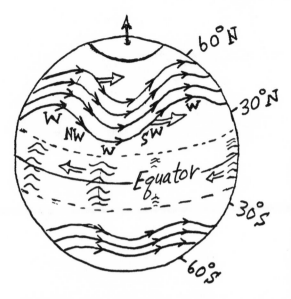

FIGURE 7-8. *Winds aloft. Throughout the mid-latitudes of both hemispheres, the prevailing winds above some 18,000 feet are from the west. These winds are the "storm tracks" or "steering winds" that pull surface weather systems around the globe. The large waves in these high winds slowly undulate and slide westward, causing the steering winds at any one place to slowly change directions between northwest and southwest—though not in a manner that is predictable over more than a week or so. In contrast, within the tropics, elongated weather disturbances called easterly waves move eastward on a fairly regular basis, temporarily altering the tradewind flow as they pass.*

winds aloft, meaning winds up at some 18,000 feet, in the upper half of the earth's atmosphere. These distinctions are important when it comes to orientation by the winds and clouds.

In the mid-latitudes of either hemisphere (30° to 60°), the winds of the upper atmosphere flow toward the east from the west. But not necessarily from due west. The band of winds aloft meanders around the globe in a serpentine path (see Figure 7-8), so the direction is just as likely to be from the northwest or southwest. Only very rarely does this band distort enough to bring these winds from east of the meridian.

The winds aloft should not be confused with the surface winds or winds just above the surface. Winds aloft are westerlies regardless of the direction of the surface winds or even changes in the surface winds. The low-pressure systems and fronts that generate the surface winds are themselves pushed eastward around the mid-latitudes of the globe by the prevailing westerlies aloft.

The value of winds aloft is their consistency. The direction of winds aloft, whether west, northwest, or southwest, is likely to remain constant for several days or longer, despite hourly and daily changes in the surface winds. If you can spot the direction of the upper winds from high clouds, you have a longer-lasting reference. In many ways, upper winds are to surface winds what swells are to waves.

The highest clouds are cirrus clouds. These are thin, wispy clouds within the winds aloft, that often appear out of a clear sky with "mare's tails" of ice crystals falling down into slower, warmer winds and streaking back as they evaporate. The orientation of the fallstreaks often shows the direction of the upper winds (see Figure 7-9).

FIGURE 7-9. *Cirrus clouds as signs of the winds aloft. Fallstreaks of cirrus cloud usually stream back, in the opposite direction of the winds aloft. This sign, however, can be difficult to read, unless they stream in the same direction in all parts of the sky, and there is also some indication of cirrus bands in line with the tails. Strong winds aloft are indicated by ragged, torn cirrus and prominent, swept-back tails, and perhaps even noticeable motion to the clouds. Weaker winds aloft have puffier, smoother, apparently stationary cirrus without tails. Generally strong winds aloft, mean the weather patterns they carry have strong surface winds.*

When cirrus clouds thicken, they sometimes aggregate into cirrocumulus that form a rippled pattern called a "mackerel sky." A similar, though bolder, wave pattern is often seen on lower, puffier altocumulus clouds. These waves in the clouds are formed by the winds aloft, just as waves on the sea are formed by surface winds. So to picture the direction of the winds aloft, think of them blowing over the clouds, making the wave patterns you see. Sometimes wave patterns in clouds divide into broad bands or streets. And sometimes some of these broad bands form a wave pattern of sorts themselves. But we should not let this broader pattern mislead us. The winds aloft are parallel to the streets and perpendicular to the shorter waves within the streets. Waves in cirrocumulus look like ripples in sand dunes, compared with altocumulus waves that look more like sheep stacked up in rows, as illustrated in Figure 7-10.

The anvil tops of towering cumulus also show the direction of winds aloft. The thunderheads build up until they reach the strong wind aloft, which blows their tops off in the direction of its flow. Sometimes you can even spot this direction from a biased shape of the tops of taller, ordinary cumulus clouds.

Cloud patterns are all temporary. A good wave pattern showing the wind direction may last only a quarter of an hour, though it could last much longer. But when it reappears in another part of the sky, you should get the same reference direction from it. The direction is most valuable when the sun is obscured — say, behind a wave-filled layer of altocumulus, or behind stratus clouds in another part of the sky. But this can't happen too often. Generally, the sun, or at least the bearing to the sun, is discernible when we can read wind directions from the clouds. The winds aloft direction is just one more reference to keep an eye on. We should use all we've got. Furthermore, even if this direction is not an aid to your steering at the time, by

FIGURE 7-10. *Waves in cirrocumulus and altocumulus clouds. Winds aloft make waves in clouds below them just as surface winds make waves in water. The direction of winds aloft is perpendicular to the waves and parallel to the bands or streets of waves. Cirrocumulus waves are more delicate, like waves in sand, than the more common altocumulus waves which appear as rows of sheep. Both patterns are transitory, forming, dissipating, and reforming again, perhaps in another part of the sky.*

117

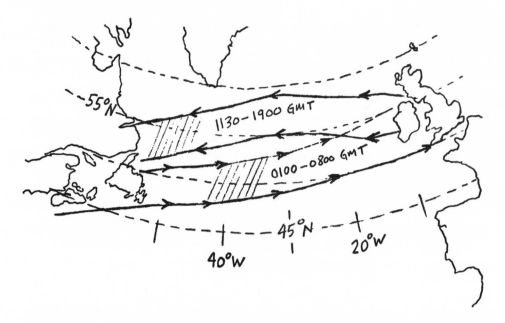

FIGURE 7-11. *Air routes over the North Atlantic. Outside of the time intervals indicated, east- or west-bound traffic may take whatever route they choose. There are no similarly scheduled lanes over the North Pacific, although the vast majority of all North Pacific crossings will be made along great-circle routes from San Francisco, Los Angeles, Seattle, or Anchorage to Tokyo or Honolulu. Air traffic sightings near airports are discussed in Section 13.1 on the signs of land.*

keeping track of it you know where to look for bad weather. Storms and fronts will approach from the direction of the winds aloft.

Birds and the directions in which they fly have a place in emergency navigation, but it's not in the middle of the ocean. You will certainly see birds no matter where you are, and it is indeed interesting to identify them, admire their flight, wish they would come aboard for a visit, and generally wonder what they are doing out there. But that's about it. Birds in the South Pacific could be headed for the Arctic Circle, or they could be just as lost as you are and maybe in more trouble. In short, isolated bird sightings when you know you are more than 80 or 90 miles offshore are not useful information for steering or for navigation. Save your hopes for help from birds till you get closer to land, when you see a lot of them. If so inclined, one might study books on sea birds, to help identify those that are known to wander the oceans, and in this way reduce the risk of raising false hopes. Birds, as a sign of land, are discussed in Section 13.1.

Airplanes are birds of another feather. Again, in some cases, they might be helpful to orientation and navigation. If you are a hundred miles or so from Bermuda or Hawaii, for example, and spot several planes during the day all headed toward or away from the same direction, then chances are you've spotted the direction to an island airport. But even in these cases, we must keep in mind that standard flight approaches or holding patterns around some airports may completely confuse airplane directions near the airport. Planes must be treated just like birds. Consider the information they suggest based on your approximate location and the number of them you see, and weigh the uncertainties carefully.

The number of plane or contrail sightings you might expect depends on your location relative to great-circle routes between major airports, though this is less certain for planes than it is for ships. Air traffic is often "weather routed" across oceans to take advantage of, or avoid, the winds aloft. Furthermore (as of 1985), air traffic across the Atlantic uses a different routing system from that used in the Pacific (see Figure 7-11), which adds an asymmetry to the topic. Of course, the number of sightings also depends on the weather.

To illustrate with a North Pacific example, the author made a 17-day voyage from Kauai to Puget Sound by a route that did not coincide with any great-circle route to the Pacific Northwest. Not a single plane was seen during the crossing. The weather was clear or partly clear about 75 percent of the time. But on a 13-day crossing from San Francisco to Maui, which did follow the great-circle route fairly closely, a plane was sighted nearly every day. On some days, as many as three were sighted. In each case, including two night sightings, the direction to Hawaii or San Francisco could be determined from the flight path. During this voyage, the weather was clear some 95 percent of the time.

Since some planes and most ships are likely to be close to great-circle routes, several sightings might give more information than just directions. If you see a lot of traffic, you might assume you are close to a great-circle route. With a pilot chart that shows these routes, you have found an approximate line of position.

Man-made satellites are a modern addition to the twilight and nighttime sky. They appear as steady lights, moving rapidly across the sky, sometimes faint but sometimes fairly bright. There is no way to use their path as a reliable source of directions. There are many satellites in the sky, going many different directions.

8

Steering in Fog
or Overcast Skies

When the sky is overcast, we usually lose the help of the sun or stars for steering, although wind and swells may still be present for temporary guides. Sometimes the sun's disk is obscured, but we can still find faint shadows if we look for them carefully. If we can find shadows, we can still use the sun for steering.

A knife blade held perpendicular to your thumb nail, or any flat-white surface, is a good way to look for faint shadows. As you rotate the blade, the shadow fans in and out just enough to give the direction of the shadow — even on days when you would swear no shadows were to be seen. But use such shadows with caution. What you are finding is the direction of the light source, which may not be the direction of the sun, depending on the uniformity of the cloud cover. A hole in the clouds off to the side of the sun may be your main source of light. There is not much you can do about this but look at the sky and make a guess. You can always find approximate directions this way; the light source can't be too far from the sun.

For more general orientation, you can often tell which side of an overcast sky the sun is on by simply noting the brighter part of the sky. The distinction is more prominent at sea than we are accustomed to on land. With the full panorama of the sky for contrast, subtle differences in shading are more discernible. During several hours on either side of either twilight, this is especially easy.

Thick weather can come with or without wind. Without steady wind or visibility to see the sea and sky, we are running out of nature's guides. But we may not have to stop just yet; we have a few manmade options to check first. Two of these, a makeshift magnetic compass and radio direction finding with an AM radio, might well keep us going through the fog. In fact, in some circumstances, either of these approaches may work well enough to be a primary source of directions, even in clear weather. But if these also fail, leaving us with no way at all to hold a steady course in a known direction, then we must simply stop and wait for the weather to clear.

8.1 How to Make a Magnetic Compass

It's a common science exercise in school. You thread a needle through a piece of straw and float it on water. The needle swings around some but finally settles down and orients in the magnetic north-south direction. That's all there is to it. And it doesn't have to be a sewing needle or straight pin. Any needlelike piece of iron will do the job: a straightened-out paper clip, a piece of bailing wire, or the pocket clip of a ballpoint pen. The only requirements are that it must be light, long, and thin, and somehow rigged to float (see Figure 8-1). Any way you can make it float will do, but try to minimize the drag in the water. You could thread the needle through small pieces of paper, bits of wood, or packing material.

Many needlelike pieces of iron will orient without extra magnetization. But you can make them work even better by rubbing them against a permanent magnet. It's not uncommon to have a magnet on board — all radio speakers contain magnets, and some screwdrivers are magnetized. A needle that has been rubbed on a magnet will orient so well that it appears to be tied to magnetic north with a spring.

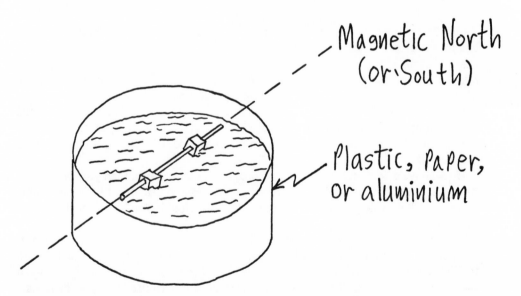

FIGURE 8-1. *A makeshift compass. The floating needle can be any long, thin piece of iron, such as a wire, strip of "tin-can" lid, straightened-out paper clip, or clip of a pen or pencil. The needle included in thin-lead mechanical pencils for cleaning the points is ideal. The water or oil container, however, should not contain iron. If a magnet is available, rub the needle on the magnet first and the compass will work much better.*

The container holding the water, however, should have no iron in its composition. Use a paper, plastic, or aluminum container. Tin cans are not good; they contain iron, which disturbs the earth's magnetic field.

A tin-can lid, on the other hand, often orients very nicely. But since it's not long and thin, it doesn't show the magnetic north-south direction. One trick you can use, providing you use it before you need it, is to draw or scratch an arrow on the oriented lid in the direction of the *North Star*. You then have a compass that points to true north from your location. You can tell if the lid orients by marking it and noting if it returns to the same direction after you disturb it.

A makeshift compass shows the magnetic north-south direction, but you have to decide which is north. The faintest shadow of the sun or shading of the sky will answer the question. And, of course, if you are to travel far by compass, you will need to know the magnetic variation for the area.

A homemade compass is not going to work as well as a ship's compass. It's un-damped, so it will swing around with the motion of the boat. You may have to hold the container in your hands to help compensate for the boat's motion. But it will work, and it is a rare boat that doesn't have the necessary materials on board to make a compass. Ways to improvise are unlimited. Take the time to play with this some, and you will be surprised to find how easy it is.

8.2 Direction Finding with a Portable Radio

Radio direction finding (RDF) is a standard technique of coastal navigation in foggy conditions or just out of sight of land. Charted radio beacons located along the coast transmit Morse-code identification letters, which can be received by special on-board RDF radios. The antenna of the RDF receiver rotates to locate the direction of the transmitting beacon. This direction can then be used for orientation just as you would use a visual bearing. Most units also receive and orient on commercial AM stations, which increases their usefulness in an emergency since these stations have a much longer range. The maximum range of most RDF stations is somewhere between 10 and 150 miles.

If you have a working RDF unit and proper nautical charts, then you can always find your way once you get into RDF range. But even if you don't have these aids, you may still be able to take advantage of this principle if you have a portable AM radio on board.

You may have noticed that an AM radio, especially an inexpensive one, gets better reception in one direction than another. When this happens, you can rotate the radio to find the strongest reception. The sensitivity of the internal antenna depends on the orientation of the antenna relative to the radio waves emitted from the broadcast station. The effect is exactly the same as the one used in navigational RDF units (see Figure 8-2).

There are two ways to orient the AM radio. You can rotate it to find either the strongest or the weakest reception. The direction of minimum reception, called the

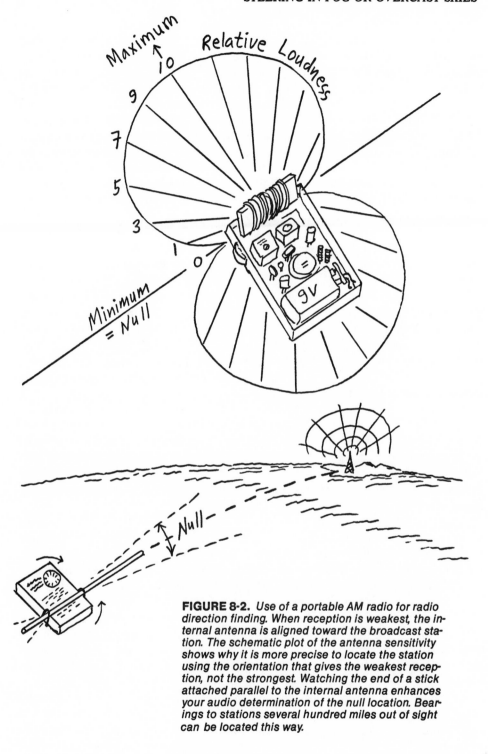

FIGURE 8-2. *Use of a portable AM radio for radio direction finding. When reception is weakest, the internal antenna is aligned toward the broadcast station. The schematic plot of the antenna sensitivity shows why it is more precise to locate the station using the orientation that gives the weakest reception, not the strongest. Watching the end of a stick attached parallel to the internal antenna enhances your audio determination of the null location. Bearings to stations several hundred miles out of sight can be located this way.*

null, is the better one to use for direction finding. The direction of the maximum reception is much less precise — at maximum reception, you can rotate the radio through 30° or more before noticing a change in loudness. The null, on the other hand, which is at right angles to the maximum, can usually be found to within a few degrees — if a null is present. Sometimes the null is so sharp that the station will completely shut off when you rotate the radio a few degrees; but at other times, or for other stations, there may be no null at all. If you can't find a null, you simply can't use that station at that time. If you can't find a null for any station from the deck of a metal boat, try a different location on deck. It may be that the boat itself is interfering with the reception, though this is rarely a problem on non-metal boats, regardless of the rigging.

To find the direction of the radio station once you've found a null, you need to know which way the internal antenna is oriented. The antenna is a coil of wire wrapped around a ferrite rod inside the radio. You have to open the radio once to check this. At the null, the ferrite rod points to the broadcast antenna of the radio station.

You won't be able to tell, however, if the rod points toward or away from the station; the rod is symmetric and the null occurs in both directions. Usually, you will know the rough direction of the station, north or south, for example, and that's all you need in order to remove this uncertainty. If you don't know your position relative to that station, look for other stations that may help. You can also eliminate this uncertainty by carrying out a standard running fix using the radio bearings as explained later in Section 13.4.

Remember that the broadcast antenna is not always located near the broadcast station. Nautical charts show the locations of many AM towers and also give the frequency and call letters of the station. But even if you are unsure of the location of the broadcast antenna, a good null still gives you a relative direction to steer by during the fog. If this is your goal, hunt around on the dial to find the station with the best null. Headed toward land, you may just find a station in the direction you want to go.

You may even be able to get more out of your makeshift RDF than just a relative direction to steer by. You might, for example, try for a true direction to a city, or even a rough position fix from the intersection of two or more true bearings. In doing this, however, there are several precautions to keep in mind. First and foremost, your pocket AM radio won't be as reliable as a regular RDF unit. The receiver and broadcast-antenna placement are not designed for this job. If it works at all, we should be grateful. Secondly, the normal precautions used with regular RDF still apply. Bearings will be most uncertain at dawn and dusk, and signals that reach you after crossing or passing by mountainous terrain are not as reliable for directions as those from unobstructed stations. These precautions apply even if the station shows a good null.

On the other hand, an island station can provide very useful directions to the island for hundreds of miles out to sea. I have received a Honolulu station at 420 nautical miles off that oriented very nicely with a $6 radio. From then on, that little radio would have taken us to Hawaii blindfolded. But as with all techniques described in this book, using an AM radio for direction finding should be practiced before you need it. For this application, cheap radios are better than higher-quality

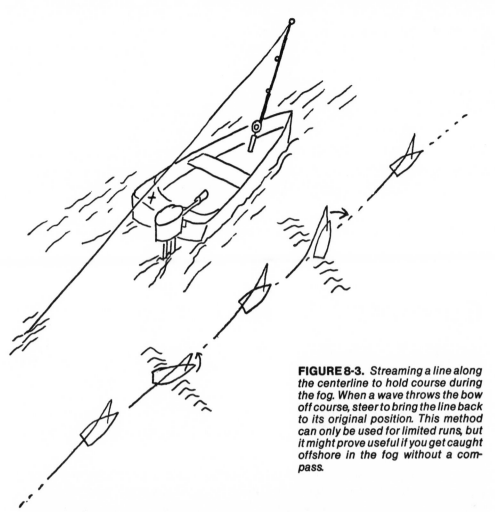

FIGURE 8-3. *Streaming a line along the centerline to hold course during the fog. When a wave throws the bow off course, steer to bring the line back to its original position. This method can only be used for limited runs, but it might prove useful if you get caught offshore in the fog without a compass.*

radios that have extra circuits and better antennas that remove the null. If you pay good money for a radio, you don't want it to shut off when you rotate it 5°.

8.3 Streaming a Line along the Centerline

A fishing line or other long, light line can be a valuable aid to steering through thick weather in some cases. It might, for example, be especially valuable to a small boat caught offshore without a compass when the fog sets in. It is something to keep in mind in any emergency situation where visibility is reduced.

Simply stream the line along the centerline, from the bow or amidships, back and over the stern. Let out a long length of line and then steer to keep the line centered on the transom. See the illustration in Figure 8-3. You can steer a long distance this way, depending on sea conditions. But you could also go in a large circle if you err in the same direction continuously. Keep an eye on the wind, if there is any, and the swells or waves for help as references. In choppy water, this trick gives you a quick way to get back to your original heading after a wave throws you off.

9
Currents

Assuming emergency orientation and helmsmanship are under control and we are diligent about recording course changes, the main uncertainty in emergency navigation is likely to be caused by currents. You can find boat speed and heading by several means, but these won't give your correct course if the water beneath you is also moving. The problem is much like trying to locate your position in a large bathroom when you know exactly where you are in the bathtub but not where the bathtub is.

Once you are well into a current, there is generally no way to detect its presence short of doing precise position fixes at timed intervals. Floating objects in a current may drift toward or away from you, but this is due to difference in leeway (windage), not to the effect of the current. Current moves everything in the water at the same rate.

Currents can exist in any body of water. For the most part, currents are driven by the winds and gravitational pull of the sun and moon. Current strengths and directions are also strongly affected by the earth's rotation and by the shape of the oceans, shoreline, and bottom, as well as the salinity of the water. For keeping track of currents, it is convenient to divide currents into three categories: ocean currents, tidal currents, and wind-driven currents — though, strictly speaking, this is a somewhat artificial classification since the three are not fully independent. The direction in which a current flows is called its set; the speed of a current is called its drift. Drift is given in knots or miles per day.

9.1 Ocean Currents

Ocean currents are the prevailing circulation of the oceans, which generally follows the prevailing circulation of ocean winds. These currents remain fairly constant over large spans of the oceans and over long periods of time, although there are seasonal variations in the set and drift of many ocean currents. There are also unpredictable, short-term variations (that is, lasting several days) in all ocean currents. The general circulation of the oceans is clockwise in the Northern Hemisphere and counterclockwise in the Southern Hemisphere (see Figure 9-1). Ocean currents are strongest along the perimeters of the oceans and are usually weak or non-existent in mid-ocean — the equator is considered here to be the perimeter that divides the southern and northern oceans.

Throughout most of the oceans of the world, the currents are not strong. A global average might be about half a knot. But there are notable exceptions. The famous Gulf Stream in the western North Atlantic and its counterpart, the Kuroshio current, in the western North Pacific average over 2 knots and can reach speeds in excess of 3 or 4 knots on occasion. Equatorial currents and countercurrents around the world are also strong. These tropical currents average over 1 knot, but they can accelerate significantly in the vicinity of island groups.

In special cases, the presence of an ocean or coastal current can be detected as we sail into or out of it. The boundaries of the Gulf Stream, for example, are marked by a distinct change in water color — from the gray-green of the Atlantic to the indigo blue of the current. The Gulf Stream is also noticeably warmer than neighboring waters, especially at higher latitudes, which means there are also more squalls and gales over the current. The Gulf Stream often carries with it large amounts of floating seaweed. And in northerly winds (against the current), the seas of the Gulf Stream are noticeably rougher than neighboring waters. Similar properties mark the boundaries of the Kuroshio current. But these currents are unique in their prominence. Other prevailing currents around the world may show some of these properties, but boundary distinctions are likely to be less prominent.

On any ocean or coastal voyage, it is the responsibility of the navigator to study the currents before and during the cruise. Ocean currents are listed in catalogues and atlases, which predict the currents at various locations and seasons. The best readily available source of ocean currents are the U.S (or British) Pilot Charts. Among other valuable data, they provide ocean currents pictorially, showing the average set and drift of ocean currents by the month or quarter.

In using any current atlas, however, it must be remembered that it provides predictions based only on the average of many observations over a period of years. At any given time, the actual current present may be different from the listed value. As a rule of thumb, consider predicted ocean currents to be correct to within plus or minus 50 percent. That is, if a current drift is listed as 12 miles a day, to be safe, assume that it could be anywhere from 6 to 18 miles a day — the average, plus or minus half the average. Generally, the predicted direction of ocean currents will be fairly close to the actual direction, within some 30° or so, but even this is not

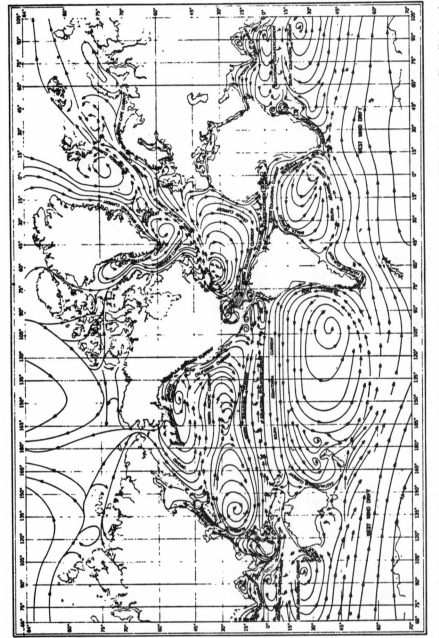

FIGURE 9-1. *Major ocean currents of the world. The patterns shown are for winter months. The figure is from Bowditch, vol. 1, which discusses each of the currents in some detail. Pilot charts (sections of which are shown in Figures 1-1 and 4-3) show the currents in more detail for individual oceans.*

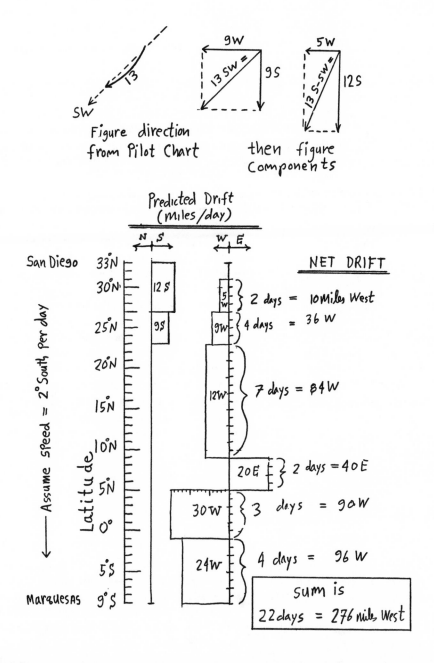

FIGURE 9-2. *A current log figured from a pilot chart. Pilot charts show currents as arrows flying with the set of the current, labeled with the drift in nautical miles per day. First lay out your planned route on the pilot chart, and record the currents and latitudes at which they change. Then figure the components of the currents as indicated in the figure, and from these make a plot or table of the results. Then with an estimated speed, you can figure your net set over different legs of the voyage. This example is for a July run from San Diego to the Marquesas at an average speed of 6 knots. The data are from U.S. and British pilot charts. Note that in this example, I would want to make some easting before I got to the southeast trades to compensate for the large westerly set.*

guaranteed. In some areas, deep countercurrents sporadically surface, making the predicted direction as wrong as possible.

From the point of view of emergency preparation, the value of studying the currents before departing cannot be overemphasized. One convenient way to do this is to lay off your intended course on a pilot chart, and then read off and list the east-west and north-south components of the current for each 5° or so of latitude along your route. This exercise gives you a close look at the currents and how they might enter into your navigation of the voyage — with or without instruments. See the illustration in Figure 9-2.

Such a study would show, for example, that on a cruise from San Diego to the Marquesas, the predominant set of the current is to the west throughout the voyage, with only a brief interruption by the equatorial countercurrent. At an average speed of 6 knots, this voyage would take about three weeks, and the net drift to the west would be about 280 miles. This is clearly enough to miss the islands if you had to make much of the crossing by dead reckoning alone and did not take currents into account.

It is only remotely possible that you might ever end up adrift without any means of power, but should this occur, your knowledge of the local currents could well determine the outcome of the adventure. With only emergency navigation to go by, it is essentially impossible to measure the currents present. You simply must have some prior knowledge on which to base a reasonable guess. Remember that currents tend to flow with the prevailing winds, so if all you can make to weather is a knot or so through the water, you must look downwind for a route to safety, even if it is further to land that way. See, for example, Dougal Robertson's account of his emergency voyage given in his book *Survive the Savage Sea* (London: Elek Books Ltd., 1973).

9.2 Tidal Currents

Tidal currents are the flow of water associated with the rise and fall of the tides. They have no influence on ocean sailing except near the coast or island channels. Open channel currents tend to increase, subside, and reverse with the tides, in contrast to tidal currents along a coast, which are more likely to rotate with much less change in strength, although there tends to be an along-shore bias to many tidal current rotations — meaning that the current direction spends more time along shore than toward or away from shore. Tidal currents along a complicated coastline may have speeds of several knots, though a knot or so might be the average along a smooth coast. In either case, since the direction rotates, you are left with little net displacement over a day's time. Generally, tide-height ranges and associated currents are larger at higher latitudes.

If your voyage ends at a river entrance, remember there can be dangerous breaking waves at river bars during the ebb cycle, especially if a strong swell is running. Approaching the back of the breakers from sea, you may hear them before you see them. Also, at highly constricted bay entrances, you may find maximum currents near high and low water on the coast, which is just the opposite of tidal current behavior near large open channels. On the ebb, for example, the constriction prevents water from leaving the bay as fast as it leaves the seaward side, so the slope of the water across the constriction builds toward a maximum near low water on the coast, which in turn causes maximum flow through the constriction.

Tidal currents along a coast are given in regional *Tidal Current Tables* (NOAA); they are also discussed more generally in the *Coast Pilots* (NOAA) for American waters and in the *U.S. Sailing Directions* (DMAHTC) for other areas.

9.3 Wind-Driven Currents

On any waters, from oceans to inland lakes, if the wind blows long enough, it starts the water moving. Current generated by local, temporary winds is called wind-driven current. The interaction between wind and surface waters is a complicated one with many parameters, so for estimates of these currents we must make do with general rules of thumb rather than precise formulas.

As a rule of thumb, if the wind blows steadily for half a day or more, it generates a surface current with a speed of approximately 3 percent of the wind strength. In open waters of the Northern Hemisphere, the direction of the current will be roughly 30° to the right of the wind direction, meaning that if the wind is a northerly (toward 180°), the wind-driven current would set toward roughly 210°. In the Southern Hemisphere, this current is to the left of the wind, since the deflection comes from the Coriolis force.

By this rule, a wind of 20 knots for half of a day generates a current of 0.6 knots. We can't count on this rule to give the speed precisely since there are too many variables involved — it works better in strong winds than in light winds, but we care about these the most anyway. The rule is certainly reliable to within 50 percent. That is, in the 20-knot example, it is unlikely that the current would be less than 0.3 knots or greater than 0.9 knots. If the wind blows much longer than a day or so, you might expect the current to build slightly. In long, heavy rains, wind-driven currents are likely to be even stronger, since brackish surface water slides more easily over the denser salt water below.

The significance of wind-driven current is not always so much in its strength, but in its effect on other currents and on our progress to weather in strong winds (Section 10.4). If we read in sailing directions, for example, that currents in some coastal area vary from 1 to 3 knots, we might guess that the upper limit (or slightly above it) applies when strong winds blow with the current and the lower limit (or slightly below it) applies when strong winds blow against the current.

9.4 Coastal Currents

We can consider the region of coastal currents to be within some 20 miles of an island or coast or, alternatively, well onto the continental shelf, if it is prominent.

Generally, coastal currents are the most difficult to predict. In these coastal regions, currents might be dominated by any one of the three types of currents or even be composed of a combination of all three (ocean, tidal, and wind-driven currents) — or they may be caused by still another effect. A strong onshore wind, for example, can sometimes pile up water against prominent headlands, which in turn creates significant currents when the wind dies and the water flows back to level the surface. In such circumstances, you might find strong currents without wind or tidal changes.

Coastal currents can vary significantly in strength at any one location and vary rapidly and irregularly from point to point along a coast. Coastal or island currents tend to be stronger closer to the shore if the current has an onshore component to its direction, as many do. Sailing directions and coast pilots are a good source of coastal current information.

In many places around the world, on-shelf coastal currents are primarily wind-driven currents. If the wind blows to the north, currents flow north; with wind to the south, currents flow south. This can be valuable information, since we can use the rule of thumb for strength estimates, but, more important, it helps in interpreting sailing directions. On the Pacific Coast shelf (Washington to California), for example, sailing directions often describe the near-coastal currents as southerly in the summer and northerly in the winter. The currents behave in this general way because prevailing winds of the region are from the north in the summer and from the south in the winter. A more informative description might be that these are wind-driven currents. The primary ocean circulation well off the shelf, however, is persistently to the south in this region throughout the year.

The sea state can often indicate a strong coastal current. A strong current flowing against the wind causes an enhanced chop and steepness to the seas, whereas a current flowing with the wind diminishes the seas just as dramatically. To recognize the effect, however, requires some experience at sea, since you must be able to conclude that the seas are not consistent with the winds. More generally, in a strong coastal current you might notice "confused" seas with not just steeper waves but also more frequent big ones, or frequent waves running perpendicular to the wind. These are dangerous conditions that often signal the presence of a focused "current jet" — a somewhat rare coastal current effect similar to the focused jet stream within the winds aloft.

10

Dead Reckoning

The word "dead" in dead reckoning derives from the abbreviation "ded," for deduced. Dead reckoning means deduced reckoning. To navigate by dead reckoning, you deduce a new position from an earlier one using on-board measurements of speed and direction. The modern abbreviation for dead reckoning is "DR." If I sail northwest for 20 miles, my DR position is 20 miles northwest of where I started. But it's not quite as simple as it sounds.

Chances are I won't be exactly 20 miles, exactly to the northwest of where I started. Currents; leeway; inaccurate helmsmanship; compass errors; log, time, or speedometer errors; and simple blunders in logbook entries can all contribute to errors in a DR position. If it weren't for these factors, we could dead reckon our way across an ocean. These errors may each be small over a short run, but on a long passage small persistent errors accumulate. An error of a few hundred miles after a voyage of a thousand miles is a small percentage error, but it could easily make the difference between finding or missing your destination.

Accurate dead reckoning requires accurate on-board instruments and diligent recording of all course changes. In an emergency, however, you may be left with no instruments at all — steering by the stars and gauging boat speed by your wake and passing debris. Nevertheless, in most circumstances, even makeshift dead reckoning will still be your most reliable means of keeping track of position for distances up to several hundred miles. In Chapters 11 and 12, we cover methods of finding and keeping track of position using the sun and stars. These celestial methods, though, require some practice and memory work to be useful. Even then, their accuracy without proper instruments will rarely be as high as careful dead reckoning for

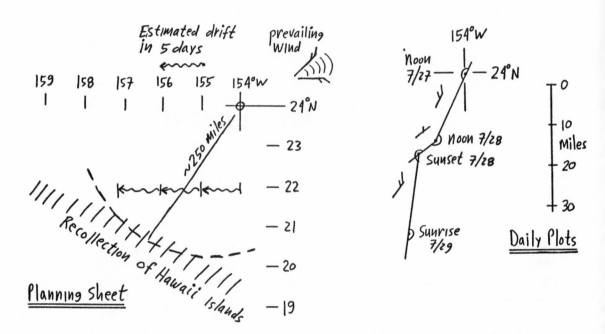

FIGURE 10-1. *Makeshift DR plots. The planning sheet shows a hypothetical emergency occurring some 250 miles north of Hawaii. The location of the islands is drawn in as recalled, as are the current drifts and prevailing winds. In this example, the immediate navigational goal would be to make at least 2° of the south in less than 15 days, to keep from drifting over the top of the islands. Daily plots help you keep track of position and monitor your progress.*

voyages of a few hundred miles. The value of celestial sights becomes apparent when you must make a long voyage — long in time or distance. In this case, the celestial sights are useful in correcting or confirming your dead reckoning.

Besides steering, which we have already covered, the main tasks in emergency dead reckoning are finding speed through the water and keeping track of course changes. It's not absolutely necessary to have a watch to do either of these, but it helps tremendously. Some sailors can tell the speed of their boat to within half a knot from the sail trim, heel, and wake. But drifting in a raft or sailing your own boat under jury rig, it is easier to judge speed accurately if you have a watch.

The main value of a watch for dead reckoning, however, is to keep track of how long you have sailed on any one course. It is better to know it was 18 hours than to guess it was about one day. Without a watch, you won't even know how long one day is. Time flies when you're having fun, but it drags on forever when you're in trouble. We can't rely on our own ability to judge time at sea when we are under stress. In a long storm, it is not uncommon to even lose track of the day. Sections 12.3 and 14.3 cover methods of checking the time and date from the sun, moon, and stars.

If you have a long voyage ahead of you, it is necessary to keep a written record or make a "DR plot" of your progress (see Figure 10-1). Without a record of some kind, it is easier to quit caring. After several course changes, you may lose track of your course and, with it, your position. Knowing where you are is not only a question of safety; it is also a morale booster. It is just one more way to keep in control of the situation.

Dead reckoning is vital to emergency navigation, but even the best dead reckoning is useless if you don't know where you started from. If you don't know where you are to begin with, you must start your dead reckoning from a position you read from the stars, and in general this means you start with an uncertainty of some 100 miles, or possibly even more if you have not practiced the celestial methods. Going to sea without wearing a watch is risky, but not knowing where you are when you have the ability to do so is downright dangerous.

10.1 Finding Boat Speed

One way to find boat speed is to time the passage of anything floating on the water. If your boat length is 30 feet and it takes 10 seconds to pass a piece of driftwood, then your speed is 30 feet per 10 seconds, or 3 feet per second. The only job left is to convert this feet-per-second speed to knots (nautical miles per hour). A nautical mile is about 6,000 feet, and an hour is 3,600 seconds. So 1 knot is the same as 6,000 feet per 3,600 seconds, or 10 feet per 6 seconds, which means 1 foot per second is six-tenths of a knot. In equation form, this reads

Speed (in knots) = 0.6 x Speed (in feet per second).

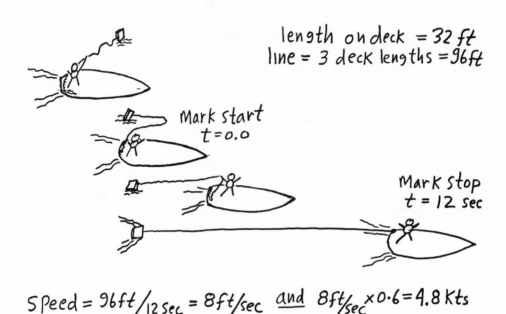

length on deck = 32 ft
line = 3 deck lengths = 96ft

Mark start
t = 0.0

Mark stop
t = 12 sec

Speed = 96ft/12 sec = 8ft/sec and 8ft/sec × 0.6 = 4.8 Kts

FIGURE 10-2. *Measuring boat speed with a chip log. With a watch and some practice, the measurements are easy and accurate.*

If you are moving at 8 feet per second, your speed is 4.8 knots. Ten feet per second is the same as 6 knots.

You can time anything that floats: debris, seaweed, even a patch of foam. Or throw the marker off the bow, preferably tied to the stern by a long, light line so you can use it again. Timing the passage is no problem if you have a watch. Without a watch, you must count off the seconds as best you can. If you haven't tried it, test yourself now with a watch to get the pace. The standard method of counting, "One thousand one, one thousand two, . . .," works pretty well. Remember that any speed measurement should be made several times. An average result is always more accurate than a single measurement.

Timing a marker as it passes the boat works well, providing the passage times are at least 5 or 6 seconds. For shorter times, results are less accurate. The way around this is to make the reference length longer using a light line. A fishing line or a light sheet is ideal (see Figure 10-2). Tie an object to the line, then measure off 50 to 100 feet of line — the longer the better, but sea conditions or available line may determine what you use. To measure the line, it's convenient to know the length of your outstretched arms, fingertip to fingertip. This length (the original fathom measurement) is about 6 feet on many people. Or use your height or the boat length. To get your speed, tie the line to the stern and cast the marker and line off the bow. Start counting when the marker passes the stern and stop when you begin to tow it. A plastic bottle partially filled with water makes a good marker. Your speed in feet per second is the line length divided by the time it takes to extend the line.

Another way to measure speed is to make an old-fashioned log line and count knots in the line as it streams over the stern — the method that gave us the word "knot" for speed. You can improvise the knot spacing to suit your needs, but here is one way to do it. Tie some object to the line that floats but still has drag in the water (like the partially filled plastic bottle). Then 20 feet or so from the object tie the first knot, maybe marked with a piece of cloth. Then every 10 feet after that, tie another knot.

Fake the line out carefully so it can run freely, then cast off the float, letting the line stream through your hand. Start counting when the first marker passes your hand and then stop the line at 6 seconds. Haul in the line and count the knots, including the fraction left at your hand. The number of knots that passed your hand in 6 seconds is your speed in knots. If five and a half knots passed by, your speed was 5.5 knots. Or better still, especially at faster speeds, count to 12 and divide the number of knots by two. With practice, this method is as accurate as a knotmeter.

For optimum accuracy, it's important to check the boat speed often. If your speed changes by 2 knots and you haven't noted it for 3 hours, you have lost 6 miles in accuracy. This doesn't have to happen very often before you develop serious position errors. It also helps to have frequent speed checks to determine your average speed. With a careful record, you can distinguish short-term fluctuations from the long-term changes that affect your average speed.

Once you have your average speed, distance run is just the average speed multiplied by the number of hours at that speed. If your average speed was 4 knots from 1000 to 1600 and 2 knots from 1600 to 2000, then in these 10 hours you have run (4 x 6) + (2 x 4), or 32 miles.

It is important to do the very best you can with your dead reckoning. Use every bit of information you have. Basic dead reckoning is your most powerful tool in an emergency. You can go a long way with it, if you keep up with it constantly. There will be errors of course (you can't avoid them all), but if you record all speed and course changes you know about, then chances are the ones you overlook will cancel each other out, as we show later in Section 14.1.

Long storms are the enemies of accurate dead reckoning. In a storm, you have a lot to think about besides navigation, and your course and speed may change significantly. It's easier to say than do, but try to record the times of course changes and occasionally estimate your speed. Then, after things calm down, do your best to put it all back together. Accurate dead reckoning is hard work, and there is certainly some luck involved. But remember the old saying, "The harder you work, the more luck you'll have."

10.2 DR Errors from Speed and Direction

An obvious goal of navigation is to know where you are. A less obvious, but equally important, goal is to know how well you know where you are. In other words, to know your accuracy. This is especially true in emergency navigation, since so much of it depends on estimates or makeshift measurements. If you figure you are 50 miles offshore, chances are you are confident it is closer to 50 than to 100. But how sure are you that it's 50 and not 70, or 30? When a critical decision must be made on the basis of your navigation, you should be prepared to estimate the accuracy of your position.

It is helpful to think of position accuracy in terms of percentages. A position uncertainty of 5 miles represents a high level of accuracy if you have traveled 100 miles, but your accuracy is poor if your position is uncertain by 5 miles after traveling only 10 miles. In the first case, the accuracy is 5 percent; in the second case, it is 50 percent. A DR accuracy of within a few percentage points would be very good, using the best on-board equipment available. With only limited instruments, or maybe none at all, we have to consider 20 percent or so as reasonable accuracy.

Also, by thinking of your DR accuracy in terms of percentages, it is easier to keep track of how position uncertainty increases over a long voyage. For example, suppose I have a compass, so I know my course accurately, but I have no log or knotmeter. If I decide I am figuring my distance traveled to an accuracy of 20 percent, it means my position grows uncertain by 20 miles for every 100 miles I travel, which is the same as a 2-mile uncertainty for each 10 miles traveled. With this accuracy, if I start out from a known position and travel what I think is 10 miles, then I can be fairly confident that I have covered at least 8 miles and probably less than 12 miles. After traveling 30 miles, I must assume that my position could be off by plus or minus 6 miles, since 20 percent of 30 miles is 6 miles. Naturally, one should be conservative when estimating accuracy.

Errors in a DR position can be caused by errors in the distance run or errors in the course direction. Speed and time-on-course errors affect only the distance run, while steering and leeway errors affect only the course direction. Currents, on the other hand, affect both the distance run and the direction.

Errors in speed can be caused by errors in the reference length used to measure the speed (boat length or line length) or by errors in timing the passage of this length. Your boat length or your height are known accurately, so line lengths can be measured with a little practice to within 5 percent accuracy.

Timing with a watch would essentially produce no error if it weren't for the uncertainties in the starting and stopping times. These add up to a possible error of at least 1 second. Put another way, it's hard to time any interval we might be interested in and obtain a result with less than 1 second of error, plus or minus. For a time interval of 5 seconds, your timing uncertainty is 1 out of 5, or 20 percent. This is the reason for trying to keep the time interval as long as possible when measuring boat speed. If you double the time interval, your percentage error in timing is cut in half, since the 1-second starting and stopping uncertainty doesn't change.

In good conditions, we may have about a 5 percent error in length and about a 10

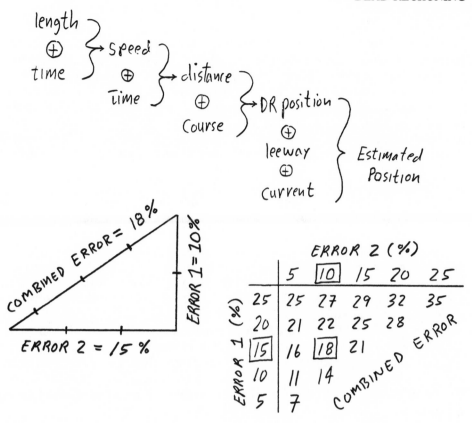

FIGURE 10-3. *Combining independent errors. Independent errors (uncertainties) expressed as percentages add like the sides of a right triangle. The final uncertainty in our estimated position is the combination of the several factors shown. A watch is extremely valuable since it essentially eliminates the timing errors that lead to distance run.*

percent error in timing. This translates into a total speed error of about 11 percent in good conditions. You may say my arithmetic is strange but it isn't. When you have two independent sources of error and one is much larger than the other, the combined error is not the sum of the two but closer to the larger of the two errors. This is a mathematical result that takes into account the possibility that the errors could be in opposite directions.

From a statistical point of view, two independent errors (uncertainties) combine as the square root of the sum of their squares — in the last example, 11 equals the square root of (5 x 5 + 10 x 10). Generally, this is not easy to figure in one's head, but this prescription (coincidentally) is the same one used to figure the hypotenuse of a right triangle. Using this analogy, we have a simple way of figuring the combined effect of two errors. As illustrated in Figure 10-3, just sketch a right triangle, using any convenient scale, with the sides proportional to the two errors. The length of the hypotenuse on the same scale is then the combined error. The example in Figure 10-3 shows that a 10 percent error and a 15 percent error combine to an 18 percent error.

Using this procedure, it is easy to see why we can simply neglect the smaller error if it is much less than about half the larger one. In finding speed, if I have a 5 percent error in length and a 20 percent error in time, I can forget about the 5 percent error. My final uncertainty in speed will be about 20 percent. On the other hand, if I must combine two errors of about the same size, the final error is about halfway between the sum of the errors and the error itself. Two 10 percent errors add up to a final error of about 15 percent (a right triangle would show the exact answer is 14 percent).

You may also wonder why we bother with this much detail. The reason is we simply can't avoid it. We must be able to realistically assess our ability to navigate some particular route and then estimate the accuracy of our position along it. What we know well and what we don't will vary with the circumstances, and we should be prepared to figure out how the particular uncertainties at hand will affect our navigation. If we must choose between heading for an isolated island 100 miles off versus a continent or string of islands 500 miles off, we had better know beforehand what our chances are of finding the isolated island.

So far, we have used one set of "good conditions" to illustrate boat-speed accuracy — with a watch, a long line, and calm or moderate seas, you can figure your speed to an accuracy of about 10 percent or so. Much better than this is hard to do, but with some effort and luck you shouldn't have to do much worse under these conditions. A 20 percent uncertainty in speed, for example, is pretty large — at 5 knots, it would mean I couldn't tell if I was going 4 knots or 6 knots.

Now, how do you know how well you are doing? For runs of less than a few hundred miles (before the stars "begin to move"), the answer, unfortunately, is that you never really do, until you make your landfall or get some other confirmation. But you can test for *consistency* by looking at the spread in the values you use to get the average. In measuring speed by log line when you know the 10-foot spacings are accurate, the only uncertainty comes from the timing. At 12 seconds, we estimate this could be about 1 out of 12, or about 8 percent. If the average of several consecutive measurements is 5 knots, then the individual speeds should vary at most by 8 percent of 5, or 0.4 knots, between 5.4 and 4.6. If the spread is larger, we may not be timing to 8 percent accuracy or our speed is not constant to within 8 percent, and we should increase the uncertainty accordingly. We can't claim a speed accuracy of 8 percent if we can't reproduce the measurement to within an accuracy of about 8 percent using this method. Of course, our speed error would be even larger (and undetected) if the knot spacing was not as accurate as we thought.

Bear in mind, however, that regardless of how the average value and the individual values turn out, you can't realistically expect, with these methods, to find average boat speed over an extended run with a level of accuracy higher than about 10 percent. You may find the speed at any one time more accurately, but it is unlikely that you can check it often enough to claim an average speed with greater than 10 percent accuracy.

Errors in distance run are figured the same way as speed errors. You combine the uncertainty in speed with the uncertainty in the time at that speed. If my speed is 5 knots with an uncertainty of 10 percent, and I run for 10 hours exactly, then the distance run is 50 miles with an uncertainty of 10 percent, or 5 miles. The time is accurate in this case.

If the speed is 5 knots with a 10 percent uncertainty, and I run for *about* 10 hours, but I couldn't say for sure that it wasn't 9 or 11 hours, then I should take into account this extra uncertainty. Plus or minus 1 hour out of 10 is another 10 percent uncertainty. So in this case, I would still figure I ran 50 miles, but now the uncertainty is about 14 percent of 50, which is 7 miles.

Again, this may appear pretty detailed for emergency navigation — on a 50-mile run it's unlikely that the difference between a 10 percent and 14 percent uncertainty will make much difference to your decision making. But we must learn to appreciate that these details are generally more important in emergency navigation than in routine work. On a long voyage, it could easily be quite important as you approach land to know whether you have been navigating with, say, 20 percent or 50 percent accuracy. In the one case, your position uncertainty would be 40 miles after traveling 200 miles; in the other, it would be 100 out of 200. Furthermore, on still longer voyages when we must rely on makeshift celestial observations, our DR position and its accuracy must be continually compared with the celestial position and its own uncertainties. The more accurate our dead reckoning is, the better we can interpret the celestial observations.

The ultimate accuracy we need, of course, always depends on what we are looking for. In the end, we must always compare our navigation accuracy with the visible range of our target. This topic is covered in Sections 13.1 and 13.2.

This discussion of errors should show why it's so important to record the times of all course or speed changes. This is one source of error that can be avoided by keeping a close watch on your dead reckoning. The value of a watch is obvious. Even if you don't know the correct time, a running watch greatly improves your dead reckoning.

Emergency steering and direction errors were discussed briefly in Section 3.3. The accuracy attainable depends on several factors, and typically it will vary from day to day and throughout the day, depending on the sea and sky. In many cases, steering errors tend to average out, which means the longer you strive for a particular course, checking and adjusting its direction regularly, the more accurate it becomes.

Taking into account the rotation of the sky, which helps average out some errors, the suggested rule of thumb for steering accuracy was about 12°, which translates into a lateral off-course position uncertainty of about 20 percent, as shown earlier in Figure 3-7. In other words, each 100 miles you travel adds 20 miles of uncertainty to the left or right of your position. This estimate assumes you know your *average* heading to with an *average* uncertainty of plus or minus 12°. This is not as difficult to achieve as it may first appear, but it does take practice. If you are not confident you are doing this well on a particular course, it would be safer to increase your direction uncertainty accordingly. Plus or minus 18° is equivalent to a 30 percent position uncertainty. A graphic procedure for estimating lateral position uncertainties from course uncertainties is illustrated in Figure 10-4.

On the other hand, if you have *Polaris* or other favorable stars to steer by, you may well do better than 12°. The best way to prepare yourself to gauge this accuracy

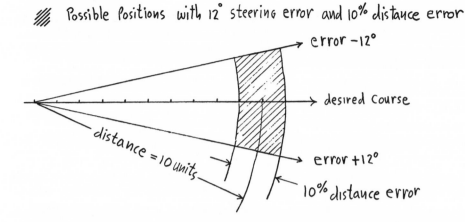

FIGURE 10-4. *Graphical way to find the position uncertainty caused by errors in steering and distance run. Without log or knotmeter, a 10-percent distance error is good work, but in many circumstances, and with some practice, we should be able to achieve better accuracy than 12° on the average course held without a compass. The distance off course we expect to be after sailing with a specific, constant course error can be determined as in Figure 3-7.*

is to practice the methods of Chapters 5 and 6 before you need them — when you have a compass and can tell precisely how well you are doing. Simply treat it as a game during your routine sailing — it is more than a trivial pursuit.

We can now make an estimate of total DR accuracy by combining direction accuracy with distance-run accuracy. Do this using the right-triangle rule discussed earlier for combining errors. If you run 100 miles at 15 percent accuracy, steering at 20 percent accuracy, your combined position uncertainty would be about 25 percent, or 25 miles. This means that after 100 miles you could be anywhere within a circle with a radius of 25 miles, drawn around your DR position (see Figure 10-5). This level of accuracy might be considered a typical one to expect with some work and careful DR records.

If our star steering is weaker, say about 30 percent accuracy (heading uncertainty of about 18°), but we work harder on boat speed and get it down to 10 percent accuracy, then we are left with about 32 percent navigation accuracy, and our circle of uncertainty increases to 32 miles after 100 miles. With good star steering or favorable stars, we might expect 20 percent accuracy on direction and, with good boat-speed measurements and careful course records, 10 percent accuracy on distance run, leaving an optimum accuracy of some 22 percent. It is unrealistic to hope for much better than that over a long run, in the best of conditions — which means no significant unknown currents and not going to weather in strong winds.

Using the recommended 25 percent navigation accuracy as a typical goal, our position would be uncertain by about 75 miles after traveling 300 miles. But, as we shall see in Chapter 11, we should be able to read our latitude from the stars to within some 60 miles with practice, so we need not let latitude become uncertain by as much as 75 miles at any time or over any run. Our longitude accuracy depends on our watch. If we know GMT, we can do even better than 60 miles on it, but if we don't know GMT, our longitude uncertainty will generally increase as our DR

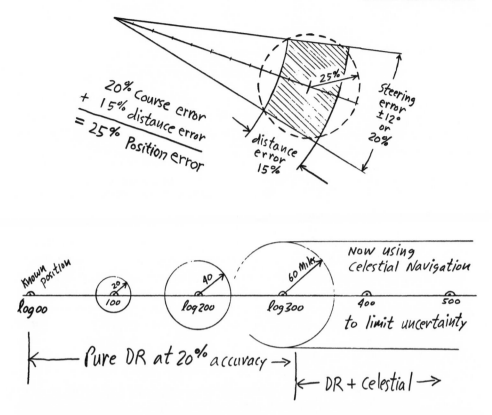

FIGURE 10-5. *Position errors as percentages and how our position uncertainty increases with distance run. By expressing steering (course) error as a percentage, we can figure position uncertainty without plotting, using the rules of Figure 10-3. This is, however, clearly an approximation, since the circle of uncertainty we figure this way does not coincide with the shaded area of uncertainty that we figure directly from course and distance. However, the convenience of the percentage method far outweighs its lack of precision. Using percentages, we can more easily tell what navigation factor is most important, and we can judge how far off course we might be after a given distance run—which is critical in determining the best route to safety. After a few hundred miles, it will pay to know the celestial methods that tell us latitude and longitude to within some 60 miles. Without knowledge of celestial methods, DR position uncertainty would continue to grow.*

uncertainty increases. Ways to minimize this if we start from a known position are covered in Chapter 12.

One final point should be stressed about accuracy in navigation, which is again a mathematical result of statistics. Always bear in mind that we have been discussing here estimates of how much your dead reckoning *could* be off as a result of measurement errors, not how much it *will* be off. Not counting unforeseen errors in a persistent direction, it is unlikely that you will be off as much as these estimates show. Roughly speaking, there is a 50 percent chance that your actual error will be less than half of the estimated amounts. If we made that 100-mile run at 25 percent accuracy over and over again, more than half the time we would be off course at the end by less than 12 miles or so, not 25 miles. But we are only going to do it once, so we can't count on anything better than we've figured.

10.3 DR Errors from Currents and Leeway

Since emergency navigation usually won't be accurate enough to measure the set and drift of typical ocean currents, the best we can do is simply guess the current using any resource we have, correct our dead reckoning accordingly, and estimate the uncertainties involved.

Once the guesses are in hand, corrections are easy to make. If the predicted current is 12 miles a day toward the southwest, at the end of each day's dead reckoning, adjust your DR position 12 miles to the southwest, and start the next day's dead reckoning from the shifted position. This is all there is to the correction, regardless of your course, or course changes, throughout the day.

Pilot charts are the most common source of current predictions. As mentioned in Section 9.1, a rule of thumb for the uncertainty in the listed currents is about 50 percent. If the current is listed as 14 miles a day, it adds an uncertainty of 7 miles a day to your dead reckoning, even after you correct your course for the 14-mile drift. You can combine this with your other uncertainties by converting it to a percentage of your day's run. On a 50-mile day, this current contributes an uncertainty of 7 out of 50, or 14 percent, to your position. If you are navigating with 25 percent accuracy (distance and direction combined), the current uncertainty increases this to about 29 percent, since $\sqrt{25^2 + 14^2} = 29$, according to the right-triangle rule.

You can use this procedure to adjust your dead reckoning underway or to estimate your potential progress across currents that lie ahead. Suppose your destination lies due south, but to get there you must sail across southeast trades and a westerly current drift of, say, 14 miles a day. To make good a course to the south against this current, you have to go east (to weather) at least 14 miles a day. To be safe, you should also figure in the current uncertainty, meaning you might have to make as much as 21 miles a day to the east. If you can't point into the wind enough to make this average easting, you may have to consider another route or destination. Or at least keep this current constantly in mind, and whenever the wind backs to the east, follow it around and get east as much as you can.

Leeway is another matter. Any boat sailing to windward slips to leeward to some extent, which causes the actual course to deviate to leeward of the boat's heading. At first glance, this resembles the effect of current, in that both speed and course are affected. But on closer examination, the effects are different.

Leeway is motion through the water, not with the water as current is, and consequently we can measure it. Also, the effect of leeway on speed is not important, because any method we use to measure speed through the water includes the leeway, or downwind, component. Only the leeway angle must be measured separately. Leeway angle (usually just called leeway) is the angle between the direction we travel through the water and the heading of the boat.

The amount of leeway depends on several factors, a principal one being the draft of the boat. A raft or other flat-bottomed craft has much more leeway than a keel boat; a shoal-draft keel boat has more leeway than a deep-keeled boat. For any vessel, though, the amount of leeway is greatest when sailing close-hauled; and on any point of sail, leeway increases with wind strength.

A high-performance sailboat in moderate winds, for example, may slip only 4° or 5° to leeward of its optimum close-hauled course (usually about 45° off the true wind direction). In strong winds (say, 20 knots or so apparent), the leeway of this boat may increase to between 8° and 10°, but in practice probably not much more than this. A less efficient sailboat may slip as much as 15° or so in these winds. There is a practical upper limit to the leeway for all vessels, because at a certain wind strength we finally give up the struggle and fall off some. And in a keel boat, leeway decreases rapidly as we fall off a close-hauled course — generally, it becomes negligible as the apparent wind approaches the beam.

In very light air, leeway is again a concern. Generally leeway is much larger than we might suspect when sailing at less than some 25 percent of our potential hull speed. A full-keeled 36-footer, for example, sailing to weather at less than 2 knots, might slip to leeward 20° or so. Again, we tend to feel the inefficiency of the boat in these conditions and fall off to get more power, which reduces the leeway. Nevertheless, we should keep these navigational consequences in mind if we ever get stuck trying to make way to windward in light air — such as crossing a vast high-pressure area in the middle of the ocean.

Leeway is the principal concern when it comes to rigging a flat-bottomed boat for sailing. Even with a jury-rigged leeboard, we can't realistically hope to make much progress to weather. Here the concern may not be so much how close we can sail into the wind, but how far we can sail off of dead downwind. It's difficult to even estimate the answer — it depends on everything; hull, leeboard, rudder, rigging, sails, wind, and seas. But you can certainly count on a large leeway when trying to make way to weather in a flat boat. In any jury-rigged craft, the leeway must definitely be measured and figured into your navigation. But don't forget the lee board; even a paddle blade makes a big difference.

The definition of leeway and the method of measuring it, however, do not depend on the type of boat or the extent of the leeway. Leeway is always the angle between the boat's track through the water and the direction the bow is pointed. In principle, the wake, or foam trail, of a boat provides the track we need. If a wake were discernible for a sufficient distance, we could measure the leeway by measuring the angle between the centerline and the wake line. But this is more of a theoretical than a practical approach in most circumstances.

A more practical method is to stream a line over the stern, that is attached somewhere near amidships on the centerline. The resistance of the water will pull the line tight in the direction of your track through the water. Your leeway is then the angle between the dragging line and the centerline — the drag line acts as a visible wake. The angle can be figured by measuring the distance along the centerline from attachment point to stern and the distance athwartships along the stern from the centerline to the drag line, as illustrated in Figure 10-6. With these dimensions, you can draw a scaled-down version of the angle to estimate its size. The measurement is not affected by currents.

This measurement is harder to do in strong winds and rough water, though these are one of the conditions we care about most. Waves throw you off course, which makes it difficult to judge the average shift of the line off the centerline. And strong winds tend to push the exposed line to leeward, which reduces the apparent leeway. As shown in Figure 10-6, your track through the water (the drag line) lies to wind-

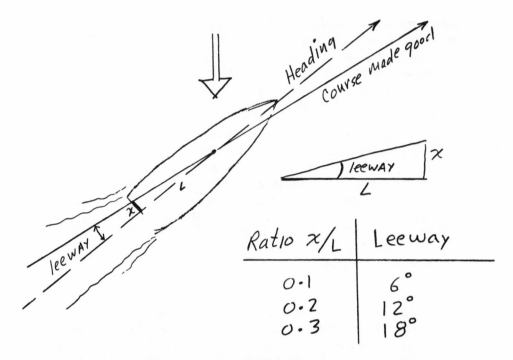

Ratio x/L	Leeway
0.1	6°
0.2	12°
0.3	18°

FIGURE 10-6. *Measuring leeway by streaming a line over the stern. As the boat slips to leeward, the line slips to weather of the centerline. The angle between the dragging line and the centerline is your effective leeway. The angle can be determined from the proportions shown—essentially the same rule used in Figure 3-7 to find course errors. In many cases, it is adequate to simply attach the line to the stern and estimate its angle above the centerline.*

ward of the stern, so when the line is pushed to leeward, the leeway angle appears smaller than it really is.

In principle, the line should be attached to the boat directly below the center-of-effort of your sail plan, or near it, but it is often difficult to get an unobstructed path from there to the stern. The attachment point is especially important if the line is heavy. The drag of the line, when it's attached forward of the center-of-effort (at the bow, for example), tends to increase your leeway, since the wind pivots the stern to leeward relative to the bow. But a line attached to the stern holds the stern to windward as the bow pivots to leeward, which reduces leeway — a heavy line attached to the stern is a sea anchor. Try different sizes and lengths, if available, to find the optimum. You need some drag in the water to keep the line taut against the wind, but any line below the water doesn't help you judge the angle; it just causes drag, slowing you down and altering the true leeway angle if the attachment point is not correct.

Once you've measured the leeway angle, it is a simple matter to include it in your dead reckoning. Just offset your recorded course to leeward by the leeway angle, and base your navigation on this corrected course. In a craft with large leeway (and a line available), you could just cast off the line occasionally, align a makeshift compass card with the line, and note the way you are going. In other words, determine your course from the drag line, not the bow of the boat.

When sailing your own boat with a normal sail plan, the best approach is to know the leeway ahead of time for various winds, seas, and points of sail. In routine sailing, this information is most easily and accurately obtained by comparing your compass course (assumed accurate) to your Loran's course–made–good output when sailing in slack water and steady winds. A well-kept logbook for one active sailing season should do the job, since you can interpolate from the data you get. Remember, we are after actual (effective) leeways, not theoretical values, which will always be much smaller. Published leeways for various yacht designs are like fuel consumption ratings for cars. They can be used to compare models, but they don't tell you what you will actually get in the stop-and-go traffic of honest waves or idling along in the windless middle of an ocean High.

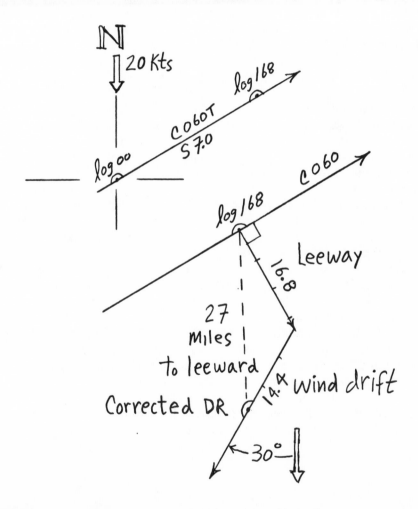

FIGURE 10-7. *Progress to weather. Here a 6° leeway is accounted for as a 10 percent offset to leeward, and an estimated wind drift of 0.6 knots is assumed to flow 30° to the right of the wind direction. These are both rough estimates, but this corrected position will certainly be closer to the true position than the uncorrected one.*

10.4 Progress to Weather

Leeway and wind-driven currents act in the same general direction, to leeward. These are two subtle effects in light-air navigation, but their combined effect in strong winds is not subtle. If you overlook these effects, your progress to windward could be significantly less than anticipated. We must be careful about such things in emergency navigation, since we can't count on getting an accurate position later on (in better conditions) to correct for what we've overlooked.

As a specific example, suppose we are close-reaching across a sustained 20-knot northerly at an average speed of 7 knots on a heading of 060° True (an apparent wind of about 25 knots at 45°). And suppose we were unaware of a 6° leeway and the wind-driven current, which in this case would be about 0.6 knots in the approximate direction of 210° True (see Section 9.3).

Dead reckoning without leeway or wind-driven current would predict a 24-hour run of 168 miles toward 060° True. The 6° of leeway, however, would cause a lateral error of 10 percent (about 17 miles) to the right of 060°, toward 150° True. And the wind-driven current would set us about 0.6 x 24, or some 14, miles toward roughly 210° True during this day's run. The net error would be about 17 miles toward 150° True and 14 miles toward 210° True; when plotted out, as in Figure 10-7, you find the actual position some 27 miles south (to leeward) of the uncorrected DR position. In the 168-mile run, this is a 16 percent error that we might have overlooked. And, frankly, even this apparently extreme example is an underestimate of the problem.

The drift of the current probably wouldn't be much larger than assumed, unless it were pouring rain all day, but the set could be more aligned with the wind than we assumed, especially at lower latitudes where the Coriolis force is weaker. With the current more aligned with the wind, the leeward error would be larger. Also, the leeway could easily be larger than assumed here. This depends on the vessel, sail plan, and heeling angle. But there is yet another problem — helmsmanship — as you confront successive waves. Boats tend to pound going to weather in big seas, and we often alter course briefly at each big wave to minimize this. If this is done by falling off slightly as the bow rises out of the water, we have a brief but persistent course alteration to leeward, which also inhibits progress to weather over a long run. Estimates of this effect would be even shakier than the others, but it is something to keep in mind when figuring progress to weather in strong winds.

Again, keeping and studying a careful Loran logbook throughout various conditions will teach you about the performance of your boat to weather in strong winds, and thus better prepare you for sailing without Loran.

11

Latitude at Sea

There are several independent ways to find latitude without modern instruments, and the principles behind these methods are easy to understand and remember. With practice, careful work, and some luck, we might count on an average accuracy of within about 50 miles, although a more conservative range of about 90 miles is a more realistic goal.

To find latitude from the stars, we must measure the angular height of a star above the horizon, or determine how close a star is to directly overhead. The measurements are the same ones used in some methods of direction finding, but now the measurements must be precise — latitude error is the same as the star-height error, and since 1° of latitude is 60 nautical miles, if a star height is wrong by 2°, the latitude figured from it will be wrong by 120 miles.

As always, repetition is the key to accuracy. Repeat each measurement several times and average the results. We must also learn to calibrate improvised instruments and to choose the best method to use. It is difficult, for example, to measure a star height of 40° with an accuracy of 30', but it is easy to measure a height of 4° with this precision. In any event, the measurements take time and concentration and are often tiring to the eyes since most require extended periods of alternating eye focus between stars and hands. You may have to temporarily alter course for a smoother ride or repeat measurements on several headings to get an accurate average.

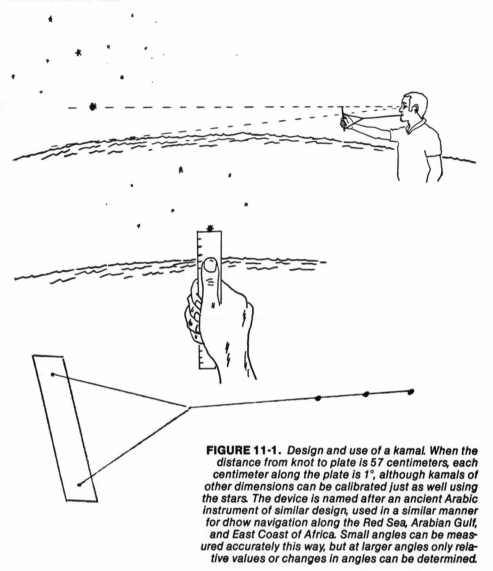

FIGURE 11-1. *Design and use of a kamal. When the distance from knot to plate is 57 centimeters, each centimeter along the plate is 1°, although kamals of other dimensions can be calibrated just as well using the stars. The device is named after an ancient Arabic instrument of similar design, used in a similar manner for dhow navigation along the Red Sea, Arabian Gulf, and East Coast of Africa. Small angles can be measured accurately this way, but at larger angles only relative values or changes in angles can be determined.*

11.1 Makeshift Altitude Measurements and Calibrations

Without a proper sextant, the most accurate and convenient angle (altitude) measurements will be of small angles, less than 15° or so. There are several reasons for this, some practical, some mathematical. With a little practice and the simplest of tools, we can measure small angles to within 30' or so. Larger angles require a different approach and the results are less accurate.

The best makeshift device for measuring small angles is a kamal, mentioned briefly in Section 6.3 for keeping track of relative angles. The device is just a flat plate or stick with a knotted string attached to it with a bridle, as shown in Figure 11-1. With the knot in your teeth, hold the plate out in front of you, so that the top edge is aligned with the star and your thumb is aligned with the horizon. We then convert this measured distance along the plate edge to an angular height above the horizon. The knotted string keeps the eye-to-plate distance constant and the bridle keeps the plate perpendicular to the string.

If you happen to have a centimeter ruler, you can make a kamal with built-in calibration. Use the ruler for the plate, and make the knot-to-plate distance equal to 57 centimeters. Then each centimeter along the edge of the plate equals 1° of angle, for angles less than 15° or so.

But we don't need a ruler of any kind to make a calibrated kamal, and even if we make one with a ruler, we should still check its calibration with the stars. First make a kamal with a comfortable string length — just long enough so that you can extend it in front of your eye without having to push your shoulder forward. This length will be about 20 inches or so for average arm lengths, but the precise length doesn't matter. We then figure the angle scale along the edge of it from the stars. And now the key point — we need to know a few of these calibration star distances from memory.

Figure 11-2 shows a few calibration distances in prominent constellations. The distances between the Pointers in the Big Dipper (5.4°) and the Guards in the Little

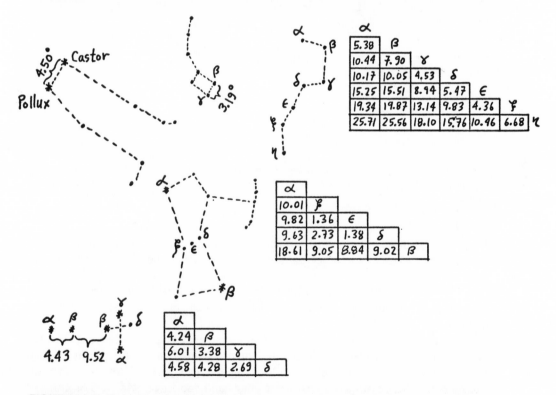

FIGURE 11-2. *Selected star-pair calibration angles. Note the alpha-beta pairs of the Big and Little Dippers (the Pointers and the Guards) form a convenient sequence to remember (5.4°, 3.2°). The stars of Orion's belt are about 1.4° apart. The inset tables contain the spacings of several pairs in the adjacent constellations. These distances are most easily determined using a programmed calculator, although they can be found graphically as in Figure 11-3.*

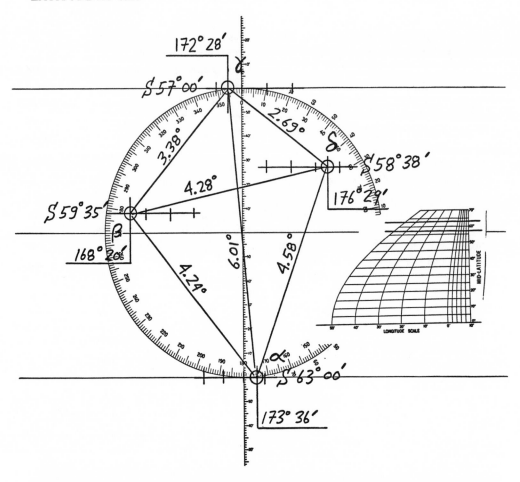

FIGURE 11-3. *Graphical determination of the star spacings of the Southern Cross. The star positions are plotted on a universal plotting sheet using declination in place of latitude and sidereal hour angle in place of longitude. Note that such a large "latitude" range requires separate longitude scales for each star.*

Dipper (3.2°) make a numerical sequence that is easy to remember. You can also figure these distances for other pairs of stars that might be more convenient for practice. The simplest way is to plot the star positions on a universal plotting sheet (see Figure 11-3), using declinations for latitudes and sidereal hour angles for longitudes. Then measure the distance between them using the latitude scale for degrees.

This, of course, must be done before an emergency requires their use. But the angular distances between close stars that you can figure this way (or measure directly with a sextant) are valuable aids in learning emergency navigation. You can, for example, use these distances to calibrate your hand and finger widths. For much of the star steering covered in Chapters 5 and 6, we need only approximate angles, and once you know the angular width of your hand, say, you can use it for these. A typical finger width at arm's length is about 2°, and an outstretched hand (thumb tip

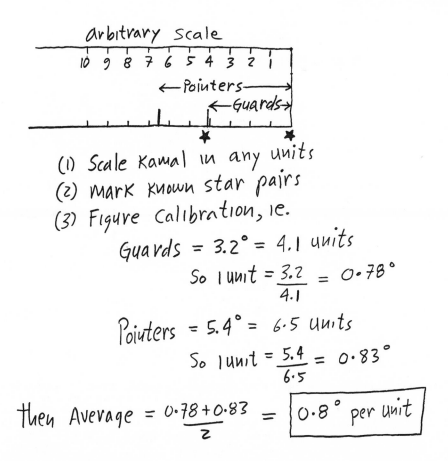

arbitrary scale

10 9 8 7 6 5 4 3 2 1

←—Pointers—→

←—Guards—→

(1) Scale Kamal in any units

(2) Mark known star pairs

(3) Figure Calibration, ie.

Guards = 3.2° = 4.1 units

So 1 unit = $\frac{3.2}{4.1}$ = 0.78°

Pointers = 5.4° = 6.5 units

So 1 unit = $\frac{5.4}{6.5}$ = 0.83°

Then Average = $\frac{0.78 + 0.83}{2}$ = $\boxed{0.8° \text{ per unit}}$

FIGURE 11-4. *Calibration of a kamal. Align the kamal with star pairs of known separation, mark their distance along the plate, and then figure the calibration scale as shown. The example shown uses the Pointers and Guards of the Big and Little Dippers.*

to little-finger tip) is about 20°. Once you have a few star distances marked on the edge of the kamal, you can figure out what the scale must be, since the angular scale is linear for small angles. The process is illustrated in Figure 11-4.

To measure larger angles, we need a more specialized piece of gear: a large, flat board some 18 inches on a side (like a locker cover or cabinet door); a section of tubing (boat pole section) or hose; two nails or screws, or some way to make holes in the board; a piece of string; and a weight. The design is shown in Figure 11-5. Let the sighting tube define the top edge of a large quadrant with a radius of 57 units, and then verify the other side of the quadrant with the horizon as shown. The string can serve as a draftsman's compass to mark the arc. To make the angle scale along the arc, use the rule that on an arc whose radius is 57 units, 1 unit is 1 degree. To use the device, align the star in the center of the tube and read the angle where the plumb line crosses the scale.

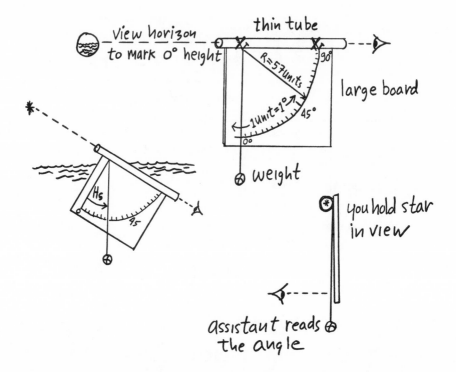

FIGURE 11-5. *Design and use of a plumb-bob sextant. Although it takes much care to rig one of these that measures exact angles, they can more reliably be used for relative angles. If the scale is spaced properly, you can, for example, tell that a star height has dropped by 0.5°, but it will be much more difficult to decide if it went from, say, 35.5° to 35.0° or 35.0° to 34.5°. In any use, however, many measurements must be taken and then averaged for a good result.*

The line will swing around as the boat rocks, and you must also keep the plate vertical so the string doesn't drag on the plate. But with patience and practice, you can measure star heights this way to within about 1° accuracy, providing the scale is constructed carefully. To make measurements alone, you must pinch the string against the plate while sighting the star and then read it. Many sights are needed for a good average. Two people, however, can do this much better than one. One holds the plate in line with the star, and the other watches the plumb line on the scale to figure its average position.

Star-height measurements made this way are not restricted to twilight — since you don't need to see the horizon to do the sights — which makes a good plumb-bob sextant extremely valuable for several applications in latitude reckoning and direction finding. But it takes a lot of work to convince yourself that it's doing the job properly. To use this with the sun, you must rig a transparent sun filter of some sort, or do the sights when skies are overcast. The sights are still potentially dangerous to the eyes, however; so unless you happen to have overcast skies or adequate materials to make a good sun shade, this device won't be of much use for sun measurements.

Relative angles can be measured by several means, and often the eye alone is very precise in judging relative sizes of small angle intervals between stars. Viewing a group of three close stars, for example, it is usually easy to judge by just looking that, say, stars two and three are twice as far apart as stars one and three. Or, compare finger widths between the stars or distances along a kamal to confirm your observation. Similarly, at twilight we might be able to easily tell that the height of star three above the horizon is the same or, just less than the distance between stars two and three.

Another trick is to align your finger or a kamal with one of the stars when one eye is closed. Then open that eye and close the other, holding your pointer as still as possible (see Figure 11-6). The pointer will shift about 6°, and this angular shift will always be the same — it is determined by the eye-to-pointer distance (arm or kamal length) and the distance between your eyes. With known star distances or a sextant available you can calibrate your "wink" — find out if your shift is 6° or 7°, or whatever — and then have this handy trick for quick small-angle measurements that can, with a little practice, be quite accurate. For example, you can find out how much you are slipping to leeward by "winking your wake."

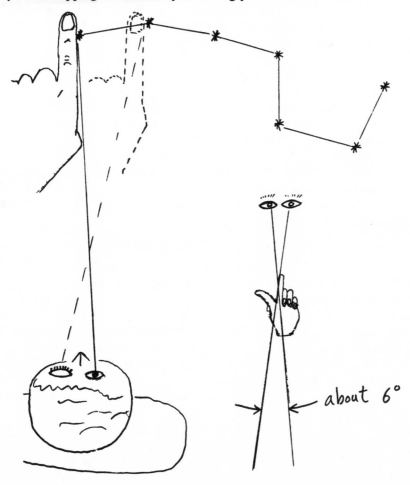

FIGURE 11-6. *"Winking" your finger at arm's length to measure angles. If you hold your finger in line with one star of a pair, and then change eyes, and your finger moves to the other star, the two stars are about 6° apart. If your finger only moves halfway to the other star, the stars are about 12° apart. Calibrate your wink using known star pairs or using a sextant and distant landmarks. A typical "wink" is about 6°. Winking a kamal edge is easier and more accurate than winking your finger.*

11.2 Makeshift Altitude Corrections

Angular height measured relative to the horizon must be corrected for several factors in order for us to be able to figure latitude from it with optimum precision. The corrections are listed in the *Nautical Almanac,* and their application is standard procedure in routine celestial navigation. The corrections are each fairly small, but their sum can be significant, especially when we happen to have a sextant and can measure sun and star heights accurately. Even without a sextant and almanac, you should not overlook these corrections in makeshift latitude sights, since we can estimate them fairly well without an almanac.

The altitude, or angular height, measured directly from a sextant or kamal is called "sextant height" (H_s). The angular height, after all corrections have been applied, is called "observed height" (H_o). We start with H_s and we want H_o. The altitude corrections can be summarized as follows:

$$H_o = H_s \pm IC - Dip - Refraction \pm Semi\text{-}diameter.$$

"IC" is the index correction. It is used only for sights with proper sextants, in which case it is read directly from the sextant after aligning the direct and reflected views of the horizon. It can be positive or negative.

"Dip" is the correction for the observer's elevated eye height at the time of the sight. It applies to all sights with conventional sextants and kamals, but not to bubble or plumb-bob sextants. It is always a small negative correction and can be figured accurately from the square root of the observer's height of eye, expressed in feet above the water:

$$Dip = 1' \times \sqrt{Height\ of\ eye\ (feet)}\,.$$

For an eye height of 9 feet, the dip is 3', so the dip correction is –3'.

"Semi-diameter" is half the angular width of the sun, and we should correct for this width in all sun sights. Latitude (or any other sunline) is figured from the height of the sun's center, but we can only measure the height to its upper or lower limb. Within an accuracy of about 0.5', the sun's semi-diameter is constant throughout the year at 16'. Therefore, the semi-diameter correction is +16' for lower-limb sights and −16' for upper-limb sights. A similar correction must be applied to moon sights, but moon sights without an almanac are not usable and almanacs include the moon's semi-diameter correction.

"Refraction" is the bending of light rags as they enter the atmosphere from the vacuum of space. It causes an error in all sights with any instruments. Refraction is largest for low sights, which makes it especially important in emergency navigation. The correction is always negative, but its size depends on the height of the sun or star. For sextant heights (H_s) greater than about 6°,

$$Refraction = \frac{60'}{H_s}$$

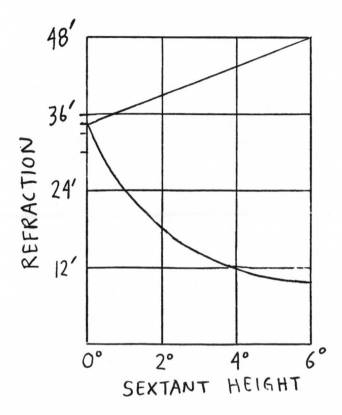

FIGURE 11-7. *Low-angle refraction corrections to sextant sights. To construct the curve of refraction corrections, draw a rectangle as shown, and swing an arc from the upper right-hand corner through a refraction of 34.5' (one eighth of a unit down from 36') at 0° sextant height. This curve reproduces the exact values to within 1' or so. At a sextant angle of 1° the refraction correction is 24', at 4° it is 12'. This trick was developed by brute force (trial and error). At larger angles, refraction equals 60' divided by the sextant height in degrees.*

At a star height of 15°, the refraction would be $60' \div 15 = 4'$, so the refraction correction is $-4'$. This approximation is accurate to within about 1' for sextant heights greater than 6°. For lower heights, the correction must be figured with a graph, since it increases rapidly as the height decreases.

To figure low-angle refraction, construct a graph as shown in Figure 11-7. Draw a rectangular graph with 3 units on the horizontal axis to represent 6° of sextant height and a vertical axis of 4 units to represent 48' of refraction. Then, from the upper right corner, swing a circular arc through a refraction of 34.5' at Hs = 0°. This arc (which will pass through a refraction of about 9' at Hs = 6°) represents the curve of corrections for various small angles. It is accurate to within 1', in principle. With little practice, even a freehand drawing can reproduce the corrections to within a few minutes. The maximum value of 34.5' is an easy number to remember, and also easy to locate on the graph since it is one-eighth of a unit down from the third mark, as shown in the figure.

11.3 Latitude from *Polaris*

A routine method of finding latitude in the Northern Hemisphere is to measure the angular height of *Polaris* above the horizon. The method works because *Polaris* lies very near the north pole of the sky, and the height of the pole is equal to the observer's latitude. Even without special corrections, the direct sextant height of *Polaris* gives you your latitude to an accuracy of about 1° at worst, and usually better than that. But we can't count on the greater accuracy unless we take into account the difference between the star's position and the pole position.

To remove this 1° uncertainty, we must make the usual altitude corrections (Section 11.2) to the sextant height (Hs) to get the observed height (Ho), and then apply a "*Polaris* correction" to account for the star's position at the time of the sight. This can be expressed as:

$$\text{Latitude} = H_o + Polaris \text{ correction.}$$

In routine navigation, we find the *Polaris* correction in the *Nautical Almanac,* but, as we shall see shortly, it is easy to estimate this correction in an emergency without an almanac.

If an emergency leaves you in the Northern Hemisphere with a working sextant and nothing else, the height of *Polaris* is your best way to find and keep track of latitude. Without a sextant, however, the optimum value of this method is pretty much restricted to latitudes between about 5° N and 15° N. At higher latitudes, the star's height is difficult to measure accurately without a sextant, although a large plumb-bob sextant (Section 11.1) might be accurate to within 1 or 2 degrees; at lower latitudes, the star is only rarely visible since it is not bright enough to shine through the haze of the low horizon. *Polaris* can't be seen in the Southern Hemisphere and there is no south star counterpart.

To figure the *Polaris* correction, recall that the declination of *Polaris* is N 89° 12', which places the star 48' off the north pole of the sky. Consequently, *Polaris,* like all stars, circles the pole once every 24 hours. The only difference with *Polaris* is that its circle (of radius 48 ') is so small that it doesn't appear to move throughout the night. To find accurate latitude, though, we must take this motion into account even though we can't see it. It's the height of the pole (the center of the circle) that is our latitude, not the height of the star. Since we can't see the pole, we have to measure the height of the star, and then figure the difference between the pole height and the star height. This height difference is the *Polaris* correction — in the past called the "regiment of the pole" — and we can read it from the relative positions of neighboring stars.

Our modern "regiment" uses the constellations of Cassiopeia and the Big Dipper, lying on opposite sides of *Polaris*. The line joining the trailing stars of Cassiopeia and the Big Dipper passes through *Polaris* and the pole, with *Polaris* on the Cassiopeia side of the pole. This line tells where *Polaris* is relative to the pole. If the line is perpendicular to the horizon with Cassiopeia on top, *Polaris* is directly above

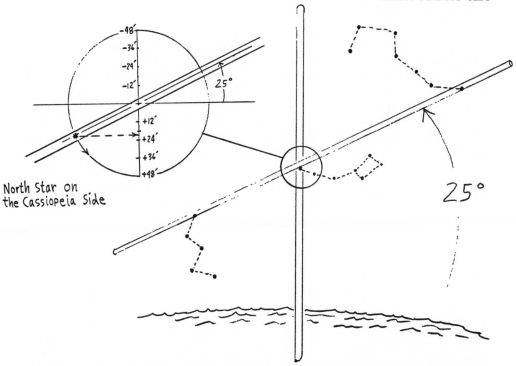

North Star on
the Cassiopeia Side

FIGURE 11-8. *Correction needed to find latitude from the height of Polaris. The line between the trailing stars of Cassiopeia and the Big Dipper passes through both the north celestial pole and the star Polaris. The star is on the Cassiopeia side. Hold sticks as shown, or by other means measure the orientation of the trailing star line, and from this figure the correction as shown.* Polaris *circles counterclockwise around the pole on a radius of 48'.*

the pole, so the correction is –48'. If the trailing star of the Big Dipper is on top, *Polaris* is directly below the pole and the correction is +48'. If the trailing-star line is parallel to the horizon, *Polaris* and the pole are at the same height, so there is no correction.

But we won't always be so lucky as to find this reference line in one of these convenient orientations during morning or evening twilight when we must do the sight. Generally, this line is tilted relative to the horizon, which puts the correction somewhere between –48' and +48'. The first step, then, is to estimate the angle this line makes with the horizon (see Figure 11-8). This can be done with a folded piece of paper or with two sticks. Align one stick with the trailing-star line and hold the other perpendicular to the horizon in line with *Polaris*. The angle between the sticks gives the orientation of the line.

Then draw a circle with a radius of 4 units to represent the path of *Polaris* around the pole, and draw a line through the center of the circle with the same orientation you observed for the trailing-star line. Now mark the circle with the position of *Polaris,* where the Cassiopeia side of the line crosses the circle. Draw in the vertical axis of the circle and mark it off in one-unit intervals. Each unit equals 12' of height difference, which is just the correction we want. To get the correction, move the star to the vertical axis without changing its height and read the correction.

Notice that we don't need to see both Cassiopeia and the Big Dipper to find this correction. The orientation of the line can be found from *Polaris* and the trailing star of either constellation. At lower latitudes, part or all of one of the constellations may be below the horizon.

Now to review the full process. Let's say we measured the height of *Polaris* with a kamal several times and the average value was 10.4°, or 10°24′. We also noted that the trailing-star line was tilted about 25° up from the horizon at the time of the sights (again the average of several measurements), with the Big Dipper above and to the right of the star. As shown in Figure 11-8, we find that a tilt angle of 25° means the *Polaris* correction is +20′. Referring back to Section 11.2 for the altitude corrections, for an eye height of about 9 feet, the dip correction is −3′, and the refraction correction for a star height of 10°24′ is − 60′ ÷ 10.4, or about −6′. So,

$$H_o = H_s - Dip - Refraction = 10°24′ - 3′ - 6′ = 10°15′$$

and

$$Latitude = H_o + Polaris \text{ correction}$$
$$= 10°15′ + 20′$$
$$= 10°35′ N.$$

With a sextant and nothing else but these makeshift corrections, we can usually find latitude to within about 10 to 15 miles at any north latitude. Without a sextant, measuring the height from a kamal (from latitudes south of about 15° N), we can find latitude this way to within about 30′ in good conditions and nearly always to better than 50′ or so. At higher northern latitudes, we are limited to accuracies of within 1 or 2 degrees, depending on our success with a plumb-bob sextant.

Practice this method of finding emergency latitude when you have a sextant and proper tables to check your results, and you will know how well you might do without them.

11.4 Latitude from Zenith Stars

The point in the sky directly overhead is called the zenith. A star that passes through the zenith is called a zenith star. Our latitude equals the declination of our zenith stars. The principle is simple and fundamental. The practical problem is deciding whether or not a particular star with known declination is passing precisely overhead. If the star is not directly overhead at its highest point (meridian passage), we must estimate how many degrees it is to the north or south of our zenith when the star crosses our meridian. If a star passes 2° to the north of our zenith, our latitude is 2° south of the declination of the star — the height of this star as it crosses the meridian would be 88° above the northern horizon. Likewise, stars with declinations south of our latitude will pass to the south of our zenith by the corresponding number of degrees. See Figure 11-9.

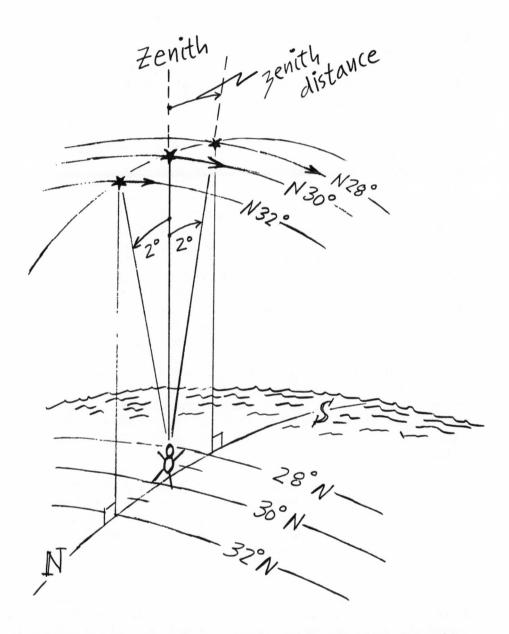

FIGURE 11-9. *Finding latitude by zenith stars. A star that passes directly overhead has a declination equal to your latitude. If a star passes 2° to the south of your zenith as it crosses your meridian, your latitude is 2° north of the star's declination. Also see Figure 5-20.*

Finding latitude from zenith stars is a well-established technique of no-instrument navigation, It has been used routinely by traditional navigators of the Pacific islands. Its practicality has been documented by several contemporary navigators (see articles by David Lewis and Marvin Creamer in the bibliography). With practice, a consistent accuracy of about 1° can be achieved. Obviously, the conditions of the sea and the stability of the vessel affect our ability to judge the overhead position of a star. But when the sky is clear enough to see zenith stars, more often than not they can be used to help find latitude. This method can be used at any time of night that known stars pass overhead, since we don't need to see the horizon to judge the zenith distance.

Another virtue of this method is that we are able to estimate its uncertainty. We do this using the angular distances between stars near our chosen reference star. We establish our zenith point in the sky, and then compare the distance from it to our chosen star with the spacings of other overhead stars in view. After a series of measurements, for example, we might conclude that a star appears to be passing 2° south of our zenith, while related measurements might make us much more confident that it is certainly more than 1° south and less than 3° south. This type of accurate information can be combined with the accuracy of our dead reckoning latitude, or with any other means we have of checking latitude, to piece together the best possible estimate of our actual latitude. If our course takes us to the south at a DR rate of 60 miles a day, zenith stars should move north at a rate of 1° per day. If they don't, we are doing something wrong with our navigation.

It is easy to spot zenith stars and zenith distances on land by sighting upward along a pole or plumb line — any string with a weight attached. But at sea we must contend with the motion of the boat. Several ways of observing overhead stars were suggested in Section 5.19 and illustrated in Figure 5-17. Sighting along the mast is one way. For this approach, you must take into account the heel of the boat and any rake or bend to the mast. You will also have to find the optimum course heading for a smooth ride. Using the mast, it is easiest to determine when a star is at the zenith, or at least at its highest point, if you are sailing east or west. But the optimum course in any particular circumstance will depend on the wind and seas.

Another approach is to just look up toward the zenith and then turn in a circle. This may not be the most precise way to judge zenith stars, but it's a convenient way to tell when to start looking in whatever way you do decide is the most accurate. By turning in a circle, we overcome our natural tendency to underestimate the height of a high star (for low stars the common tendency is just the opposite, to overestimate the height).

Though it is sometimes frustrating and tiring to the eyes and neck, the author has found that a plumb line can also be quite useful for this measurement at sea. The optimum arrangement found was a line about 3 feet long attached to a holding stick. From a comfortable reclined position, hold the stick overhead and sight the star along the weighted line. The weight must be steadied continuously, but eventually an accurate average position can be determined. Or better still, find a place to rig the holding stick so you can lie under it without having to hold it. A pointer attached to the top of the string can be used for zenith angle calibration (see Figure 11-10).

To make the calibrator, use the rule that 1 unit equals 1° at a distance of 57 units.

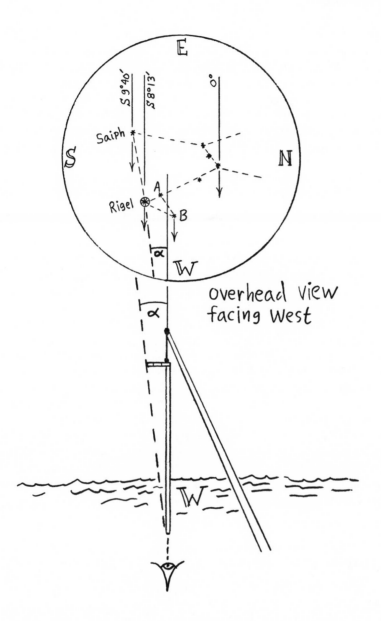

FIGURE 11-10. *Using a plumb line to spot zenith stars. Here the plumb line is a straight stick attached to a longer stick by a short string. The pointer at the top of the stick represents an angle of 4° that can be used to judge the relative positions of overhead stars. Or better still, use a kamal to measure distances among close pairs (as made up among Rigel, Star A, and Star B) and then use these relative distances to judge the location of the zenith. Here, we are located just north of Orion's knees (Rigel and Saiph), about halfway between Star A and Star B. From the measured spacings of these stars, we can determine our latitude relative to the known declination of Rigel. The zenith point is located by imagining the center of the pattern made by the motion of the plumb line against the background of stars. The plumb line must frequently be steadied by hand.*

163

For example, at an eye-to-pointer distance of 28.5 inches (57 x 0.5 inches), each half-inch along the pointer is 1° of zenith distance. A 2-inch pointer would be 4° across. We need this information to judge how far off the zenith a known star passes. Another convenient way to do this is to use a kamal to measure the distances between stars near your chosen reference star. It is easier to note that your reference star is, say, south of the zenith by half the distance between two other stars also in view at the time, than to make an unaided guess at its zenith distance. With a calibrated kamal you can fairly accurately measure the distances between any two close stars.

Try not to get discouraged when you first look up at the stars and find that your reference point (masthead or plumb line) is moving all over the sky, because it will do just that, even in fairly calm waters (see Figure 5-17). But as you watch it, you should be able to detect a repeated pattern. Your reference point is the center or an edge of the pattern, and you can measure the extent of the pattern using a kamal or other angle calibrator. Your job then is to estimate the number of degrees between the star and the reference point as the star passes through its highest point in the sky. With some practice you can gain help with this judgment by "winking" the zenith star (Section 11.1) as it crosses your reference marker.

The best way to remember the declinations of important stars along your route is to associate the stars with the islands or coastal landmarks they cross. Examples are shown in Figure 11-11. At the beginning of any long voyage (before a navigational emergency arises), check the sky throughout the night to see which stars are in season. Then, from an almanac, pick a few prominent stars that cover the latitude range of your voyage and memorize their declinations by checking a chart to see what landmarks they cross. Then, if you should be left to navigate by the stars, you are prepared. Even without an emergency, this provides an interesting record of the sky along your route. You can use the progression of zenith stars to mark the progress of the voyage. Learning the stars becomes almost automatic if you use celestial navigation routinely. After several sight reductions of the same star, we often memorize its declination even if we didn't intend to.

11.5 Latitude from Horizon-Grazing Stars

If a bright star of known declination crosses the meridian at altitudes of some 15° or less during twilight, we have a unique and accurate means of finding latitude without a sextant. Star candidates for this method must be bright, since only bright stars can be routinely seen low on the horizon. Furthermore, if we consider the typical sailing domain as 60° N to 60° S, these stars must have fairly high declinations if we are to see them cross the meridian at low altitudes. In short, considering brightness and location, there are only six or seven dependable candidates for this method. Nevertheless, these few stars alone offer remarkably extensive coverage when we consider their full potential.

This method is nothing more than conventional latitude by meridian passage ap-

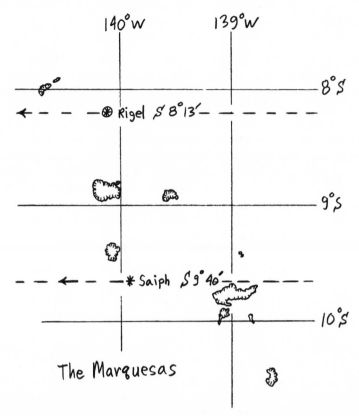

FIGURE 11-11. *Taurus and Orion passing over islands of the mid-Pacific, with details of the Marquesas. Note that stars near Orion's raised hand are zenith stars for Hawaii, as Orion's bow is for the Line Islands, and Orion's knees are for the Marquesas. Mintaka, the leading star of Orion's belt, circles the earth over the equator. About halfway between Rigel and Saiph would be a good target latitude for a winter voyage to the Marquesas.*

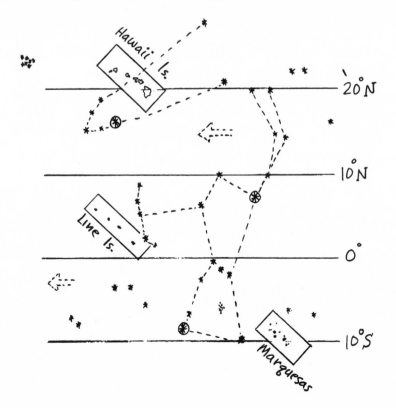

plied to low-altitude stars. The principle is the same as the one used for latitude from zenith distance in Section 11.4. A star crossing the meridian to the south at an observed height of 10° up from the horizon has a zenith distance of 80° down from the zenith. Our northern latitude must be 80° north of the southern declination of the star. If we can measure the height of the star near the meridian, we can figure our latitude. The geometry was illustrated in Figure 5-20.

Any westbound star that crosses the meridian low on the horizon must have a declination name (north or south) contrary to our latitude — when we are in north latitudes, it must be a southern star, and vice versa. To figure latitude in this special case of meridian passage, first figure the "polar distance" of the star:

$$\text{Star's polar distance} = 90° - \text{Star's declination}.$$

The the rule for figuring latitude from meridian passage of westbound stars of contrary name is

$$\text{Latitude} = \text{Star's polar distance} - \text{Star's maximum H}_o.$$

The name of your latitude (north or south) is always opposite that of the star.

As a specific example, suppose we see *Canopus* (declination S 52° 41') low on the southern meridian at twilight, from an eye height of 6 feet. Using a kamal, we measure its sextant height (Hs) to be 5° 30'. From Section 11.2, the dip correction is about –2' and the refraction correction is about –10 , so

$$\begin{aligned} H_o = H_s - \text{Dip} - \text{Refraction} &= 5°30' - 2' - 10' \\ &= 5°\,18', \end{aligned}$$

and

$$\begin{aligned} \text{Polar distance} &= 89°60' - 52°41' \\ &= 37°19'. \end{aligned}$$

We then find

$$\begin{aligned} \text{Latitude} &= \text{Polar distance} - \text{maximum H}_o \\ &= 37°19' - 5°18' \\ &= 32°01'\,\text{N}. \end{aligned}$$

Canopus is the second brightest star in the sky, so it is a prime candidate for this method.

An especially nice example of this method is shown in Figure 11-12. If your known bright star has any star nearby in line with the pole, then you can tell at a glance when the star crosses the meridian — the pair will "stand up."

This method can also be applied to circumpolar stars moving eastward across the meridian at the bottom of their circular path around the pole. The procedure is the same. Use a kamal to find the height of the star when it crosses or nears the meridian. In the Northern Hemisphere, you want the height of the star when it lies below

FIGURE 11-12. *Scene from a navigator's dream. The lower star of the Southern Cross, Alpha Crucis or Acrux, has declination almost exactly S 63° 00'; the upper star, Gamma Crucis or Gacrux, has declination almost exactly S 57° 00'. These are easy references to remember, and since they are in line with the South Pole, this means they are almost exactly 6° apart. In this view we know they are on the meridian because they are standing up, and we can tell by eye alone that Acrux is one cross-length, or 6°, above the horizon. So its zenith distance is 84°, and our latitude is 84° north of 63° S, or 21° N. Or using the latitude rules from the text: Its polar distance is 27°, and its maximum height is 6°, so our latitude is 27° minus 6°, or 21°.*

Polaris. In the Southern Hemisphere, we don't have this luxury, but it's still easy to spot stars headed eastward. Viewed from any southern latitude, the stars that move eastward are the ones lying to the south with heights less than your latitude. The same is true looking north from northern latitudes.

For eastbound circumpolar stars, the height on the meridian will be the minimum height of the star as it dips below the pole. The rule for latitude from meridian passage of eastbound circumpolar stars is:

$$\text{Latitude} = \text{Star's polar distance} + \text{Star's minimum } H_o.$$

To see a circumpolar star, you must be in the same hemisphere as the star, so latitude always has the same name as declination. Note that the two latitude rules are the same except for the sign of observed height; we add minimum observed height for eastbound stars, but subtract maximum observed height for westbound stars. If you do it wrong, you get nonsense (relative to your DR latitude), which is your signal to try it the other way. This symmetry is the reason for the form of the latitude rules.

For example, I see *Capella* (declination N 45° 58') lying below *Polaris* at twilight, and I measure its sextant height (Hs) to be 3° 20' above the horizon from an eye height of 9 feet. So,

$$H_o = H_s - \text{Dip} - \text{Refractions} = 3°20' - 3' - 13'$$
$$= 3°04',$$

and

$$\text{Polar distance} = 89°60' - 45°58'$$
$$= 44°02'.$$

We then find

$$\begin{aligned}
\text{Latitude} &= \text{Polar distance} + \text{minimum } H_o \\
&= 44°02' + 3°04' \\
&= 47°06'\text{N.}
\end{aligned}$$

Unfortunately, there are not many bright candidates in the Northern Hemisphere for this circumpolar trick other than *Capella* and *Vega;* but on very clear nights, other northern stars may be useful if we happen to know the stars or have a list of star declinations. Sailing just south of the southern tropics, however, there are several bright stars for this application.

Considering both the westbound (called upper-transit) and eastbound (called lower-transit) applications of this method during both morning and evening twilight, opportunities for this type of sight are fairly numerous, even though there are only seven bright stars to choose from. The latitude ranges and available dates for these stars are shown in Figure 11-13 and in Table 11-1.

One factor that extends their usable dates is the low altitude of the stars at meridian passage. Since the stars are low, their height changes very little near the meridian, so we need not actually catch the star crossing the meridian during twilight to get an accurate latitude from its height. For example, a star might be headed toward the meridian at the start of twilight and still be some 5° from reaching it at the end of twilight, when it's too dark or too light to continue measuring its height. But since its arc is so flat, even at 5° off the meridian, its height will be well within 30' or so of its meridian height. This factor has been taken into account in the dates shown in Table 11-1. The information presented is not intended to help in an actual emergency application of this procedure; its goal is just to demonstrate the frequency of the opportunities, showing when and where you might practice it.

Remember that even the brightest stars will not appear bright when low on the horizon. But if the low horizon is blank except for one faint star, you can bet it's a bright one or you wouldn't see it at all. And since bright stars are well-known stars, seeing one at all is usually enough to identify it. In exceptional cases with crystal-clear skies and about a three-quarters moon high in the sky — a bright full moon is often too bright — this type of sight is possible during the night using a moonlit horizon, but this is a pretty rare combination of events. If you happen to see it, take advantage of it, but don't wait for it.

With confidence that you are getting accurate readings from a plumb-bob sextant, this method can be extended to the meridian passage of any star with known declination. The latitude rule given above for lower transit is valid for any star height, but the upper-transit rule, as presented above, is only for stars of contrary name. For same-name stars, or near the equator when you don't know your "name," use the latitude rule for the sun given in Section 11-7.

Although we are essentially limited to twilight sights for accurate latitude, the principle of this method provides a much more general way to discover your approximate latitude. Sailing south from high northern latitudes, for example, I would not see *Canopus* at any time during the night — this star with high southern declination would stay below the horizon all night long. But as I continue south, at some latitude *Canopus* will appear on the horizon at some time during the night — providing, of course, it's the right season for it. When I first see *Canopus,* regardless of the time of night, I can figure out how far south I must be.

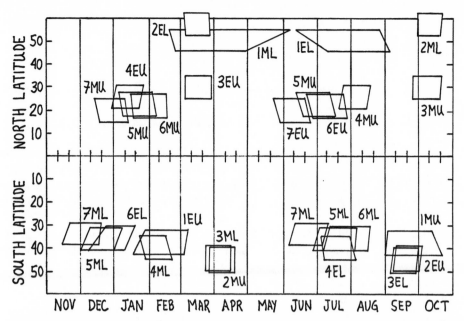

FIGURE 11-13. *Opportunities for finding latitude from horizon-grazing stars. Outlined areas mark where and when a bright star will appear low on the meridian during twilight. See Table 11-1 for specific values and abbreviations. Acrux, shown low on the horizon in Figure 11-12, is star 7. The view shown in that figure must be either during morning (M) twilight of mid-December to mid-January, or evening (E) twilight of late-May to late-June. These computer calculations show that this method has a good chance of being useful in many parts of the world. It does not work near the equator, since there are no bright stars near either pole.*

TABLE 11-1. OPPORTUNITIES FOR LATITUDE FROM HORIZON-GRAZING STARS.[a]

Star & Transit	Latitude and Dates for a height of about 2°		Latitude and Dates for a height of about 12°	
1 EL:	46° N	July 11 to Sept. 04	54° N	June 12 to Aug. 25
1 ML:	46° N	Feb. 24 to April 27	54° N	Feb. 19 to June 07
1 EU:	42° S	Jan. 17 to March 04	32° S	Jan. 29 to March 07
1 MU:	42° S	Aug. 31 to Oct. 22	32° S	Sept. 03 to Oct. 13
2 EL:	53° N	March 06 to March 27	63° N	March 03 to March 25
2 ML:	53° N	Sept. 29 to Oct. 21	63° N	Sept. 29 to Oct. 22
2 EU:	49° S	Sept. 08 to Sept. 30	39° S	Sept. 10 to Oct. 01
2 MU:	49° S	March 27 to April 17	39° S	March 27 to April 17
3 EL:	39° S	Sept. 06 to Sept. 30	49° S	Sept. 05 to Sept. 29
3 ML:	39° S	March 23 to April 16	49° S	March 24 to April 16
3 EU:	35° N	March 04 to March 28	25° N	March 05 to March 28
3 MU:	35° N	Sept. 26 to Oct. 19	25° N	Sept. 26 to Oct. 20
4 EL:	35° S	July 05 to July 31	45° S	July 08 to Aug. 04
4 ML:	35° S	Jan. 24 to Feb. 16	45° S	Jan. 29 to Feb. 21
4 EU:	31° N	Jan. 02 to Jan. 26	21° N	Dec. 30 to Jan. 23
4 MU:	31° N	July 25 to Aug. 18	21° N	July 21 to Aug. 14
5 EL:	32° S	Dec. 10 to Jan. 08	42° S	Dec. 01 to Dec. 31
5 ML:	32° S	July 03 to Aug. 06	42° S	June 03 to Aug. 06
5 EU:	28° N	June 12 to July 12	18° N	June 19 to July 18
5 MU:	28° N	Jan. 04 to Feb. 04	18° N	Jan. 09 to Feb. 06
6 EL:	31° S	Dec. 18 to Jan. 18	41° S	Dec. 09 to Jan. 10
6 ML:	31° S	July 13 to Aug. 17	41° S	July 06 to Aug. 17
6 EU:	27° N	June 21 to July 23	17° N	June 28 to July 28
6 MU:	27° N	Jan. 13 to Feb. 15	17° N	Jan. 17 to Feb. 16
7 EL:	29° S	Nov. 22 to Dec. 18	39° S	Nov. 15 to Dec. 12
7 ML:	29° S	June 11 to July 11	39° S	June 06 to July 07
7 EU:	25° N	May 23 to June 20	15° N	May 29 to June 25
7 MU:	25° N	Dec. 14 to Jan. 10	15° N	Dec. 18 to Jan. 13

Star	Relative Brightness	Sight Abbreviations
1. *Capella*	9	E = Evening Twilight
2. *Vega*	10	M = Morning Twilight
3. *Canopus*	25	
4. *Achernar*	6	L = Lower Transit
5. *Hadar*	5	U = Upper Transit
6. *Rigil Kentarus*	10	
7. *Acrux*	4	

[a]For example, "1 EL" means Evening Lower transit sight of Capella, which is possible at any latitude between about 46° N and 54° N on any date between about July 11 and August 25.

To do this, I use the basic formula for meridian passage of westbound stars:

Latitude = Star's polar distance − maximum H$_o$.

When the star first appears, its height must be near 0°, so my latitude must be roughly equal to the star's polar distance. The declination of *Canopus* is S 52° 41′, so the latitude at which *Canopus* first appears is 90° − 52° 41′, or about 37° 19′ N. If I see *Canopus* at all, at any time during the night, I know for certain that I am at least as far south as 37° 19′ N. The same reasoning applies when a star first fails to appear during the night as you sail away from it; but "seeing" is always better proof than "not seeing." Again, because of their brightness and location, the stars listed in Table 11-1 are the prime candidates for such latitude readings, but now with the advantage that their useful dates are greatly expanded since it doesn't matter at what time of night we see them.

11.6 Latitude from Double Transits of Circumpolar Stars

With a working plumb-bob sextant at higher latitudes, we can find latitude from circumpolar stars whenever the night is at least 12 hours long. All we need is the minimum height of a star as it dips under the pole headed east and the maximum height of the same star as it climbs over the top of the pole headed west. The average of these is the height of the pole, which is our latitude:

$$\text{Latitude} = \frac{(\text{maximum H}_o + \text{minimum H}_o)}{2}.$$

For example, suppose we are in southern latitudes (in the summer) and note that a medium-bright star lies to the south during the early evening. We watch its height with a plumb-bob sextant (or kamal) to discover that its lowest height was about 13°. Then just before first light in the morning, it has circled halfway around the pole and is now passing through its maximum height of about 67°, which we must read with a plumb-bob sextant. Our latitude must be (13° + 67°) ÷ 2 = 40° S. This method requires chance circumstances, but not particularly rare ones, since we can use any circumpolar star. We do not need to know its declination.

11.7 Latitude from the Sun at LAN

In celestial navigation, it is standard procedure to find latitude from the meridian passage of the sun, whereas it is highly uncommon to use the meridian passage of stars for latitude, as described in the last three sections. In emergency navigation, the reverse is true. Though we can use the sun for directions, without a proper sextant it is usually impossible to measure the height of the noon sun accurately enough to find a useful latitude from it.

The problems are the sun's height and brightness. The only exceptions might be an emergency at a high north latitude in December or January or a high south latitude in June or July. In these cases, the noon sun might be low enough to measure with a kamal and jury-rigged sun shade. If you have a sextant, though, the noon sun is a valuable way to find latitude anywhere, especially in the Southern Hemisphere where latitude cannot be found from the pole height. In exceptional cases in overcast skies, a plumb-bob sextant with sun shade might provide approximate latitude, but the sights are still potentially dangerous to the eyes. The procedure is not recommended.

To get latitude from the height of the sun at meridian passage, we need to know the sun's declination, which changes slowly from day to day. It is listed in almanacs, but we can also figure it fairly accurately from the date. The rule for finding latitude from the sun's height on the meridian depends on where you are relative to the sun. To cover all cases, including a large uncertainty in DR latitude very near the equator, it is simplest to give signs (+ or -) to latitude, declination, and zenith distances as follows:

North latitude is (+).	South latitude is (−).
North declination is (+).	South declination is (−).
Looking north to the sun,	Looking south to the sun,
zenith distance is (+).	zenith distance is (−).

With these signs, the rule for latitude is:

$$\text{Latitude} = \text{Declination} - \text{Zenith distance,}$$

where

$$\text{Zenith distance} = 90° - \text{maximum } H_o.$$

To determine maximum observed height, measure sextant height every minute or so as the sun crosses the meridian at midday, and then apply the altitude corrections (Section 11.2) to the maximum sextant-height value.

For example, looking south to the noon sun, we find its maximum observed height to be 70° when the sun's declination was S 21°. The zenith distance is $-(90° - 70°) = -20°$, and the declination is $-21° - (-20°) = -21° + 20° = -1° = 1°$S. And a second example: looking north to the noon sun, its maximum observed height was 60° when its declination was N 15°. The zenith distance is $+(90° - 60°) = +30°$, and the declination is $+15°$, so latitude = declination − zenith distance $= +15° - (+30°) = -15° = 15°$S.

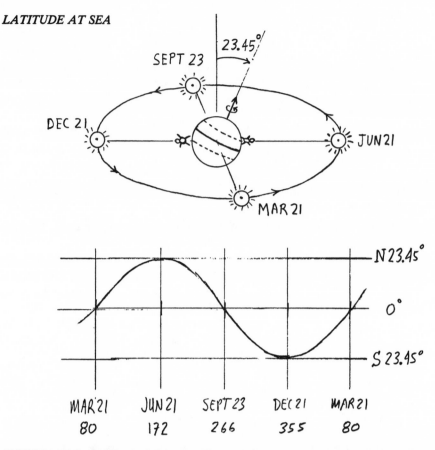

FIGURE 11-14. *Declination of the sun. The sun's declination varies from N 23.45° (23° 27') to S 23.45°. We use the decimal form here to emphasize the unique number sequence that makes the maximum value easy to remember. The turning points are at the solstices, June 21 and December 21, the longest and shortest days of the year. The sun crosses the equator on the equinoxes, March 21 and September 23, at which times the lengths of day and night are the same. The declination changes most rapidly near the equinoxes (some 24' per day) and most slowly near the solstices. The seasonal oscillation of the declination occurs because the tilt of the earth's axis remains constant as it circles the sun—here shown in reverse, with the sun circling the earth.*

To figure the declination of the sun, we first need to figure where we are within the present season by counting days. We then convert this position to an angle, since the sun's declination varies throughout the year in a circular pattern. The seasons are marked by the equinoxes and solstices, as shown in Figure 11-14, so figure the angle alpha as follows:

$$Alpha = \frac{S}{S+E} \times 90°,$$

where

$$S = \text{the number of days to the nearest solstice,}$$
$$\text{and}$$
$$E = \text{the number of days to the nearest equinox.}$$

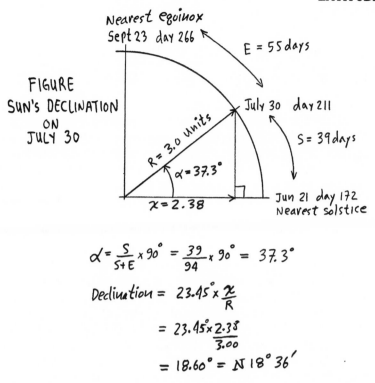

FIGURE
SUN'S DECLINATION
ON
JULY 30

Nearest equinox
Sept 23 day 266

E = 55 days

July 30 day 211

S = 39 days

R = 3.0 units

$\alpha = 37.3°$

$x = 2.38$

Jun 21 day 172
Nearest solstice

$$\alpha = \frac{S}{S+E} \times 90° = \frac{39}{94} \times 90° = 37.3°$$

$$Declination = 23.45° \times \frac{x}{R}$$

$$= \frac{23.45° \times 2.38}{3.00}$$

$$= 18.60° = N\ 18°\ 36'$$

FIGURE 11-15. *Figuring the sun's declination from the date. Count days to find your angular location within the season, construct the angle and measure the ratio of sides as shown, and use this ratio to scale the maximum value of 23.45°. The radius R can be any length. Note how the declination changes slowly as the angle (the date) rises above the solstice, but then it changes more rapidly as you approach the equinox. Plotted very carefully, this method is accurate to within 10' or so, although an accuracy of 20' to 30' is a more practical goal. A calculator solution is: Declination = 23.45° × Cos(alpha). The exact value for July 30 at noon is N 18° 29' plus or minus 6', depending on our location within the leap-year cycle. The declination on a given date varies some 10' within this cycle, but each date has the same declination every four years. Sunrise and sunset times repeat in the same manner.*

Then draw a quadrant of a circle, using a makeshift compass card (Section 3.3), and measure the ratio of X/R, as shown in Figure 11-15. You can use any units you like for the length measurements since we need only the ratio. The sun's declination is then found from:

$$Sun's\ declination = 23.45° \times (X/R).$$

We must, though, still remember when the declination is north (summer half of the year) and when it is south (winter half of the year), as shown in Figure 11-14. This procedure is accurate in principle to within about 10', but some precision is bound to be lost in the drawing. With reasonable care, accuracy to within 30' should be possible. With a sextant and no almanac, the first step would be to spend some time generating a declination table, rather than planning on figuring it separately each time you need it.

11.8 Latitude from the Length of Day

For most of the year, the length of daylight (sunrise to sunset) depends on your latitude. Sailing south during summer, the days get shorter; sailing south during the winter, the days get longer. Only near the equinoxes is the length of the day the same for all latitudes. On the equinoxes, March 21 and September 23, the sun rises at 0600 and sets at 1800 (solar time) everywhere on earth — equinox means "equal nights," because the day and night have the same length at this time. The length of day changes most rapidly with latitude near the solstices, June 21 and December 21, the longest and shortest days of the year.

For several months on either side of each solstice, the length of day changes fast enough with latitude that we can actually determine our latitude from a measurement of the length of the day. To do this, we need a watch and a set of tables that list the times of sunrise and sunset for various latitudes. A set of these tables is included in the back of the *U.S. Tide Tables*. The watch does not have to be set properly on any specific time zone. We need to measure only a time interval, not specific times.

To measure the length of the day, note the time (to the second) when the sun's upper edge first appears on the eastern horizon and again when it finally disappears below the western horizon. The length of daylight is the difference between these two times. If the sun comes up at 09:15:30 and sets at 20:16:50, the length of the day was 11:01:20.

This is a simple measurement when we can see both the sunrise and sunset. But, as mentioned in Section 6.3 on local apparent noon, it is not often that we can see the precise time of sunset or sunrise on the actual sea horizon, even in the middle of the ocean. The rim of the horizon is frequently obscured by clouds. Luckily, to use this method we do not have to see both the sunrise and sunset. We need to see only one of them — but it's easier and more accurate if we do see both.

The trick is to use a kamal to measure the time of local apparent noon (LAN), as described in Section 6.3. LAN always occurs exactly halfway between sunrise and sunset, so if we know the time of LAN, we need to measure the length of only half a day. To see how this works, we define five special times: T_{sr} = the time of sunrise; T_{am} = the time the sun is at some arbitrary low height on the kamal in the morning; T_{pm} = the time the sun is again at this height in the afternoon; T_{ss} = the time of sunset; and T_{lan} = the time of LAN, which we can figure as follows:

$$T_{lan} = \frac{(T_{am} + T_{pm})}{2}$$

Now we can find the length of day three ways, depending on what we see. Length of day = $T_{ss} - T_{sr}$, if we see both the sunset and sunrise; or length of day = $(T_{lan} - T_{sr}) \times 2$, if we see the sunrise only; or length of day = $(T_{ss} - T_{lan}) \times 2$, if we see the sunset only. In the last two cases, we are simply finding the length of half a day and multiplying by two. Furthermore, these times need not be from the same day. We can use times one or two days apart, providing we have not moved significantly. These time measurements were illustrated in Chapter 6, Figure 6-8.

Once you have the length of day, go to the sunrise-sunset tables for the proper date and your approximate latitude. For that date and latitude, subtract the tabulated sunrise time from the sunset time and compare this length of day with your measurement. Then do the same for the next larger and next smaller latitudes listed in the table. Once you have found a day length that is longer and a day length that is shorter, than the one you measured, you can interpolate the results to find your latitude. You may also have to interpolate for the proper day since all dates are not given.

If your sunrise-sunset tables (tide tables) happen to be outdated, it doesn't matter. The times of sunrise and sunset are the same each year, for all practical purposes.

This method of finding latitude works best at higher latitudes, above about 30° or so, during the two months before and after each solstice. Nearer the solstices, it works fairly well at all latitudes. This method does not work at all for a couple of weeks on either side of each equinox. However, the question of how well this method might work under particular circumstances can always be tested ahead of time. Simply look up the number of minutes the length of day changes for 1° of latitude for your date and approximate latitude. If this figure is high, say 5 minutes or more, then you have a sensitive latitude measurement. If this time is low, 1 or 2 minutes per degree, then this method will not be precise, but it will still give your latitude to within a few degrees, and possibly even better if you have a good view of sunrise and sunset. If the length of day changes by less than 1 minute per degree, this method will not be useful.

We have also assumed, so far, that the vessel is not moving. When headed west we run away from the sun in the morning and chase after it in the afternoon. As a result we stretch out the length of daylight when traveling west. Likewise we shorten the length of daylight when headed east at any latitude, which of course, affects this method since we can change the length of day without changing latitudes. This is an easy problem to correct, however, once the principles and basic chart work are understood.

When headed west during this measurement, shorten your measured day length by 4 minutes for each 1° of longitude (or 1 minute for each 15′ of longitude) you made to the west — regardless of your latitude change during the day. When headed east, lengthen the day by the same amount. Then use this corrected time to find your latitude in the sunrise-sunset tables. No correction for latitude change is required, but if your latitude does change, the latitude you figure from the length of day will be halfway between what it was at your sunrise and sunset. At steady course and speed, you will find what your latitude was at midday (see Figure 11-16).

As an example, on July 5 my DR latitude was 39° N to within 2° or so, in west longitudes. Sunrise was recorded as 05:48:20 watch time, and my course was north-west (315 T) at 6 knots and steady throughout the day. Sunset was recorded as 20:38:12 watch time. The measured day length was 20:38:12 – 05:48:20, or 14:49:52, which equals 14.8 hours. At 6 knots, I ran about 89 miles toward 315 T from sunrise to sunset, which corresponds to a westing of 63 miles when the course is plotted. At latitude 39° there is about 47 miles to each 1° of longitude (explained in Figure 12-9, next chapter); so my longitude increased by 63 miles x (1°/47 miles), or 1.34°. This calls for a longitude correction of 1.34° x (4 minutes/1°), or 5.36 minutes which equals 5 minutes and 22 seconds. The corrected day length is then

SUNRISE AND SUNSET, 1985

Date	34° N. Rise	34° N. Set	36° N. Rise	36° N. Set	38° N. Rise	38° N. Set	40° N. Rise	40° N. Set
	h m	h m	h m	h m	h m	h m	h m	h m
July 5	04 54	19 15	04 49	19 20	04 43	19 26	04 37	19 32
10	04 57	19 14	04 51	19 19	04 46	19 25	04 40	19 30
15	05 00	19 12	04 54	19 17	04 49	19 22	04 43	19 28
20	05 03	19 10	04 58	19 14	04 53	19 19	04 47	19 25
25	05 06	19 06	05 02	19 11	04 57	19 16	04 52	19 21
30	05 10	19 03	05 05	19 07	05 01	19 11	04 56	19 16

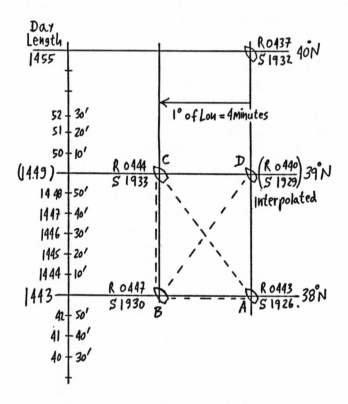

FIGURE 11-16. *How sunrise and sunset times change with location on July 5. Sailing west, sunrise and sunset times increase by 4 minutes for each 1° of longitude covered. Sailing toward the latitude of the sun's declination, the sun rises later and sets earlier, shortening the length of the day, but not in a way that is easy to predict. To find latitude from the length of day, we must correct the measured day length for our change in longitude. Sailing 1° west from A to B, the sunrises (R) at 0443 and sets (S) at 1930, for a measured day length of 1447. The corrected day is 1447 minus 4 minutes, or 1443, which, from the tables, we learn must have been at latitude 38° N. The answer we get will always be halfway between our latitude at sunrise and our latitude at sunset, which in this case are the same. Sailing 1° east from B to D, the sunrises at 0447 and sets at 1929, for a measured day length of 1442. The corrected day is 1442 plus 4 minutes, or 1446, which from the tables we learn must have been across a mid latitude of 38° 30' N. Check other routes among the points shown to see more of how this works.*

14:49:52 – 5 minutes and 22 seconds, or 14:44:30. The tables tell me that on July 5 the day length at latitude 38°N is 1443 and at 40°N it is 1455. I can plot these out as shown in Figure 11-16 to discover that my latitude at noon on July 5 was 38° 15′ N.

If I had not made the longitudinal correction, my latitude would have been wrong by about 1°. This is an important correction. This method works best at higher latitudes where longitude changes more rapidly with east-west progress. The conversion between distance run and longitude interval as discussed in Chapter 12 on longitude.

11.9 Keeping Track of Latitude

The first way to keep track of latitude is dead reckoning (DR). Sailing due south or north, your latitude changes by 1° for each 60 nautical miles you cover. Sailing due east or west, your latitude doesn't change. On a diagonal course, you will need a makeshift chart to figure out your latitude change.

To make a chart, draw a vertical line for the latitude scale and a horizontal line for the longitude scale. The intersection of these two lines marks your initial position. Then choose a convenient miles scale for the voyage you anticipate. One inch or one finger width could be 1 mile or 60 miles, depending on how far you have to go. Since 60 miles equals 1° of latitude, you can use your chosen scale and this conversion to mark off the latitude scale in degrees and then draw in the latitude lines. See the example in Figure 11-17.

As you sail from your initial position, keep track of your DR position on the makeshift chart. With this type of chart, you can read your latitude in degrees, but you will have to keep track of your longitude in terms of miles east or west of your initial longitude (Section 12.4 tells how to figure your longitude in degrees with this type of chart.)

We should always keep track of our DR latitude as accurately as possible and compare it to our star measurements at every opportunity. These two independent sources of latitude measurements support and strengthen each other. The methods of finding latitude from the sun and stars that we have discussed so far are most valuable when we start navigating from an unknown position. In this case, we must "discover" our latitude. But if we are starting from a known latitude, it is a much easier job to simply keep track of our latitude with the stars as we move away from the known position. In this case, we have to measure changes in latitude only.

The principle behind measuring changes in latitude is simple. If we sail south, stars on the southern meridian rise, and those on the northern meridian descend. And their height changes by the exact amount that our latitude changes. The reverse occurs as we change latitudes to the north.

For measuring latitude changes, we can use any star that happens to be on the meridian at twilight. We can use northern or southern stars, and we can use stars of any height — but, again, we will generally get more accurate results from lower

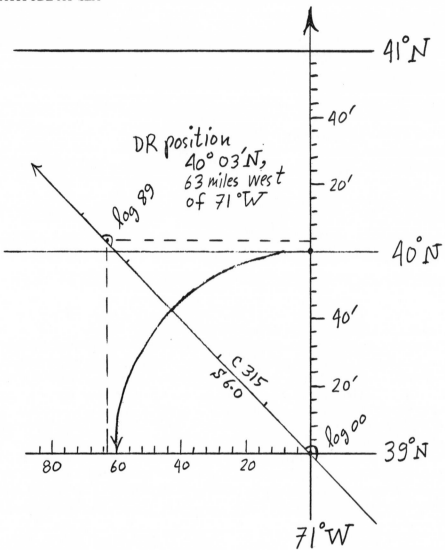

FIGURE 11-17. *A makeshift plotting sheet. A northwest run of 89 miles yields a westward progress of 63 miles. DR latitude can be read directly from this chart, but longitude **degrees** must be figured separately, as explained in Section 12.4 and Figure 12-9.*

stars. The big advantage is that we do not need to know the names or the declinations of the stars we use. We only have to be able to spot the same stars each night. It does help the bookkeeping, though, to make up names for the stars we use.

The procedure is to rig a kamal to mark the height of a star as it crosses the meridian at twilight. The height of the star can even be fairly high, since we don't care about exact angle measurements for this application, only relative ones. As the voyage progresses, we can watch the position of the star change on the kamal, as illustrated in Figure 11-18. We can then compare the change in position (a length

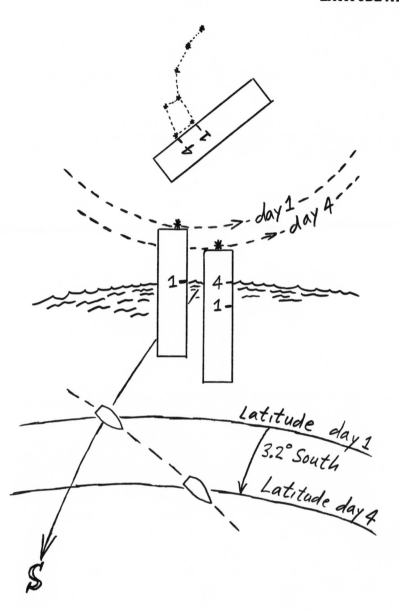

FIGURE 11-18. *Progress to the south noted by descending stars. Here a kamal is used to mark the height of a star crossing the northern meridian at twilight on day 1 and again on day 4. During these four days, the star descended the width of the Guards, so we know we have made good 3.2° to the south. This measurement tells nothing about longitude directly, although it might tell you something about your general dead-reckoning accuracy. If your DR agrees with the 3.2° of southing, you know there is no strong north-south component to your drift, which in some circumstances might give supporting, though not definite, information on longitude reckoning. If the current set is most likely to the southeast in this region, for example, you have learned that its drift must be small, or it would have thrown off the DR latitude.*

along the kamal) with one of the standard references like the distance between the Guards, Orion's belt, or others discussed in Section 11.1. If a particular star on the northern meridian descends as the voyage progresses by an amount equal to the distance between the Guards, we know we have traveled about 3.2°, or 192 miles south.

This is a very powerful method of keeping track of latitude. You can use the northern and southern meridian at morning and evening twilight. This method provides one of the best reasons for learning several reference distances between pairs of stars.

12

Longitude at Sea

Longitude is time and time is longitude. If we know GMT, we can find our longitude from any place on any date. And equally important, if we know our longitude at the time of an emergency, we can find GMT (if we didn't know it), and then use it to keep track of longitude as we move on. Left in an unknown position with nothing but GMT, we find longitude from the sun. In contrast, left in an unknown position with everything but GMT, we find longitude from the moon (Section 14.3).

But we need slightly more than just a timepiece to find longitude from the sun. We need special information, listed in almanacs or easily figured from sunrise-sunset tables. Or, without either of these, we can figure it from the date using a makeshift prescription.

The principles behind the methods are easy to see, using the sun's meridian passage at LAN as an example. The sun appears to move westward around the earth once a day, crossing over 360° of longitude every 24 hours, which means the sun moves west at a rate of 15° of longitude per hour. If I see the sun on my meridian now, then someone at a longitude 15° west of me will see the sun on his meridian exactly 1 hour later, regardless of his latitude. If I happen to be at longitude 60° W and the sun crosses the Greenwich meridian (longitude 0°) at 1200 GMT, then the sun will pass me at exactly 1600 GMT, since it takes 4 hours to cover 60° of longitude at 15° per hour (see Figure 12-1). And that is the extent of the theory. If we know when the sun passes Greenwich and we can determine when it passes us, we can figure out our longitude as the number of hours between these two times multiplied by 15. Whenever the sun passes us after passing Greenwich, our longitude is west. If the sun passes us on the way to Greenwich, our longitude is east.

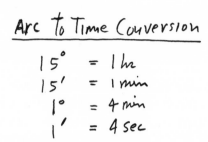

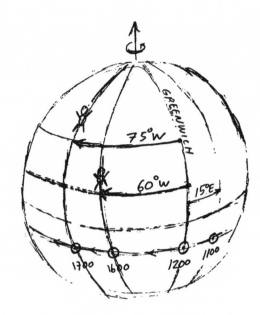

FIGURE 12-1. *As the earth turns daily on its axis the sun moves west at 15° of longitude per hour. On a daily basis, the sun's latitude remains essentially constant, although on a yearly basis it varies slowly back and forth across the tropics.*

This principle can be applied to the time of LAN, as just described, or to the time of sunrise or sunset. In either case, we compare a measured time with the corresponding time at Greenwich, and the difference is our longitude. The time at Greenwich must be looked up in tables or figured from the date using a rule.

GMT is fundamental to emergency longitude. Wear a watch and keep track of GMT, and with very little practice you can always find your longitude. Even if you don't know GMT or where you are to begin with, a watch is still extremely valuable for keeping track of longitude, as we shall see. Unlike latitude, we must have a watch to check DR longitude against celestial motions.

12.1 Longitude from Sunrise or Sunset

The easiest way to find emergency longitude is to time the sunrise or sunset. To use this method, we need to know GMT and we also need sunrise-sunset tables from an almanac or tide tables. This method can be used anywhere on any date, providing that you can indeed see the sun rise or set over the true sea horizon. But since the rim of the horizon is often obscured by low clouds, this method will not be useful everyday even when the other means are there. Sunrise time depends on latitude, so we must find our latitude first before we can find our longitude this way.

The time of sunrise we want is the moment the top of the sun's disk (upper limb) first appears on the sea horizon. The time of sunset is the moment the sun's disk disappears completely. To find longitude, note the watch time of sunrise or sunset to the second, and convert this time to GMT by correcting for the time zone of the watch and the current watch error. Then look up the tabulated time of sunrise or sunset for your date and latitude (which might require an interpolation). Subtract the predicted time from the observed time and convert the time difference to degrees. This difference is your longitude. The conversion rate is 15° per hour, but smaller divisions are also useful and easy to figure:

$$15° = 1 \text{ hour} \qquad 15' = 1 \text{ minute}$$
$$1° = 4 \text{ minutes} \qquad 1' = 4 \text{ seconds.}$$

In west longitudes, the observed GMT will be later than the tabulated time. In east longitudes, it will be earlier.

As an example, let's say I am wearing a watch set to Pacific daylight saving time, which is 7 hours behind GMT. The watch gains 0.5 seconds a day, and it was set to the proper time on July 4. It is now August 4, my latitude is 36° N, and I note that the time of sunset is 21:49:31 by my watch. What is my longitude?

From July 4 to August 4 is 31 days, so my watch on August 4 is about 15 seconds fast. The correct GMT of sunset, therefore, is 21:49:31 plus 7 hours minus 15 seconds, or 28:49:16 — which is actually 04:49:16 the next day, but this doesn't matter since we care only about time differences, not times. In the tables (Figure 12-2), I find that on August 4 at latitude 36° N, the time of sunset is listed as 1902. This tabulated time is the GMT of sunset observed from longitude 0°. The time difference is 28:49:16 minus 19:02:00, or 09:47:16, which can be converted to degrees as follows: 9 hours = 135°; 47 minutes = 11° 45'; 16 seconds = 4'. Summing these parts, my longitude is 146° 49' W.

Remember, it is always the time zone of your watch that matters, not the time zone you happen to be in. With accurate time and sunrise-sunset tables, this method

TABLE 4.-SUNRISE AND SUNSET, 1985

Date	30° N. Rise	30° N. Set	32° N. Rise	32° N. Set	34° N. Rise	34° N. Set	36° N. Rise	36° N. Set	38° N. Rise	38° N. Set	40° N. Rise	40° N. Set
	h m	h m	h m	h m	h m	h m	h m	h m	h m	h m	h m	h m
Aug. 4	05 20	18 51	05 17	18 55	05 13	18 58	05 09	19 02	05 05	19 06	05 01	19 11
9	05 24	18 47	05 20	18 50	05 17	18 54	05 13	18 57	05 09	19 01	05 05	19 05
14	05 27	18 42	05 24	18 45	05 21	18 45	05 17	18 52	05 14	18 55	05 10	18 58
19	05 29	18 37	05 27	18 40	05 24	18 43	05 21	18 45	05 18	18 48	05 15	18 52
24	05 32	18 32	05 30	18 34	05 28	18 37	05 25	18 39	05 23	18 42	05 20	18 44
29	05 35	18 26	05 33	18 28	05 31	18 30	05 29	18 32	05 27	18 34	05 24	18 37
Sept. 3	05 38	18 21	05 36	18 22	05 35	18 24	05 33	18 25	05 31	18 27	05 29	18 29
8	05 41	18 14	05 39	18 16	05 38	18 17	05 37	18 18	05 35	18 19	05 34	18 21
13	05 43	18 08	05 42	18 09	05 42	18 10	05 41	18 11	05 40	18 12	05 39	18 13
18	05 46	18 02	05 46	18 02	05 45	18 03	05 45	18 03	05 44	18 04	05 43	18 04
23	05 49	17 56	05 49	17 56	05 49	17 56	05 48	17 56	05 48	17 56	05 48	17 56
28	05 51	17 50	05 52	17 49	05 52	17 49	05 52	17 49	05 53	17 48	05 53	17 48

FIGURE 12-2. *Section of the sunrise-sunset tables from the* U.S. Tide Tables. *These times are essentially the same from year to year so out-dated tables can be used. Similar tables appear on the daily pages of the* Nautical Almanac.

Find Sunset time on
Aug. 7 at 37° 20′N

	36°N	(37° 20′N)	38°N
AUG 4	1902		1906
(AUG 7)	(1859)	(19:01:40)	(1903)
AUG 9	1857		1901

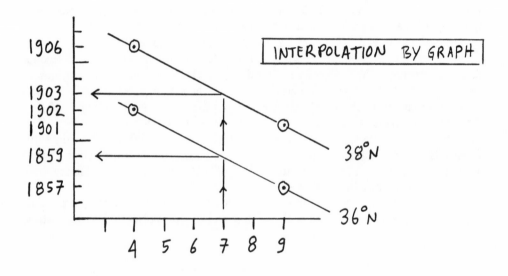

INTERPOLATION BY GRAPH

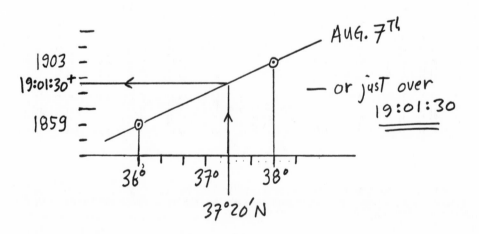

AUG. 7ᵀᴴ

— or just over
19:01:30

37°20′N

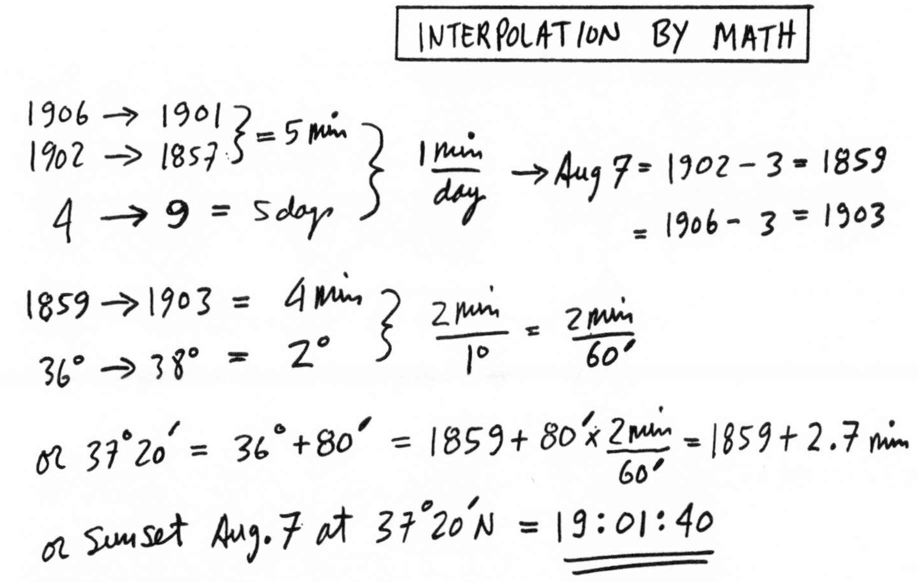

$$\boxed{\text{INTERPOLATION BY MATH}}$$

$\left.\begin{array}{l} 1906 \rightarrow 1901 \\ 1902 \rightarrow 1857 \end{array}\right\} = 5\,min$

$\left. \begin{array}{l} 4 \rightarrow 9 = 5\,day \end{array} \right\}$ $\dfrac{1\,min}{day} \rightarrow Aug\ 7 = 1902 - 3 = 1859$

$\qquad\qquad\qquad\qquad = 1906 - 3 = 1903$

$\left. \begin{array}{l} 1859 \rightarrow 1903 = 4\,min \\ 36° \rightarrow 38° = 2° \end{array} \right\}$ $\dfrac{2\,min}{1°} = \dfrac{2\,min}{60'}$

or $37°20' = 36° + 80' = 1859 + 80' \times \dfrac{2\,min}{60'} = 1859 + 2.7\,min$

or Sunset Aug. 7 at $37°20'N = \underline{\underline{19:01:40}}$

FIGURE 12-3. *Interpolating sunrise-sunset tables for date and latitude. The tabulated values used are from Figure 12-2.*

is very reliable. You can count on a longitude accuracy of 20' or so if you interpolate the sunrise tables and if you know your latitude well. Furthermore, with the tables you can always figure how sensitive this method is to your latitude accuracy. Suppose the tables show that, for your date and latitude, the sunset time changes by 2 minutes for a 1° change in latitude. In this case, if your latitude is uncertain by 1°, the sunset time at Greenwich that you get from the tables will be uncertain by 2 minutes, so the longitude you figure from it will be uncertain by 30'. Longitude error due to a timing error is always the same. If your watch time is wrong by 1 minute, your longitude will be wrong by 15'. Usually we must interpolate the sunrise-sunset tables for both latitude and date as shown in Figure 12.3.

12.2 Longitude from LAN (the Equation of Time)

We find longitude from the time of LAN just as we do from sunrise or sunset, but for this method we do not need to know our latitude. An almanac or sunrise-sunset tables are very helpful, but if need be we can do without them also.

First use a kamal (or sextant, if you have one) to measure the GMT of LAN, as discussed in Sections 6.3 and 11.8. Then compare the measured GMT of LAN with the GMT of LAN at Greenwich — which we must look up or figure from the date —

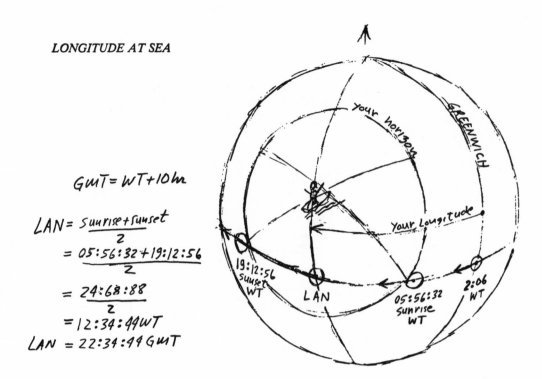

$$GMT = WT + 10^m$$

$$LAN = \frac{sunrise + sunset}{2}$$

$$= \frac{05:56:32 + 19:12:56}{2}$$

$$= \frac{24:68:88}{2}$$

$$= 12:34:44 \, WT$$

$$LAN = 22:34:44 \, GMT$$

FIGURE 12-4. *Measuring the time of LAN from observed Watch Times of sunrise and sunset. The Watch Time (WT) is 10 hours behind GMT.*

and proceed to find longitude as you do with sunrise or sunset times. We can get the GMT of LAN at Greenwich from sunrise-sunset tables by finding the time halfway between the tabulated sunrise and sunset on the proper date, interpolating if necessary. Just use an approximate latitude for this, since the time of LAN does not depend on latitude. To figure the midday time, just add the tabulated sunrise time to the sunset time and divide by 2. You can even use outdated tables, since these values do not change much from year to year.

As an example, on August 4 at approximate latitude 30° N, I determine the GMT of LAN to be 22:34:44 from the time halfway between the observed sunrise and sunset times as illustrated in Figure 12-4. From sunrise-sunset tables (Figure 12-2), I learn that sunrise on August 4 at latitude 30° N is at 0520 and sunset is at 1851. So LAN at Greenwich is

$$\frac{(05:20:00 + 18:51:00)}{2} = \frac{(21:11:00)}{2} = 12:05:30.$$

The time difference between the observed GMT of LAN and the corresponding time at Greenwich is 22:34:44 − 12:05:30, or 10:29:14. And to find longitude, I convert this time difference to degrees:

$$
\begin{aligned}
10 \text{ hours} &= 10h \times 15°/1h &&= 150°, \\
29 \text{ minutes} &= 29m \times 15'/1m &&= 7°15', \text{ and} \\
14 \text{ seconds} &= 14s \times 1'/4s &&= 3.5'.
\end{aligned}
$$

Summing the parts, my longitude is 157°18.5′ W. Practical results will certainly not be accurate to this precision, although one can improve on a single Greenwich time obtained from sunrise tables by averaging values from several latitudes at the same date, as shown in Part A of Figure 12-5.

TABLE 4.—SUNRISE AND SUNSET, 1985

Date	0° Rise	0° Set	5° N. Rise	5° N. Set	10° N. Rise	10° N. Set	15° N. Rise	15° N. Set	20° N. Rise	20° N. Set	25° N. Rise	25° N. Set
	h m	h m	h m	h m	h m	h m	h m	h m	h m	h m	h m	h m
Sept. 3	05 56	18 03	05 53	18 05	05 51	18 08	05 48	18 11	05 45	18 14	05 42	18 17
8	05 54	18 01	05 52	18 03	05 50	18 05	05 48	18 07	05 46	18 09	05 43	18 12
13	05 53	17 59	05 51	18 01	05 50	18 02	05 49	18 03	05 47	18 05	05 45	18 07
18	05 51	17 57	05 50	17 59	05 50	17 59	05 49	18 00	05 48	18 00	05 47	18 01
23	05 49	17 56	05 49	17 56	05 49	17 56	05 49	17 56	05 49	17 56	05 49	18 01
28	05 48 +17 54		05 48 +17 53		05 49 +17 53		05 49 +17 52		05 50 +17 51		05 51 +17 50	

$$= \frac{22:102}{2} \quad\Big|\quad = \frac{22:101}{2} \quad\Big|\quad = \frac{22:102}{2} \quad\Big|\quad = \frac{22:101}{2} \quad\Big|\quad = \frac{22:101}{2} \quad\Big|\quad = \frac{22:101}{2}$$

$$= 11:51.0 \quad\Big|\quad = 11:50.5 \quad\Big|\quad = 11:51.0 \quad\Big|\quad = 11:50.5 \quad\Big|\quad = 11:50.5 \quad\Big|\quad = 11:50.5$$

1   2   3   4   5   6

AVERAGE OF 6 VALUES IS 11:50.67 = 11:50:40   (A)

1985 SEPTEMBER 28, 29, 30 (SAT., SUN., MON.)   191

G.M.T.	SUN G.H.A.	SUN Dec.	MOON G.H.A.	MOON v	MOON Dec.	MOON d	MOON H.P.	Lat.	Twilight Naut.	Twilight Civil	Sunrise	Moonrise 28	Moonrise 29	Moonrise 30	Moonrise 1
	° ′	° ′	° ′	′	° ′	′	′	°	h m	h m	h m	h m	h m	h m	h m
28 00	182 17.9	S 1 54.8	11 11.2	16.0	S 6 00.7	14.0	55.0	N 72	03 38	05 02	06 09	18 08	17 38	17 06	16 22
01	197 18.1	55.8	25 46.2	15.9	5 46.7	14.0	55.0	N 70	03 52	05 06	06 07	18 06	17 43	17 19	16 49
02	212 18.3	56.7	40 21.1	16.0	5 32.7	14.0	55.0	68	04 03	05 10	06 05	18 04	17 47	17 30	17 09
03	227 18.5	57.7	54 56.1	16.0	5 18.7	14.0	55.0	66	04 11	05 13	06 04	18 02	17 51	17 39	17 25
04	242 18.7	58.7	69 31.1	16.1	5 04.7	14.1	55.0	64	04 19	05 15	06 02	18 01	17 53	17 46	17 38
05	257 18.9	1 59.7	84 06.2	16.1	4 50.6	14.0	55.0	62	04 25	05 17	06 01	17 59	17 56	17 53	17 50
06	272 19.1	S 2 00.6	98 41.3	16.1	S 4 36.6	14.1	54.9	60	04 30	05 19	06 00	17 58	17 58	17 58	17 59
07	287 19.3	01.6	113 16.4	16.2				N 58	04 34	05 20	05 59	17 57	18 00	18 04	18 08
08	302 19.6	02.6	127 51.6					56		05 22	05 59	17 56	18 02	18 08	18 15
09	317 19.8	03.6						54			05 58	17 56	18 04	18 12	18 22
10	332 20.0	04.5			35.1	13.4	54.3	S 50	18 09		05 57	17 56	18 06	18 16	
11	347 20.2		44.5	8	08.5	13.3	54.3	52	18 09	18 46					86 28
12	2 20.4		80.2	16.4	8 21.8	13.3	54.3	54	18 10	18 46	19 20				86 16
13	17		225 01.0	16.4	8 35.1	13.3	54.2	56	18 12	18 49	19 36	05 55	05 58	06 04	86 04
			225 01.0	16.3	8 48.4	13.2	54.2	58	18 13	18 53	19 41	05 54	05 57	06 00	86 04
			239 36.3	16.4	9 01.6	13.2	54.2	S 60	18 15	18 57	19 49	05 57	05 57	05 57	05 57
		S 2 58.9	254 11.7	16.3	N 9 14.8	13.2	54.2								
	31.8	2 59.9	268 47.0	16.3	9 28.0	13.1	54.2	Day	SUN Eqn. of Time 00ʰ	SUN Eqn. of Time 12ʰ	SUN Mer. Pass.	MOON Mer. Pass. Upper	MOON Mer. Pass. Lower	Age	Phase
21	122 32.0	3 00.9	283 22.3	16.2	9 41.1	13.1	54.2		m s	m s	h m	h m	h m	d	
22	137 32.2	01.8	297 57.5	16.3	9 54.2	13.0	54.2	28	09 11	09 21	11 51	23 55	11 34	14	O
23	152 32.4	02.8	312 32.8	16.2	10 07.2	13.0	54.2	29	09 31	09 41	11 50	24 35	12 15	15	
	167 32.6	03.8	327 08.0	16.1	10 20.2	12.9	54.2	30	09 51	10 01	11 50	00 35	12 55	16	
	S.D. 16.0	d 1.0	S.D. 14.9		14.9		14.8								

EXACT VALUE
from
NAUTICAL ALMANAC

= 12:00 − EₒT

= 11:59:60
  − 09:21

= 11:50:39
  (B)

(C) MAKESHIFT PRESCRIPTION (Fig. 12-7) GIVES   11:50:30

FIGURE 12-5. *Comparison of three ways to find the GMT of LAN at Greenwich. (A) From sunrise-sunset tables, using the average of several latitudes to get a more precise value for a given date. (B) The exact value from the* Nautical Almanac, *found by adding or subtracting the tabulated Equation of Time (at 12 h GMT) to 12:00:00. Note the "Mer. Pass." time listed is what we want, but it is only listed to the closest minute. It does, though, tell us if we should add or subtract. (C) From the makeshift prescription illustrated in Figure 12-7.*

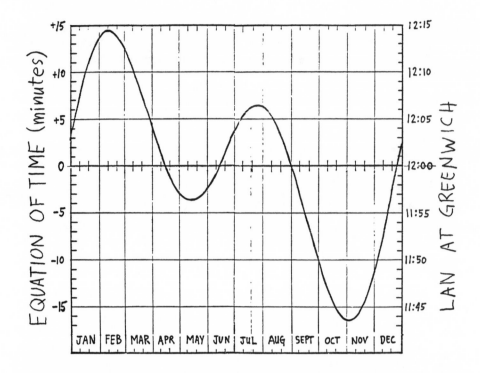

FIGURE 12-6. *The Equation of Time and the GMT of LAN at Greenwich, which is 12:00:00 corrected for the Equation of Time.*

You can determine the time of LAN from the observed times of sunrise and sunset (LAN is halfway between the two), or you can use a kamal to measure the times of equal heights of the sun, as described in Section 6.3. When the sun is low, you can often get these times quite accurately before the sun is too bright to look at. When using a kamal, take the halfway times between several heights and average the results, as illustrated in Figure 6-8 of Chapter 6. Your longitude will only be as accurate as your LAN time. With practice, you should be able to get this time to within a minute or so, corresponding to a longitude accuracy of 15' if you know the GMT of LAN at Greenwich. With a sextant, you can find the time of LAN from morning and afternoon heights quite easily to within 30 seconds when not moving very fast in the north-south direction.

The LAN method of longitude requires more careful measurements than the sunrise method does, but it typically can be used more often since it is not limited by horizon clouds. The greater advantage, however, is that we can use this method without special tables if need be. We can figure the time of LAN at Greenwich from the date, but we can't figure the time of sunrise or sunset without tables.

The GMT of LAN at Greenwich varies from 1144 to 1214 throughout the year due to the tilt of the earth's axis and our (slightly non-circular) orbital motion around the sun. The variation is gradual, but the annual pattern it follows is complex as shown in Figure 12.5. The difference between 1200 and the GMT of LAN at Greenwich is called the "equation of time." It is listed in almanacs (see Part B of Figure 12.5) or can be figured from the date using the following prescription.

How to figure the equation of time

On Valentine's Day, February 14, the sun is late on the meridian by 14 minutes (LAN at 1214); 3 months later, it is early by 4 minutes (LAN at 1156).

On Halloween, October 31, the sun is early on the meridian by 16 minutes (LAN at 1144); 3 months earlier, it is late by 6 minutes (LAN at 1206).

These four dates mark the turning points in the equation of time. We can assume that the values at the turning points remain constant for 2 weeks on either side of the turn, as shown in Figure 12-7. Between these dates, assume the variation is proportional to the date.

There is some symmetry to this prescription, which may help you remember it:

| 14 late | 3 months later | goes to | 4 early |
| 16 early | 3 months earlier | goes to | 6 late |

— but I admit it is no catchy jingle. Knowing the general shape of the curve and the form of the prescription, however, has been enough to help me remember it for some years now. It also helps to have been late sometimes on Valentine's Day. An example of its use, when interpolation is required, is shown in Figure 12-7.

The accuracy of the prescription is shown in Figure 12-8. It is generally accurate to within a minute or so, which means that longitude figured from it will generally be accurate to within 15' or so.

This process for figuring the equation of time may appear involved at first, but if you work out a few examples and check yourself with the almanac it should fall into place. If we are going to memorize something that could be of great value, this is it. When you know this and have an accurate watch, you will always be able to find your longitude. You don't need anything else. With this point in mind, it is worth the trouble to learn it.

Also remember that the LAN method tells you what your longitude *was* at LAN, even though it may have taken all day to find it. To figure your present longitude, you must DR from LAN to the present. Procedures for converting between distance intervals and longitude intervals are covered in Section 12.4.

For completeness we should add that, strictly speaking, this method assumes your latitude does not change much between the morning and afternoon sights used to find the time of LAN. A latitude change distorts the path of the sun so that the time halfway between equal sun heights is no longer precisely equal to LAN. Consider an extreme example of LAN determined from sunrise and sunset when these times are changing by 4 minutes per 1° of latitude (above latitude 44° near the solstices). If we

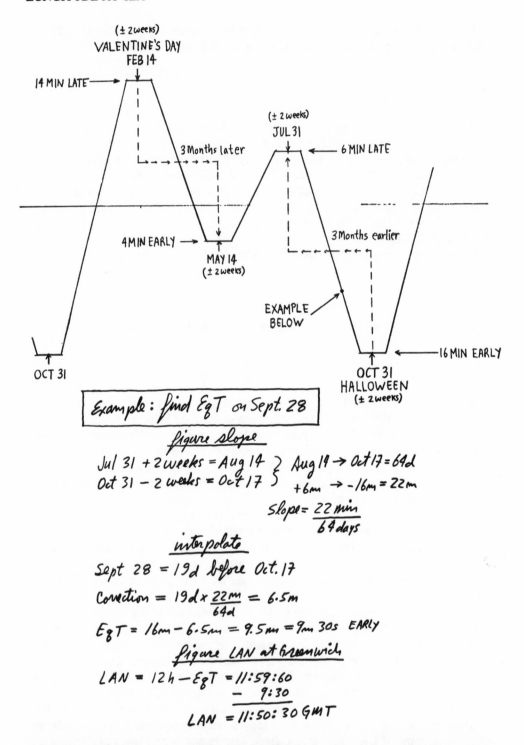

(± 2 weeks)
VALENTINE'S DAY
FEB 14

14 MIN LATE

3 Months later

4 MIN EARLY

MAY 14
(± 2 weeks)

(± 2 weeks)
JUL 31

6 MIN LATE

3 Months earlier

EXAMPLE
BELOW

OCT 31

OCT 31
HALLOWEEN
(± 2 weeks)

16 MIN EARLY

Example: find EqT on Sept. 28

figure slope

Jul 31 + 2 weeks = Aug 14 ⎫ Aug 14 → Oct 17 = 64d
Oct 31 − 2 weeks = Oct 17 ⎭ +6m → −16m = 22m

Slope = $\dfrac{22\ min}{64\ days}$

interpolate

Sept 28 = 19d before Oct. 17

Correction = 19d × $\dfrac{22m}{64d}$ = 6.5m

EqT = 16m − 6.5m = 9.5m = 9m 30s EARLY

figure LAN at Greenwich

LAN = 12h − EqT = 11:59:60
            −   9:30
LAN = 11:50:30 GMT

FIGURE 12-7. *Makeshift prescription for finding the Equation of Time (EqT). Values at the turning points are assumed constant for two weeks on either side. Intermediate values must be interpolated as shown. The rule begins with "14 minutes late on Valentine's Day..."*

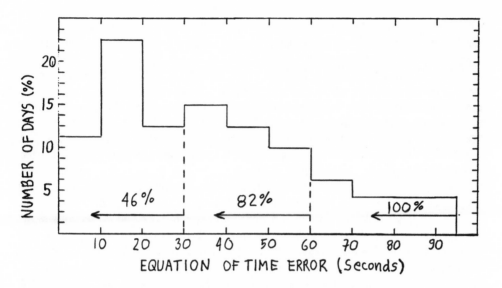

FIGURE 12-8. *Errors in the makeshift prescription for the Equation of Time. For 82 percent of the year the values are accurate to within 60 seconds. The maximum error is 95 seconds, which occurs during 4 percent of the year.*

sail due south 2° between sunrise and sunset, the sunset time will be wrong by 8 minutes, which makes the halfway time of LAN wrong by 4 minutes. The longitude error would be 60′, or 1°. But it is only a rare situation like this that would lead to so large an error. It is not easy to correct for this when using low sights to determine the time of LAN. For emergency longitude, we can overlook this problem.

In preparing for emergency navigation before a long voyage, it is clearly useful to know the equation of time. Generally, it will change little during a typical ocean passage. Preparing for emergency longitude calculations from the sun involves the same sort of memorization required for emergency latitude calculations. For example, departing on a planned 30-day passage starting on July 1, you might remember that the sun's declination varies from N 23° 8′ to N 18° 35′ and that the time of LAN at Greenwich varies from 1204 to 1206. Then, knowing the emergency prescriptions for figuring latitude and longitude, we can derive accurate values for any date during this period.

12.3 Finding GMT from a Known Position

We have found longitude from time. We now find time from longitude. At the time of an emergency, I might know my longitude but not the time zone or current error of the only watch available. The task then is to use the sun and known position to set the watch. From then on, I could use the watch to keep track of longitude as I move away from the known position.

Take the following example. Without moving from the known position during the day, I find the time of LAN to be 11:15:30 by the only watch available, and I know I am at longitude 67° 25′ W. From sunrise-sunset tables or from the prescription of Section 12.2, I figure that the equation of time for this day is minus 13 minutes and 30 seconds, so the GMT of LAN at Greenwich is 12:00:00 minus 00:13:30, or 11:46:30. I am west of Greenwich by 67° 25′, which equals 04:29:40 when converted to time at the rate of 15° per hour. Therefore, the GMT of LAN at my longitude should have been 11:46:30 plus 04:29:40, or 15:75:70, which equals 16:16:10. Since the watch read 11:15:30, it is slow on GMT by 16:16:10 minus 11:15:30, or 05:01:40. This watch is set on time zone plus 5 hours and is 1 minute and 40 seconds slow. From now on, I know GMT is the watch time of this watch, plus 5 hours, 1 minute and 40 seconds. With the necessary tables, you could discover the same thing using the observed time of sunrise or sunset.

In a case like this, you almost certainly won't know the watch rate — how much time it gains or loses each day. Without knowing its rate, as time goes by and you move away from the known position, you will gradually lose track of the time. Modern quartz watches, however, are quite accurate. On average, one might gain or lose only 15 seconds or less per month. So it is probable that the uncertainty caused by an unknown watch rate would remain small for a long time. With a modern quartz watch, it would definitely be smaller than the uncertainty in the measured time of LAN or in our makeshift prescription for the equation of time.

Obviously, this procedure is of no value if you don't have a good watch or you don't know where you are to begin with. The key to good emergency navigation is prudent navigation before an emergency occurs. Know where you are to the best of your ability at all times, and wear a good watch.

12.4 Keeping Track of Longitude

The accuracy of emergency longitude calculations from the sun and GMT depends on both our knowledge and measurement skills. In special cases, the accuracy may be high and the measurements easy. With accurate time, careful work, and some luck, we should be able to achieve an accuracy to within 50 miles or so from an unknown position. But with uncertainties in watch error, sun-height measurements, and the equation of time, we must consider that an accuracy to within some 90 miles is a more realistic goal — which is about the same level of accuracy we might expect for latitude without especially favorable conditions.

And to stress another point again, we can generally travel a long distance from a known position by careful dead reckoning before our position uncertainty increases to 90 miles. In many situations, our time and effort are better spent on careful dead reckoning than on trying to discover our position from the sun or stars. Eventually,

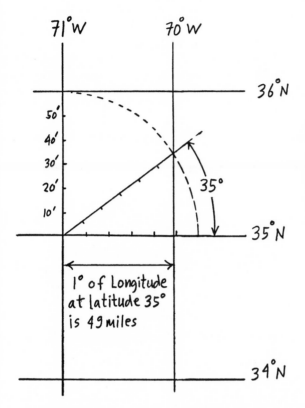

FIGURE 12-9. *A makeshift plotting sheet. Swing a 6-unit arc between the mid latitude and longitude, then draw an angle equal to your mid latitude as shown. The next meridian goes through the intersection of the arc and the angle. The procedure is identical to that used in conventional universal plotting sheets.*

though, it is the interplay between dead reckoning and direct measurement that will be the key to keeping tract of latitude and longitude on a long voyage.

Changes in latitude are easy to figure from distance run, since 1° of latitude always equals 60 nautical miles. Changes in longitude are not as easy to reckon because the number of miles to a degree of longitude changes with latitude. Throughout the tropics, we can assume that 1° of longitude also equals 60 nautical miles, but as our latitude increases from there, the number of miles to a degree of longitude begins to decrease — and the farther we get from the tropics, the faster it decreases. Because of this complication, we could end up keeping track of position with a hybrid notation such as latitude 35° 10′ N, longitude 58 miles west of 68° 30′ W.

This hybrid system works fine for recording progress, but to figure your distance off a known longitude such as a coastline or island, or to keep track of longitude with the sun, you need to convert east-west miles to longitude degrees and minutes. With a pilot chart or any chart showing your latitude region, you can read longitude miles directly from the chart scales. Or we can figure this without a chart.

Without a chart you can use the procedure illustrated in Figure 12-9. Draw a

FIGURE 12-10. *Makeshift chart showing a diagonal run of 89 miles with one course change. Westing in miles can be read directly using the latitude scale, but the longitude interval must be figured from the conversion factor of 49 miles per 1° of longitude at 35° latitude, which was found in Figure 12-9.*

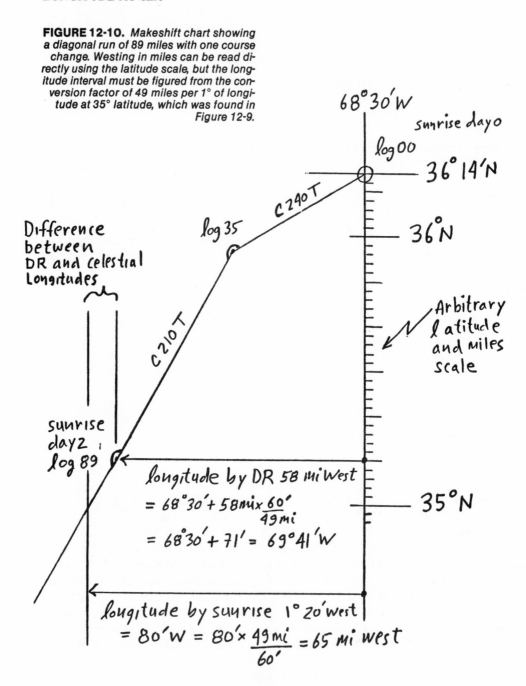

68°30'W

sunrise day0

log 00

36°14'N

C 240 T

log 35

36°N

C 210 T

Difference between DR and celestial Longitudes

Arbitrary latitude and miles scale

sunrise day2
log 89

longitude by DR 58 mi West

$= 68°30' + 58$ mi $\times \dfrac{60'}{49$ mi$}$

$= 68°30' + 71' = 69°41'W$

35°N

longitude by sunrise 1°20'west

$= 80'W = 80' \times \dfrac{49\,mi}{60'} = 65$ mi west

quadrant of a circle with a 6-unit radius to represent 60 nautical miles. Then from the center of the circle lay off an angle above the base equal to your latitude (north or south). At the point where the latitude angle intersects the circle, draw a line straight down to the base of the quadrant. The distance along the base from this line to the center of the circle is the number of miles per degree of longitude when measured with the same units used for the radius. By varying the latitude angle, you can see how the length of a longitude degree decreases with increasing latitude.

As an example of the use of this procedure, suppose that I am near 35° N in west longitudes and find that after a two-day run my longitude has increased by 1° 20' according to GMT of sunrise. Using the quadrant, I find that 1° of longitude at latitude 35° equals 49 miles. Using 1°20' = (80/60)° we figure the length of the longitude interval as (80/60)° x 49 miles/1° = 65 miles. In other words, direct measurements from the sun indicate that I have traveled 65 miles to the west during these two days, and this is the value I must compare with my dead reckoning. Or, to convert the other way, if I figure I am 58 miles west of 68° 30' W at 35° N, my longitude must be 68° 30' + (58 miles x 60'/49 miles) = 68° 101' = 69° 41' W.

When comparing longitude figures with dead reckoning, remember that the comparison is independent of latitude changes. In the last example, I could have traveled due west, or I could have moved 100 miles to the south during the two days. What I am checking with this comparison is only my east-west progress. Consequently, for an arbitrary course direction, you must first plot the number of miles traveled along your actual course and then project that distance onto the east-west axis, before you can make the comparison as shown in Figure 12-10. A similar projection onto the north-south axis must be made for latitude comparisons.

Without GMT we can't find longitude, but any good watch that's running can still help us keep track of longitude over a long voyage — even from an unknown or only poorly known position. Suppose that you have a good watch but don't know its time zone or error, and your position is only a rough guess. What can you do?

First find your latitude — you don't need time for that and it might help improve your longitude guess. Then use your longitude guess (no matter how unlikely it might be) to find the time zone and error of the watch, as explained in Section 12.3 — it won't be right, but that doesn't matter. Now as you move away from that position, just proceed with your dead reckoning and longitude measurements from the sun as if you did know GMT from the watch. Knowledge of your actual longitude will never improve over your original guess since your time isn't right, but you can still check for strong east-west currents or leeway over an extended voyage by comparing longitude changes according to dead reckoning with those deduced from the sun.

This is certainly no substitute for knowing the correct time, but it is far better than dead reckoning alone if you have a long voyage to make. Suppose, for example, that we are in a strong westbound current of some 2 knots, but don't know it — though we might suspect a current once we find our latitude, if we are familiar with the waters. But let's say we aren't. The intended course we hold is due north and we dead reckon accordingly. Now, how long can we go before the sun tells us we are being set? The answer is about two days, and in three or four days we should know pretty well by how much. Even with nothing but the prescription for the equation of time, we can find longitude to within 50 miles or so, and this current is setting us about this much each day.

13

Coastal Piloting without Instruments

The critical part of ocean navigation rarely takes place in the middle of the ocean. It's the beginning and end of a voyage that typically pose the biggest challenge, usually because they are potentially the most dangerous. We assume we have made our voyage under emergency navigation, so we complete it by covering some of the basic points of negotiating the landfall. The visible range of lights and land is fundamental, as it determines what navigational accuracy we need to find our destination. Knowing that we might not see these till we are much closer than we anticipated is also fundamental, as are the natural signs of the ocean environment that might help us out.

In some cases, we can read the subtle signs of nearby land from the air, sky, and water before the actual land is sighted. These signs could help us set a course to safety. Signs of land include clouds, birds, insects, flotsam, sea state, and such man-made indicators as aircraft, and agricultural or industrial pollution that we can see or smell. Except for clouds, these aids are potentially most valuable when our target landfall is low, since they won't expand the detectable range of land by much more than 10 or 20 miles, if that. In clear weather, we will probably see anything taller than 500 feet or so before these signs are apparent. Clouds are an exception because they effectively raise the elevation of the land.

Once the land is in sight, our primary piloting goal is to keep track of distance off as we make the approach. We can do this in several ways without conventional instruments.

13.1 Signs of Land at Sea

Stationary cumulus clouds often indicate the presence of hills or mountains. This sign is most prominent in an otherwise cloudless sky, but sometimes cumulus cloud caps are also apparent among moving or thinner clouds. Cloud caps build as the land heats, so look for these to first appear in mid-morning, becoming more prominent as the day progresses. Unfortunately, all cumulus clouds build with the day's heat, so these land indicators may be most valuable sometime before midday. Stationary cumulus clouds are useful land indicators at all latitudes. Of all the signs of land at sea, cumulus clouds over islands or mountain peaks must be ranked among the most important since they can be seen the farthest (see Figure 13-1). Nevertheless, we must always consider our basic dead reckoning and other uncertainties before turning to head for the clouds.

In temperate latitudes where the winds aloft can be strong, there is an especially prominent cumulus cloud that is a convincing indication of land. These are mountain wave clouds (altocumulus lenticularis), which occasionally form over mountain ridges in strong winds. They look like flying saucers (see Figure 13-2), and although they are usually stationary over the peak, they occasionally break loose and keep their remarkable shape as they drift downwind. This is a fairly rare cloud form, but an almost certain sign of land. Since prevailing winds aloft are from the west, we would expect these mostly when headed westward toward a mountainous coast.

Birds can provide valuable guides to nearby land in some circumstances, but their use is heavily dependent on local knowledge. You must know the habits of local birds to use the direction of their flight for bearings. And still weigh the uncertainties carefully before turning to follow a bird.

Some bird signs may be more encouraging than others. *Several* birds flying in the same direction at sunset, and again *several* birds flying from the same direction in the morning, begins to be pretty good evidence of land — especially if you have identified the birds and you know they sleep on land. Bird flight during the day is generally unreliable, but there may be local exceptions. It is reported (Gladwin, 1974), for example, that in the waters of the central Caroline Islands, a white tern flying with a fish sideways in its beak is headed for land no matter at what time of day it is sighted. Presumably it has caught a fish too big to eat at sea and is headed for land to finish it off.

The distance offshore at which a particular bird might be seen depends on the species and location. It also, of course, depends on the randomness of their flight. Sea stories and bird studies should be considered with caution when your safety is at stake. It is likely that many land-based birds that roam the seas during the day home in on land at sunset by sight, just as we do. But since they are higher, they can see farther. From a height of 200 feet, they can see land of the same height from some 25 miles off. Studies of bird navigation in the Pacific islands show the following birds to be the most useful for land bearings, with their approximate ranges offshore given in parentheses: terns and noddies (10 to 20 miles), boobies (30 miles), and frigate birds (50 miles). But there are random exceptions even among these that might lead us astray. David Lewis, for example, saw 12 boobies 700 miles west of the

Maybe?

Above: FIGURE 13-1. *Cloud caps over an island and coastal mountain range. Stationary cumulus clouds often build over peaks during mid-morning and may be a sign of land not yet in sight. These clouds can, however, also obscure peaks that would otherwise be in view, so the best chance for spotting peaks on the horizon is during early morning.* **Below: FIGURE 13-2.** *Mountain wave clouds flowing to leeward of a coastal mountain range. These clouds are characterized by their smooth, flying-saucer like appearance. They can be isolated or in a sequence as shown here. They are a fairly rare cloud, formed by strong winds aloft, but if seen on the windward horizon they are a convincing sign that land lies ahead.*

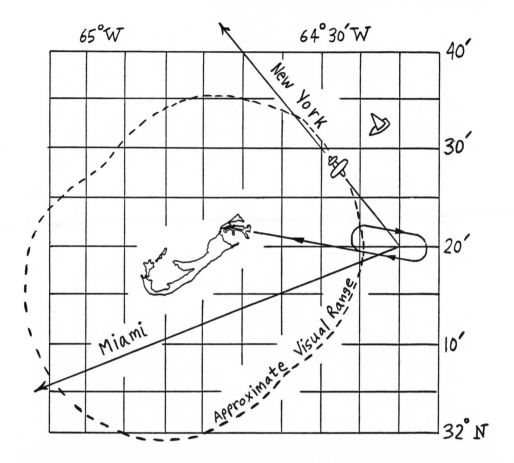

FIGURE 13-3. *Possible air traffic approaches to a holding pattern off Bermuda. The holding pattern shown is from an aircraft chart, but routes to it won't necessarily be as shown here. These are purely schematic to show that plane sightings just out of sight of an island might give misleading bearings to the island. Not likely, just possible.*

Line Islands on the first no-instrument voyage of the *Hokule'a* from Hawaii to Tahiti (private communication, 1985).

Airplane sightings for orientation were discussed in Section 7.3. Near a major airport, they might be extremely valuable for homing in on your target, but they should be treated like clouds and birds. Consider the information they suggest, but balance it against your basic dead reckoning and other information and the corresponding uncertainties. Remember that planes usually land and take off into the wind regardless of their routes. See Figure 13-3. Generally speaking, planes and contrails are overrated in the sailor's folklore of how to find an island in a bind, whereas the use of an AM radio to home in on an island station, as discussed in Section 8.2, is often overlooked in such discussions.

The first appearance of insects might also be a sign of nearby land. On one occasion, the author noticed a fly on board one day before sighting Hawaii in clear

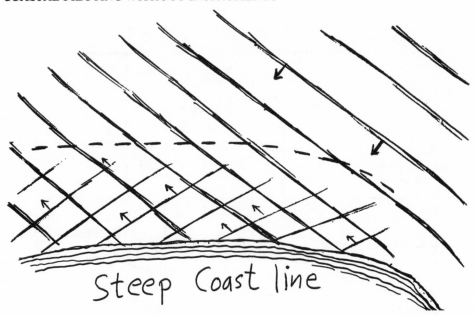

FIGURE 13-4. *Reflected swell pattern. Near a steep coastline, an onshore swell is reflected back out to sea, often causing a prominent crossed swell pattern that can be detected several miles or more from the coast. In reduced visibility, or in exceptional cases in clear weather, the approach of land may be signaled by the appearance of the reflected swell—especially if your local knowledge tells you that there can be no other source of swells from that direction.*

weather. On another crossing, Hawaii was spotted, but the next day was socked in and we lost sight of the islands. During that day, a flying insect of some kind appeared. These, though, are isolated examples. Most landfalls are likely to be bug-free. Nevertheless, it would be good procedure to wait for clear weather if you are socked in close to an island destination when insects first appear on board.

Traditional navigators of the Pacific islands are reported to have routinely used swell patterns to locate islands in their waters. This, however, is a subtle art. It generally requires a region of prevailing swells and a highly trained eye to spot recurrent features or deviations in prevailing patterns. Obviously the typical oceangoing navigator will not derive as much benefit from swell patterns in unfamiliar waters. One exception might be the first appearance of a prominent crossed-swell pattern fairly near an island or shoreline.

If the swells have been steady for some days from one direction, and all swells in the area have always been from that direction, and you now begin to detect weaker swells coming from almost the opposite direction, then quite possibly these new swells have been reflected off a shoreline ahead of you (see Figure 13-4). The crossed-swell interference pattern is often clean and prominent for several miles offshore when the primary swell is reflected off a long, steep shoreline. Think of the primary and reflected swells as billiard balls bouncing off a wall when you are trying to figure the direction to the shoreline. This effect can be seen in any waters with prominent swells. It may well be detected out of sight of land in reduced visibility.

The same general type of swell patterns develop when a swell is refracted or diffracted around an island or headland (see Figure 13-5), but the direction to the

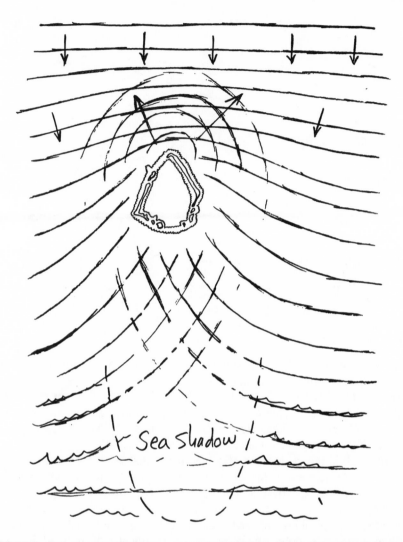

Sea shadow

FIGURE 13-5. *Refracted swell pattern near an isolated island or atoll. As the swells approach an obstruction they curve, as if to wrap around it. Approaching a very low island from windward, the first sea signs of land might be the appearance of a weak reflected swell. The curvature of the swells might be detectable from the masthead, but these are subtle signs at best in most cases. Approaching from the leeward side, the sea-shadow region of diminished waves and swell might be more convincing evidence of low land not far ahead. Detectable changes in swell patterns might extend some dozen miles or so on each side in exceptional cases, with a single prominent swell running downwind. These subtle signs are something to watch for when looking for such an isolated landfall, but we should not count on them to guide us there.*

island and the prominence of the interference pattern are harder to read. In foul weather, though, it might still serve as a sign to wait for clear horizons.

Another opportunity to detect land from swells that does not require special training occurs when we sail into the lee of an island that is interrupting the swell pattern. If you know a low island lies somewhere to windward and the swell (or seas in

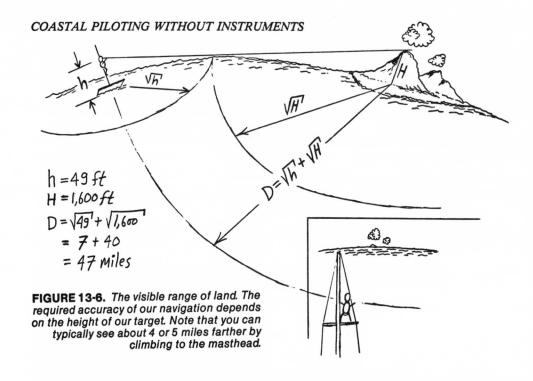

$$h = 49 \, ft$$
$$H = 1,600 \, ft$$
$$D = \sqrt{49} + \sqrt{1,600}$$
$$= 7 + 40$$
$$= 47 \, miles$$

FIGURE 13-6. *The visible range of land. The required accuracy of our navigation depends on the height of our target. Note that you can typically see about 4 or 5 miles farther by climbing to the masthead.*

general) that you have been crossing for some days disappear or become noticeably weaker, although the wind is unchanged, then you may have entered the "seashadow" of the island (see Figure 13-5). This is almost certainly the case if you continue on and the swell reappears, and you go back and it disappears. So long as the land mass is large enough, swells can be interrupted by even the lowest islands or atolls, so this could well be a sign of land not yet visible.

Another subtle effect that can also be quite valuable on occasion is the color of land, reefs, or banks reflected onto the clouds above them. This generally requires the right degree of sky cover — enough breaks to let direct sunlight through, but enough cover to form a reflective surface above the water. Shallow waters of tropical or subtropical lagoons or banks, for example, can sometimes show up quite clearly as a turquoise color on the undersides of the clouds above them.

The first smells or signs of smoke on the horizon are also signs of land to windward, as are freshly broken branches or a general increase of flotsam after a storm. As a rule, however, we should not count on any natural or unnatural signs to guide us to land. Figure the accuracy of your navigation and the visible range of the land, covered in the next section, and let these determine your choice of target.

13.2 Visible Range of Lights and Land

Before we can do any piloting, we must be in sight of land or a navigational light, or at least have a usable radio bearing. Understanding the visible range of distant objects is fundamental to navigation, emergency or otherwise. Several factors enter into this.

First, the curvature of the earth limits our range of sight regardless of the clarity of the atmosphere. If a mountain peak is "H" feet high and we are standing "h" feet above the water, then we will first see the tip of the mountain on the horizon (in clear weather and calm seas) when we are "D" nautical miles from the peak, when you figure D from the equation:

$$D = \sqrt{H} + \sqrt{h}.$$

Figure 13-6 illustrates, graphically, this equation. This is a handy formula, even though it does require a square root — squaring a few guesses will do the job. A hilltop 3,600 feet high can be seen just on the horizon at some 63 miles off when we are standing 9 feet above water (square root of 3,600 + square root of 9 = 60 + 3 = 63). A low island whose tallest feature is a palm tree 64 feet high cannot be seen from a 9-foot elevation until we are 11 miles off (8 + 3). Standing on the spreaders at a height of 49 feet, we might spot this island at about 15 miles off (8 + 7). Obviously the accuracy required of our navigation depends on what we are looking for.

This visible-range formula gives an approximation of the mathematically correct results tabulated in the *Light List* and other books (the formula results are 15 percent smaller than the tabulated ones). The simple square-root formula, however, not only does away with the tables, it is more reliable than the tables. The slightest chop on the water or a slight haze around the land will reduce its visible range by much more than 15 percent. Even the shorter range figured from the formula should be considered optimistic.

Often, even when we are sailing in clear skies, islands or coastlines we are looking for are veiled in mist or local rain showers. Cloud caps also obscure the upper heights of peaks even in locally clear weather. Visible-range calculations tell us only when the tops should first come into view, so with many clouds about, we might not see the land even when it is above the horizon. For this reason, our best chance of spotting land might be during mid-morning, before cloud caps build.

Nautical charts show the average elevation of coastal lands, in addition to peak heights and locations. With the visible-range formula and a chart — or even a rough recollection of, or guess at, the elevations — we can estimate the visible range of land. When using mountain peaks, remember you are figuring the distance to the peak, not to the coastline. If we want to find an island, the formula tells us roughly how accurate our navigation must be. To be conservative, though, I would want to be able to do somewhat better than that if the island were an isolated target.

When looking for navigational lights, the same formula and procedures apply. A light located 144 feet above the water can be seen from an elevation of 16 feet at a distance of 12 plus 4, or 16 miles. The brightness of the light and clarity of the atmosphere, however, also limit the visible range of lights at night.

The type of visible range we have discussed so far is called "geographic range." It tells when an object is above the horizon, and so places a limit on visible range, regardless of the clarity of the atmosphere or the brightness of the light. But being within the geographic range of a light does not guarantee our seeing it at night. We see bright lights farther than dim ones, and even a bright light can be extinguished by fog or rain.

Nautical charts and the *Light List* specify the brightness of lights by giving their "nominal range," which is how far we can see the light on a clear night when not

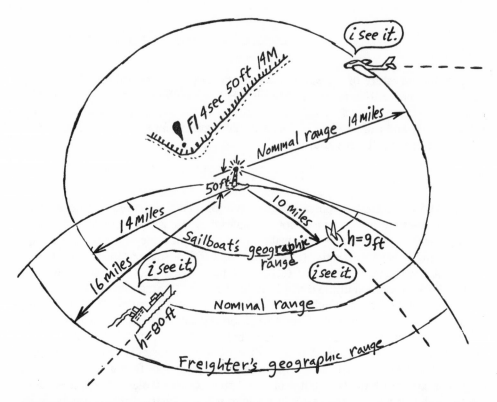

FIGURE 13-7. *Geographic range and nominal range compared. The nominal range of a light is a measure of its brightness. In a sailboat, it is often the height of the light that limits its range of visibility, not the brightness of the light.*

limited by geographic range. Consider a light that is 81 feet high with a nominal range of 14 miles. If we were standing 9 feet above the water, the geographic range of the light would be 3 plus 9, or 12, miles. Once we reach 12 miles off, we could see this light on clear nights, since the nominal range is larger than 12 miles. On the other hand, if we were standing on the spreaders at an eye height of 49 feet, the geographic range to this light would be 7 plus 9, or 16, miles. Once we reach 16 miles off, we could (in principle) see this light during the day, but not at night. Viewed from the spreaders, the light is above the horizon, but it only shines out to 14 miles. We would have to be 14 miles off to see it from the spreaders at night. From the deck, the limitation was geographic, but from the spreaders it is the brightness of the light. See Figure 13-7.

In reduced visibility, we must replace the light's charted or tabulated nominal range with its "luminous range," which we must compute. The procedure is easy; the problem is figuring how much the visibility is reduced. The atmospheric visibility is defined as how far we can see unlighted objects in daylight. Even during daylight, this is not easy to figure at sea, but we need it at night, which makes it still more uncertain. But even a rough guess, such as 10 miles (clear weather), 1 mile, or 0.1 mile, will help us plan the approach. One trick is to simply note, late in the day or at early twilight, whether you can discern a horizon, a line between sea and sky. If you can, the visibility (in nautical miles) must be greater than the square root of your eye height (in feet). If you can't see a horizon, the visibility must be less than square root of "h."

Once we have estimated the atmospheric visibility, we can find the luminous range

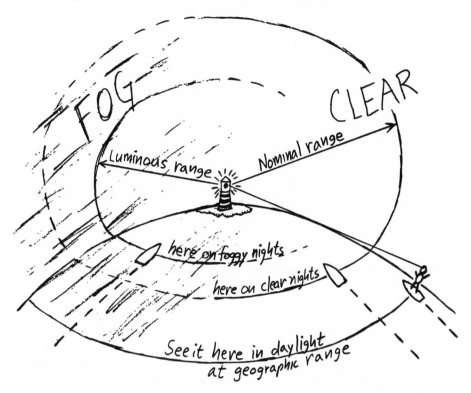

FIGURE 13-8. *Nominal range and luminous range compared. In reduced visibility, we must compare the geographic range of a light with its luminous range to see which determines the visible range. Luminous range can be figured from a table in the* Light List *or by using the formula given in the text.*

of the light from the luminous-range diagram in the *Light List,* or we can figure it without this aid in an emergency, using this formula:

$$\text{Luminous range} = \frac{\text{Visibility}}{10} \times (\text{Nominal range}) + 1 \text{ mile.}$$

This formula can be used for visibilities down to about half a mile.

For example, consider a light with a charted nominal range of 22 miles. If you estimate the prevailing atmospheric visibility to be 4 miles, the luminous range is 0.4 x 22 + 1 = 9.8 miles. In other words, a "22-mile" light is reduced to about a "10-mile" light when the visibility is 4 miles. See the illustration in Figure 13-8. Another example worth noting: A 5-mile light in 5-mile visibility can be seen only from about 3.5 miles (0.5 x 5 + 1 = 3.5).

This luminous-range formula is a simple approximation to a complex table. It is correct to within 20 percent or so, which is good enough, since we will never know the visibility any better than that. The formula is, in fact, adequate for routine navigation as well. When looking for a light in reduced visibility, figure the geographic range and the luminous range, and the visible range is the smaller of the two. Naturally, if we can't reasonably estimate the nominal range of the light in question, we can't do any of this preparation.

Remember that white lights may appear reddish or somewhat orange when first seen on the horizon, and the true flashing characteristic of a light may not be apparent until you are fairly close to it. If a light sequence includes colored and white flashes, you usually see the white ones at a greater distance than the red or green ones.

You can sometimes see the glow or loom of a bright light in the sky long before you see the light itself. What is happening here is that the height of the light is being increased to the height of the clouds or haze above it, so the geographic range is bigger. Cities or towns also light up the sky. Frequently, the loom of a city is sufficiently bright and localized to use it for a bearing to the city from a long way off. The loom of Miami, Florida, for example, can be seen routinely from some 60 or 70 miles offshore (John Dowd, private communication).

13.3 Finding Distance Off

When a known navigational light is visible from a high point on the boat but not from a lower one, then you can assume your distance off the light is fairly near the geographic range of the light viewed from the higher elevation. This method of judging distance off is called "bobbing the light." It works best in calm water and clear skies, when the geographic range is well within the nominal range — i.e. for low bright lights. Distance off figured this way won't be precise, because no geographic range formula or table is precise, but you must be fairly close to this geographic distance off for this phenomenon to occur.

Besides being able to see farther, another good reason to watch for lights from a high elevation, such as standing on the boom, is the chance of bobbing a light. Then you can jump down to bob the light when it first appears. If you spot it first from below, you may have missed this chance. In any event, if you can see the light at all, you must be within its geographic range, and this alone gives some data on distance off.

Throughout this book, we have stressed the value of small-angle measurements made with a kamal. We can put this skill to further use in finding distance off in sight of land. The procedure is to measure the angular width or height of some landmark and then figure distance off (quite accurately) from this angle and the size of the landmark. We can do this in an emergency with nothing but a stick and a string, but this method is more than an emergency trick. Given our choice of any equipment to use for finding distance off, we might still choose a stick and a string, once we are accustomed to this procedure. The method is easy and accurate. The design and calibration of a kamal are covered in Section 11.1.

First identify from the chart and surroundings (or from your local knowledge and the surroundings) one wide landmark with prominent edges, or two nearby objects that are at roughly equal distances from you and less than 15° or so apart when viewed from your vantage point. They could be, for example, two sides of a large rock, two rocks, two towers or stacks, two peaks, two sides of a bay or valley, or two edges of an island. Then use a kamal held sideways to measure the horizontal angle between the two sides. The angle we get from the kamal would be the same as the difference between the magnetic bearings to the two sides, but generally we can measure these small angles directly much more precisely than we can the individual bearings.

Then figure your distance off the center of the two objects from the following formulas:

$$\text{Distance off (in miles)} = 60 \times \frac{\text{Target width (in miles)}}{\text{Kamal angle (degrees)}},$$

or

$$\text{Distance off (in miles)} = \frac{\text{Target width (in feet)}}{100 \times \text{Kamal angle (degrees)}}.$$

The two forms of the formula are equivalent since 1 nautical mile is very nearly 6,000 feet. See Figure 13-9.

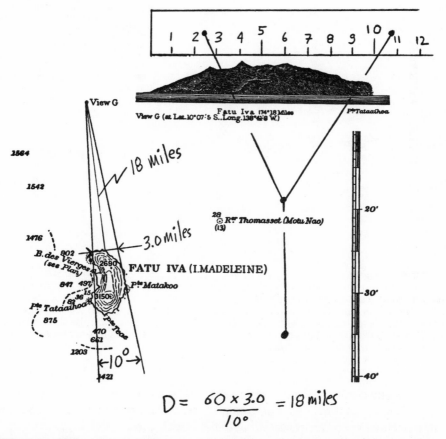

FIGURE 13-9. *Finding distance off by horizontal angle. Use a calibrated kamal (or sextant if you have one) to measure the horizontal angle subtended by the object from your perspective; then measure the width of the object from that perspective on a chart; and then use the range formula given in the text to find distance off. Note that you are finding your distance to the point at which you measured the width. You can find your position from a bearing and a distance off, or from two distances to two separated features (at the intersection of two circles of position).*

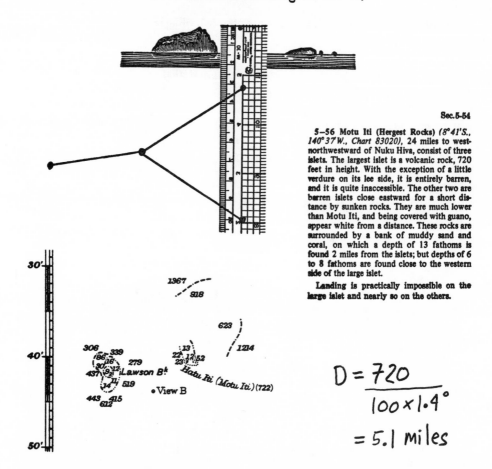

051° 5 Miles   Hatu Iti
View B (at Lat. 8°44'S..Long. 140°40'7 W.)

Sec. 5-54

5–56 Motu Iti (Hergest Rocks) *(8°41'S., 140°37'W., Chart 83020)*, 24 miles to west-northwestward of Nuku Hiva, consist of three islets. The largest islet is a volcanic rock, 720 feet in height. With the exception of a little verdure on its lee side, it is entirely barren, and it is quite inaccessible. The other two are barren islets close eastward for a short distance by sunken rocks. They are much lower than Motu Iti, and being covered with guano, appear white from a distance. These rocks are surrounded by a bank of muddy sand and coral, on which a depth of 13 fathoms is found 2 miles from the islets; but depths of 6 to 8 fathoms are found close to the western side of the large islet.

Landing is practically impossible on the large islet and nearly so on the others.

$$D = \frac{720}{100 \times 1.4°}$$

$$= 5.1 \text{ miles}$$

FIGURE 13-10. *Finding distance off by vertical angle. Use a calibrated kamal or sextant to measure the vertical angle from the tip of the object to the shoreline below it; then look up the height of the object in feet from a chart, Light List, or sailing directions. And then use the range formula given in the text to find distance off. Note that you are finding your distance to the peak of the object, not to the shoreline. The inset text describing this islet is from DMAHTC Pub. No. 80, Sailing Directions for the Pacific Islands, Volume 3. This reference differs with the charted height of this rock by 2 feet.*

This method works for any distance off as long as you are sure of the actual width of the feature you measured. For example, I see two prominent peaks on an island to the south that are 6° apart according to the kamal. From the chart, I measure these peaks to be 2.5 miles apart when viewed from the north. My distance off the peaks is (2.5 x 60) ÷ 6 = 25 miles. With practice, you can often determine horizontal angles to adequate precision by "winking" your finger (Section 11.1).

As you get closer to land, you can use the same procedure to find distance off from a vertical kamal angle (see Figure 13-10). Use a kamal to measure the angular height of a landmark above the shoreline, then figure distance off from:

$$\text{Distance off (in miles)} = \frac{\text{Target height (in feet)}}{100 \times \text{Kamal angle (degrees)}}$$

For this application, however, you must be within view of the true shoreline, which means your answer to distance off should not be much larger than the square root of your eye height. Standing on deck at an eye height of 9 feet, this will work for distances of 3 miles or so. You can stretch it some, maybe up to 50 percent, out to distances of 5 miles or so, but the result will not be accurate till you get within geographic range of the shoreline. As an example, I see a hilltop 2° above the shoreline, according to a kamal. The charted elevation of the hill is 460 feet, so my distance off is 460 ÷ (100 x 2) = 2.3 miles.

Note that the formula for vertical angle is the same as that for horizontal angle. In each case, we are simply dividing the target size (in hundreds of feet) by the kamal angle (in degrees) to get distance off (in nautical miles). For close-in navigation, vertical angle is often more convenient than horizontal angle, because your target is well located. Elevations of peaks and lights are charted, or given in pilots and sailing directions.

While holding a straight course along or toward a shoreline, you can find your distance off any landmark you see by "doubling the angle on the bow." And for this method you don't need a chart or any special knowledge of the landmark. First note the angle of a landmark relative to your heading ("the angle on the bow"), and then keep track of the distance you must travel along your course line in order to double this angle. Your distance off the landmark is then equal to the distance you traveled to double the angle.

For example, I note that a prominent rock lies 30° on my port bow as I begin to keep track of my distance run (which would be the case if I were headed toward, say, 270, and the rock's bearing was 240). When the rock has moved aft to 60° on the bow (bearing 210), I figure that I have traveled 2 miles. Therefore I am now 2 miles away from the rock. In routine navigation with a binnacle compass, this is often a convenient measurement to make using the compass pins at 45° and 90°. Sighting over the center pin when sailing along a shoreline, you can get your distance offshore without leaving the helm.

Without a compass, you must improvise the angle measurements. Any type of makeshift compass card will do, or you can use a folded piece of paper, since we don't need to know what the angle is, only that we doubled it. There are many ways to improvise (see Figure 13-11).

An obvious advantage of this method is that you can find distance off any landmark, and you don't need a chart of the area to do it. You must, though, be close enough to land that bearings to the landmark change within a reasonable time relative to anticipated currents in the region. The error in this method is very roughly equal to your DR error over the time of the run. If it took 1 hour in 1 knot of current, you could be off by about 1 mile. If doubling the bow angle will take too long for your needs, you can apply the running fix method — discussed in the next section — to visual bearings, which also does not require a chart.

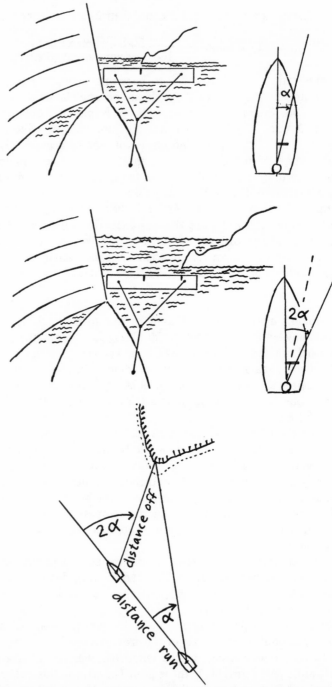

FIGURE 13-11. *Doubling the angle on the bow. Record the angle on the bow and then hold a straight course till the angle has doubled. Your distance off will then be equal to the distance you had to run in order to double the angle. Here the bow angle is shown measured with a kamal, but a portable compass card or simple folded piece of paper would do as well. Remember that these are relative angles; a kamal used this way is not accurate for measuring specific numerical values of these larger angles.*

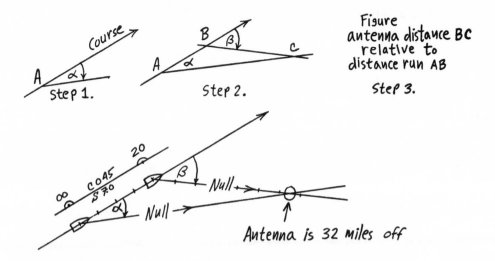

FIGURE 13-12. *Running fix from radio bearings without a chart. (1) Draw your course line and lay off the first bow angle to the antenna that you find from the null direction. (2) At any point B, draw in the second bow angle so that a triangle is formed on the page. (3) Figure the antenna distance relative to the distance run, as shown. The intersection angle at the antenna determines the quality of the fix. Radio bearings are often difficult to determine precisely, so you might have to run some distance to make this angle large enough to use. Put another way, if the antenna is very far off, this will only give you a very approximate fix. This procedure is a generalization of the bow-angle method of Figure 13-11 that does not require us to travel so far as to double the bow angle in order to find distance off. We could use this method for visual bearings if needed.*

13.4 Running Fix from Radio Bearings

Without instruments in the fog, we don't have much to pilot by except possibly a makeshift radio bearing from an AM radio. We won't necessarily know where the broadcast antenna is, but we can still keep track of relative position using an unknown antenna location. We must, though, be close enough to the antenna that bearings to it change within some reasonable time in relation to uncertainties in local currents. Also the station must be somewhere other than dead ahead, not one we are homing in on — though we could head off course and use this trick to find distance off the antenna, if it were necessary.

Doing this in the fog without a compass, we also need some way to hold a steady course direction, as discussed in Chapter 8. In sea fog we might have a steady wind direction to help with this. In radiation fog it might be calm enough to use a trailed line. The value of this type of running fix, however, is not necessarily limited to fog. We can receive AM broadcasts a long way out of sight of land.

First note the angle on the bow to the AM station using the procedures of Section 8.2. You can use actual bearings if you have them, but we don't need them. Then hold a steady course and keep track of distance run until the radio bearing on the bow changes by 15° or more (to be useful, this method requires a good null).

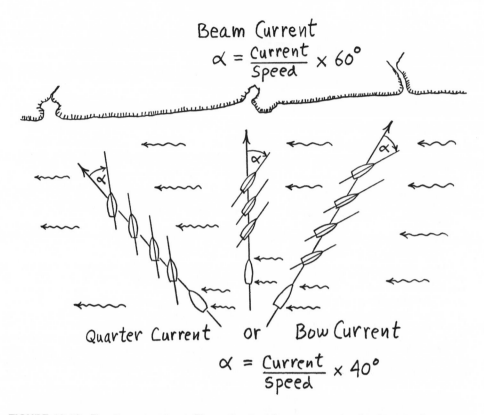

Beam Current
$$\alpha = \frac{Current}{Speed} \times 60°$$

Quarter Current or Bow Current

$$\alpha = \frac{Current}{Speed} \times 40°$$

FIGURE 13-13. *Figuring current set. The estimates shown are approximations to the proper vector solutions. These convenient approximations are more than adequate in most cases, since we rarely know the current strength or direction well enough to do any better. With current on the bow, boat speed is retarded by roughly three quarters of the current speed, which is about what you gain with current on the quarter. This estimate of set angle assumes boat speed is at least two or three times greater than the speed of the current.*

Presumably you will be headed toward land, so the bearing should move aft as you proceed — if it doesn't, you may have learned something important. With the two angles on the bow and the distance run between them, we can figure our distance off the AM antenna with the plotting work illustrated in Figure 13-12.

Draw a line to represent your course line and lay off the first bow angle. Then, at some arbitrary distance up the course line from there, lay off the second bow angle so that a triangle is formed on the page. The two bearing lines will intersect at the unknown antenna location, forming the smallest angle of the triangle, equal to the difference between the two bow angles. Your distance off the antenna is the line you just drew to complete the triangle, which you can read using the distance run along the course line between bow angles to set the scale. With this procedure, you can keep track of your position relative to the antenna. This is potentially a very powerful technique in some coastal regions or near island chains with several AM stations available. For example, it could help locate your position when in sight of a coastline, yet still too far offshore for good visual bearings.

13.5 Course Made Good in Current

Current corrections to dead reckoning in mid-ocean were discussed in Section 10.3. Although there are notable exceptions, currents are generally stronger in coastal waters, which makes our navigation of them here more critical. If we overstand an island channel entrance in strong tradewinds because we didn't reckon the currents properly, for example, we may have quite a problem on our hands in beating back to it. In the ocean we might get by with correcting our daily runs, but along a coast we might want more immediate information, such as course made good in current or heading to steer to hold a desired course. Though these are not strictly the same problem — the amount we point into a current to track straight does not always equal the amount we get set if we don't — they are nevertheless fairly close in most cases. Considering the uncertainties involved, we can use the same solution for both.

The amount we get set if we do nothing or the amount we should point into a current to track straight we will call our "set." To figure the set we need an estimate of the water speed ("current") and our own speed through the water ("speed"). The set then depends on whether we go straight across the current with it hitting our beam, or diagonally across the current with it hitting our bow or quarter sections (see Figure 13-13). The results are easy to figure without plotting. For current on the beam:

$$\text{Set} = \frac{\text{Current}}{\text{Speed}} \times 60°,$$

and for current on the bow or quarter,

$$\text{Set} = \frac{\text{Current}}{\text{Speed}} \times 40°.$$

This is a simplified solution to a vector problem, but we rarely know current strength or direction well enough for a more accurate solution. Note that current on the bow or quarter sets us off course by the same amount; the only difference is how fast we go. Current on the bow slows us down; current on the quarter speeds us up.

As an example, I figure I am making about 5 knots through the water in the direction I want to go but anticipate entering a current of about 2 knots on my port bow as we get closer in. My set will be about $(2 \div 5) \times 40° = 16°$. If I do nothing, I will be set right about 16°. If the winds allow it, I could head up-current to the left by 16° and should track straight along my previous course.

Note that this approximation for set angle only works well for current speeds less than three-quarters of the boat speed.

14

What to Do
with What You've Got —
A Summary

So far we have covered emergency navigation using few, if any, conventional aids. A watch and sunrise-sunset tables are the only specific items we took advantage of. In most cases, the supplemental value and application of other aids are obvious, should they be available. A proper marine sextant, for example, would greatly improve position and direction finding even in the absence of other standard aids or tables. Likewise, an almanac opens up much more of the sky for use in steering and position fixing.

Having only one specific aid is one thing, losing only one specific aid is another. With a bit more work, we can do away with any one of the aids we often consider vital without losing much accuracy or efficiency in navigation. These contingency procedures are easy once we are familiar with the emergency methods we have covered so far. Navigators unfamiliar with emergency procedures will find that an almanac is the one aid that is most difficult to do without — which is worth noting, since the almanac is also the one that is least likely to have a back-up.

14.1 Routine Navigation with Everything

When it comes to celestial navigation, having everything essentially means having a compass, sextant, GMT, a *Nautical Almanac,* sight reduction tables such as

DMAHTC Pub. No. 249 or 229, plotting sheets, and tools. A 2102-D Star Finder (or the British equivalent N.P. 323) is extremely valuable in routine and emergency navigation, but it is not strictly essential.

A thorough back-up system might include a spare compass, two rated waterproof quartz watches, a Davis Mark III plastic sextant, a copy of the Davies *Concise Tables for Sight Reduction,* a few universal plotting sheets, a protractor and ruler (C-Thru models 376E and B-70), pencils, erasers, notebook, and a pilot chart. These items were pictured in Chapter 1, Figure 1-2. The concise Davies tables are small and lightweight, and include a long-term almanac for sun and stars. This back-up system will get you anywhere the primary system will, though it may take more work — the plastic vernier sextant is small and lightweight but neither as accurate nor as easy to use as a high-quality metal one, and the sight-reduction procedure required with "concise tables" is more involved than it is with Pub. 249 or 229.

For primary or back-up navigation, however, it is not the style of equipment that is important, but what we do with it. Even if our primary navigation is SatNav or Loran, the recommended procedures for routine offshore navigation are the same — and, of course, we still need back-up celestial gear; no foreseeable electronic development will change this.

The main goal of routine navigation should be accurate dead reckoning, regardless of what other aids or systems we use. The reason is simple. We may well have to navigate by dead reckoning alone, no matter what other aids we have on board. Even the best SatNav, Omega, or Loran systems are not 100 percent dependable in a small boat at sea, and we can't do celestial fixes when the sky or horizon is obscured. It is fairly common to have to make a landfall with dead reckoning and radio bearings alone.

To develop accurate dead reckoning, we must keep an accurate logbook of course changes and log readings, and then carefully compare our DR position with our celestial or electronic fixes each day. One convenient way to do this is to convert the difference between each fixed position and the corresponding DR position into an effective "current" by dividing the distance between the two positions by the time run since the last fix. Then keep a separate record of these error currents and the prevailing wind conditions. To evaluate our dead reckoning and plan ahead, we need this estimate of the *rate* at which we might go off course in specific wind conditions. See Figure 14-1.

For example, if my DR position was 26 miles southwest of my fix, and the last fix was taken 13 hours ago, then the sum of my errors is equivalent to a "current" of 2 knots to the southwest. This could be due to real current, instrument errors, or just a blunder in a logbook entry. Nevertheless, making this check regularly, you will soon spot any consistent errors that might indicate a faulty log or compass. Logbook blunders will also stand out. When beating to weather, remember the several "invisible" factors that retard progress, discussed in Section 10.4. In any conditions, though, this procedure shows us very clearly how well we could navigate by dead reckoning alone if we should have to. A sample DR log is shown in Figure 14.2.

If this "current" turns out to be roughly the same each day, we could include it in our future dead reckoning, even if we are not certain where it comes from. On the other hand, if this error current turns out to be a knot or so in random directions,

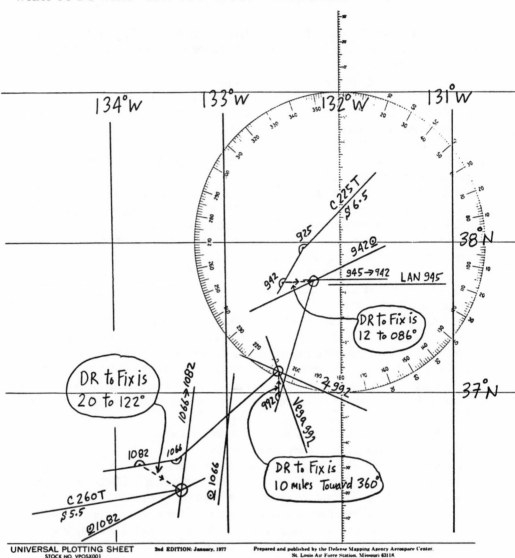

UNIVERSAL PLOTTING SHEET   2nd EDITION: January, 1977   Prepared and published by the Defense Mapping Agency Aerospace Center.
STOCK NO. VPOSX001   St. Louis Air Force Station, Missouri 63118.

Above: FIGURE 14-1. *Dead reckoning errors marked on a plotting sheet. The celestial fix taken at log reading 942 was 12 miles to the east of the 942 DR position. It is good practice to keep a record of these DR errors on the plotting sheet. A red arrow from DR to fix is one way to highlight this important information. This DR plot is for a section of the logbook shown in Figure 14-2.* **Opposite: FIGURE 14-2.** *Section of a logbook showing DR errors and error currents. The fix at log 942, for example, was taken 24.0 hours after the last fix. During this time the DR had gone wrong by 12 miles, which means there was, in effect, an error current of 0.5 knots to the east during that leg of the voyage. This "current" could be from any source, including logbook entry errors or errors in the fixes themselves. Unless the ocean currents are large, it is unlikely that these "currents" reflect actual motion of the water. This 12-mile correction to the DR plot was made after sailing 153 miles, which means it corresponds to a DR error of 8 percent in the terminology used in the text. Other data recorded in the logbook, but not shown here, include compass course, knotmeter speed, wind speed and direction, barometer, sea conditions, speed made good, and sails set.*

Log reading	Time/date	Fix position	Type of fix	Distance and bearing DR to Fix	Hours to last fix	Error current (knots)	Average Speed (knots)	Miles logged	DR error percentage
0075	0400/4	48-23, 124-45	Bearing Fix						
0272	0900/5	46-00, 128-10	Rfix sun-Venus	11 T 215	29.0	0.4	6.8	197	6
0480	1530/6	44-04, 131-11	Rfix sun	17 T 012	30.5	0.6	6.8	208	8
0634	1400/7	41-38, 132-03	Rfix sun	07 T 300	22.5	0.3	6.8	154	5
0789	1330/8	39-02, 130-55	Rfix sun	30 T 095	23.5	1.3	6.6	155	19
0942	1330/9	37-45, 133-14	Rfix sun	12 T 086	24.0	0.5	6.4	153	8
0992	2130/9	37-09, 132-32	Vega-Jupiter	10 T 360	8.0	1.3	6.3	050	20
1082	1400/10	36-22, 133-24	Rfix sun	20 T 122	16.5	1.2	5.5	090	22
1161	0530/11	35-17, 133-48	Venus-2 star	19 T 084	15.5	1.2	5.1	079	24
1181	1100/11	34-58, 133-55	sun-moon	02 T 280	5.0	0.4	3.6	020	10
1285	1600/12	34-08, 135-12	Rfix sun	07 T 035	29.0	0.2	3.6	104	7
0364	0600/13	33-15, 136-16	moon-venus	15 T 122	14.0	1.1	5.6	079	19
1412	1700/13	32-28, 136-13	Rfix sun	06 T 110	11.0	0.5	4.4	048	13
1696	0930/15	29-56, 139-54	Rfix sun-moon	28 T 320	40.5	0.7	7.0	284	10
1730	1330/15	29-30, 140-23	Rfix sun	07 T 162	4.0	1.8	8.5	034	21
1865	0600/16	28-34, 142-40	moon-*-Venus	03 T 270	16.5	0.2	8.2	135	2
1923	1430/16	28-12, 143-21	Rfix sun	17 T 032	8.5	2.0 \	6.8	058	29
1981	2200/16	27-52, 144-12	Jupiter-Vega	08 T 105	7.5	1.1	7.7	058	14
2265	1100/18	25-44, 149-09	Rfix sun	11 T 285	37.0	0.3	7.7	284	4
2343	2200/18	25-15, 150-26	Vega-Alkaid	05 T 360	11.0	0.5	7.1	078	6
2401	0700/19	24-42, 151-11	Venus-3 star	07 T 057	9.0	0.8	6.4	058	12
2486	2200/19	24-12, 152-30	Altair-Jupiter	15 T 360	15.0	1.0	5.7	085	18
2573	1530/20	23-17, 153-32	LAN (lat, lon)	11 T 074	17.5	0.6	5.0	087	13
2614	2200/20	22-49, 154-06	Jupiter-2 star	07 T 310	6.5	1.1	6.3	041	17

then we should consider that after two days of pure dead reckoning we could be some 48 miles off course, but probably not much more than this, even over longer runs, if the "set" of the errors is truly random. See Figures 14-3 and 14-4.

With the increasing use of Loran and SatNav for offshore sailing comes a tendency to overlook the basics of navigation. We might be tempted to navigate by simply recording the electronic fix in the logbook every few hours or so. This is a dangerous practice. Unless the electronics are also monitoring and recording compass headings and logged runs — which requires more sophisticated gear that is not so common — then we are learning nothing about our dead reckoning accuracy. If

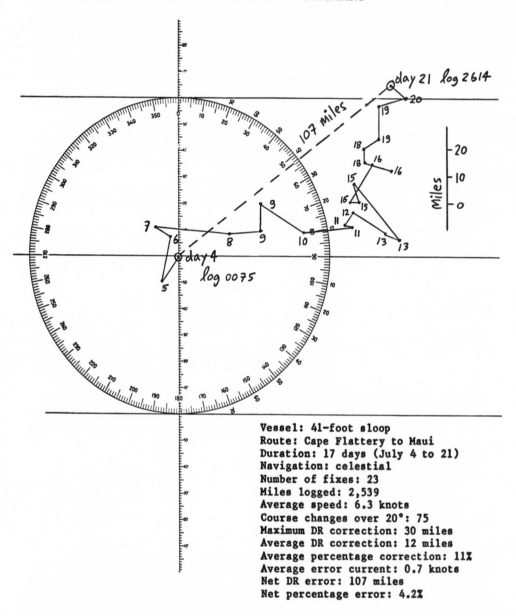

Vessel: 41-foot sloop
Route: Cape Flattery to Maui
Duration: 17 days (July 4 to 21)
Navigation: celestial
Number of fixes: 23
Miles logged: 2,539
Average speed: 6.3 knots
Course changes over 20°: 75
Maximum DR correction: 30 miles
Average DR correction: 12 miles
Average percentage correction: 11%
Average error current: 0.7 knots
Net DR error: 107 miles
Net percentage error: 4.2%

FIGURE 14-3. *Vector plot of DR errors. The individual DR errors logged in Figure 14-2 are plotted sequentially here to show how the vessel would progressively have gone off course if these corrections had not been made. If no fixes had been taken on this voyage, the boat would have been 107 miles off position at log reading 2614. In this particular example, however, it would not have been off its course line, since these errors accidentally left the vessel very near its actual course line at the time. Note that even though the individual errors averaged some 11 percent (taking into account distance covered on each leg), the net error was only 4 percent, which shows how random DR errors tend to cancel out over a long run—in part because these "DR errors" also reflect errors in the celestial fixes. This is shown even more dramatically in Figure 14-4 for another voyage. The average DR error current was 0.7 knots (taking into account time spent on each leg), which is somewhat higher than is typical for a sailboat keeping a careful DR log—the winds were unusually erratic for this trip.*

Vessel: 50-foot sloop
Route: Kauai to Cape Flattery
Duration: 18 days (August 2 to 21)
Navigation: celestial
Number of fixes: 19
Miles logged: 2,736
Average speed: 6.5 knots
Course changes over 20°: 46
Maximum DR correction: 30 miles
Average DR correction: 13 miles
Average percentage correction: 7%
Average error current: 0.5 knots
Net DR error: 10 miles
Net percentage error: 0.3%

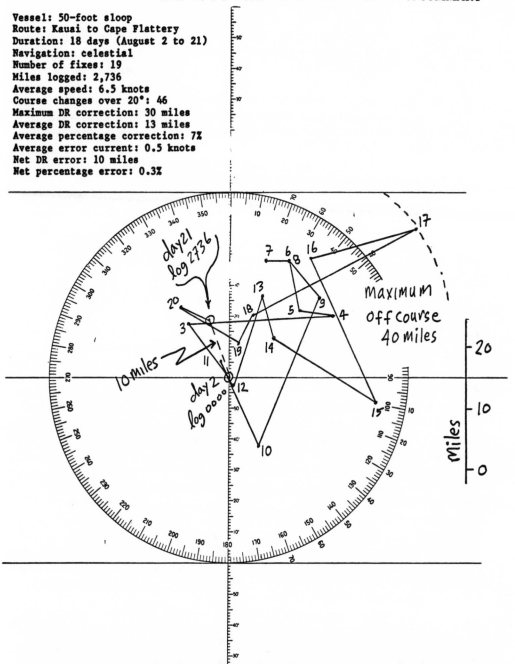

FIGURE 14-4. *Another vector plot of DR errors. Here the DR errors cancel almost completely. This is in part luck, but not entirely. The predicted ocean currents over this route nearly cancel, so they were not expected to contribute. But more important, the boat's log and compass were accurate, and a careful logbook was kept. Any confirmed course change over 5° was logged— the 46 changes listed above reflect only the number of times the course changed 20° or more, either at once, or after four 5° entries. Even with this care, corrections as large as 30 miles were made, though some large corrections followed weather legs in daylong storms, with steady winds of 30-35 knots.*

the electronics fail under these conditions, we must start the "real" navigation with no recent data on the boat's instruments or a crew not trained to make logbook entries, and probably from an unknown position. In short, our position is going to get worse before it gets better.

Another procedural point important to emergency preparation is how we handle timekeeping. It is best to navigate by the watch we wear and use the radio each day to check the watch, recording its watch error in a chronometer log but not resetting it. This way, if we lose radio time signals, we still have a well-rated watch. Setting your watch every few days by radio, or using a stopwatch and the radio time signals themselves for timing celestial sights, is dangerous since you would lose accurate GMT with the loss of the radio. With a rated watch, we can always figure out GMT, no matter where we are or what other aids we might lose. For any long passage, GMT is without a doubt the most valuable aid to have.

When sailing with Loran in areas of good Loran coverage, frequent log entries for Loran values of course and speed made good will provide valuable checks on effective leeway, current reckoning, and instrument calibrations.

14.2 Position by Radio Contact

With two-way radio contact to land or another vessel, we are essentially never lost. A vessel in sight could tell us our position, but even out of sight, a vessel or land station in VHF-radio contact could help pinpoint our position, since the range of VHF (very high frequency) signals is limited (approximately) to line of sight — the geographic range from antenna to antenna. To estimate your maximum separation, use the geographic range formula of Section 13.2, with "H" equal to the contact's antenna height (which they provide) and "h" equal to your antenna height. The intensity and clarity of the signal are also some indication of the distance off.

Furthermore, in an emergency, the Coast Guard can locate a transmitting antenna by radio direction finding (RDF). This can be done on any marine frequency, VHF for short-range communications or single-sideband (SSB) for long-distance communications. This service, however, should be reserved for a true emergency since it could require an expensive coordination of land, sea, and airborne operations. There are other things to try first if we are lost but not in danger.

For one thing, we can always get GMT if we have radio contact. We could even be told the equation of time and from this figure our longitude from the time of LAN (Section 12.2). Our contact could also possibly tell us our approximate latitude from the length of day we report, if we didn't have the sunrise-sunset tables to figure it out ourselves. Or they could tell us our approximate latitude by looking up the declinations of the overhead stars we describe. For any help of this kind, though, we should know what to ask for — radio operators, or even skippers of other vessels, are not likely to be trained in these special cases of celestial navigation. On the other hand, knowing these principles, we are prepared to help others, should we receive such an emergency call. The radio call, by the way, would be PAN, PAN, PAN, not MAYDAY.

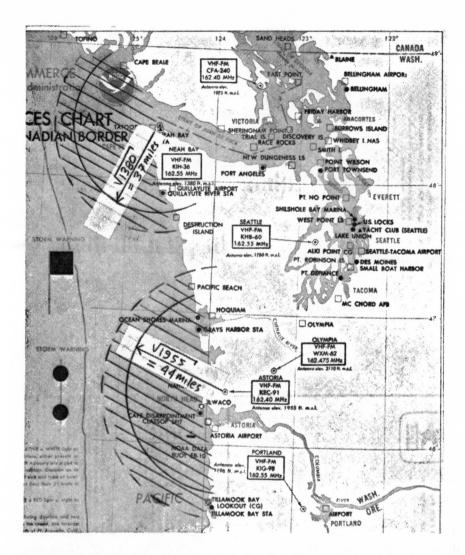

FIGURE 14-5. *Section of a Marine Weather Services Chart. These charts list all weather services in the area, and include broadcast antenna locations and elevations. They are available for all U.S. waters. You can figure the approximate radio range of the individual stations in miles (if not shown on the chart) by taking the square root of the antenna height in feet. In this application you might extend this approximate geographic range by 20 percent or so, as shown—practical radio ranges tend to be closer to the larger theoretical values than visual ranges are, although the reception may be broken near this limit, as waves and the rocking of your own antenna interrupt the signal. For example, if you can hear the KEC-91 weather broadcast, then you are likely within the shaded region shown around it. If the signal is strong, you are probably well within it; if broken, you are more likely near the limit of reception. This particular chart section is from NOAA, Pub. MSC-10 - Point St. George, CA to Canadian Border. The corresponding chart for Hawaiian waters (MSC-13) is an especially valuable aid, since it includes a map of surface wind patterns around the islands.*

Once an approximate position was established, we could be informed of any nearby traffic that might further identify our position by radio contact. Some VHF radios include built-in RDF capability. With these, you can home in on another vessel or even get bearings to the antennas used for coastal weather broadcasts (their locations and heights are shown on NOAA Weather Service Charts, an example of which is shown in Figure 14-5).

14.3 Everything but GMT

In general, we rightfully consider GMT the most vital non-tangible aid to celestial navigation. But with practice, more work, and some reduction in longitude accuracy, we can even do without it — providing we have everything else. In short, an experienced celestial navigator can indeed find longitude from an unknown position without GMT. Even with GMT, knowledge and practice of this technique lend confidence and versatility to our navigation. It is not likely that a well-prepared vessel would end up losing track of GMT with everything else in place, but stranger things have been known to happen at sea.

The main virtue of this method is that celestial navigators already know how to do it, even if they don't know they do. It requires only standard equipment and procedures of routine celestial navigation. The historically better known method of calculating longitude from lunar distance is not so attractive these days, unless you happen to have the special tables required, or a calculator and a list of special formulas. With this special preparation, however, the lunar distance method is potentially more versatile and accurate. For details see John Letcher's book listed in the bibliography. The better, more practical approach to count on in an emergency, is to learn to use the height of the moon to find GMT since it doesn't require special measurements or procedures. The moon is the only celestial body that moves through the stars fast enough for its location among the stars to be used to determine time. The procedure requires only that the moon be in the eastern or western quadrant during twilight, which is fairly common. If it is not, we can wait a few days until it is. This doesn't guarantee the optimum conditions for this procedure, but it is usually sufficient. Furthermore, it will be obvious when you do this how well it might work when it is really called for.

First make your best guess at GMT and set the watch you have to that time. We can set the watch as accurately as we know our longitude, using the watch time of LAN (Section 12.3) — with a sextant, this is easy to do, taking sights a few hours before and after LAN. Then, with your watch set to this approximate time, take a careful round of moon and star sights at twilight, using an easterly or westerly moon and any two stars that would give a good fix if you did know GMT. Take the sights in rotation — first star, moon, second star — then repeat the round until you have at least four good sights of each one. Do this as quickly as you can without sacrificing accuracy.

Next we must graphically rule out the bad sights and pick a simultaneous height for each — as if we had taken all three simultaneously. This is still just standard procedure, though not necessarily done this way by all navigators. On one sheet of graph paper, plot sextant heights versus watch times for each object. Then draw a best-fit line through the sights of each object, disregarding any obviously bad sights. And finally, pick a time to use, and read off the simultaneous heights of the three objects from the lines drawn through the sights. This graph effectively averages the sights and takes into account any motion of the boat between sights. We get the heights we need from the lines, even though we didn't take any sights at that particular time. We now have three good heights at one time, although we know the time is not precise. Next we find out how much that time is off.

Do the sight reductions of each sight in the usual manner, using your best guess of a DR position at the sight time, and carefully plot the lines of position (LOPs). The two star lines will intersect near your proper latitude, but the moon line will not go through this intersection if our time is wrong. The trick now is to adjust the watch error until the moon line agrees with the star lines, and from this we get our proper longitude and the watch error.

If the moon is fast (moon line west of the star fix), the watch is slow and vice versa. In either case, your true position is on the moon side of the star fix. From the plotted LOPs, read the longitude difference between the star fix and the moon line (where it crosses the latitude of the star fix), and figure your first guess of the watch error as 2 minutes for each 1' of this longitude difference. Now we do the sight reduction of these same sights again with the corrected GMT and a new DR position adjusted to match what we have found so far. Your new latitude is the star-fix latitude, and your new longitude is the star-fix longitude adjusted by the first-guess watch error. For each minute of watch error, move your longitude 15' from the star-fix longitude toward and past the moon line.

After these second sight reductions, the moon line will cross closer to the star fix, and we repeat this process until it coincides. The process is straightforward, but requires careful plotting. Using standard universal plotting sheets with parallels drawn 3 inches apart, it will likely be necessary to first plot on a condensed scale, with 3 inches equal to 6° of latitude, until you get the watch time to within 20 minutes or so, and then progress on up to 3 inches equal 60', 6', and then possibly even 0.6' of latitude as the watch error diminishes.

The sextant sights must be accurate for this to yield accurate longitude and GMT. The moon moves relative to the stars only about 12° per day, which is 0.5' per minute. Turned over, this gives the 2 minutes of time for each 1' of star-moon longitude difference that we use for the rough watch-error correction. Consequently, a 1' error in sextant height could cause a 2-minute error in time, which is a 30' error in longitude. But even this is optimistic, since the moon is unlikely to be moving in the optimum direction when we take the sights. In other words, if we can find our longitude to within 30' or so from an unknown position without GMT, we are doing well. With care, though, we shouldn't have to do much worse than that.

This very neat procedure was first described by John Letcher in 1964, though others (including Sir Francis Chichester) discovered it independently later on. John Letcher's book, *Self-Contained Celestial Navigation with H.O. 208* (Camden, Maine: International Marine Publishing Co., 1973), includes several numerical examples and variations of the procedure. Refinements, extensions, and limitations of the method have been added (Kerst 1975, Luce 1977), but for emergency use, the simplest form of this procedure is all we need. It will be clear as we practice it that careful sights, sight reductions, and plotting are vital for optimum accuracy. In an emergency, though, we don't need the level of accuracy we expect in routine sailing.

As an example, consider a vessel that somehow ends up without a radio or GMT after several days of storm sailing with poor navigation records. After things settle down, a LAN sight gives a midday latitude of 35° 30' N, but accurate longitude is not known. The best guess for midday longitude is about 74° W. Using this longitude guess and the observed watch time of LAN, the watch is set to GMT. The vessel is ghosting south-southwest at some 2.5 knots, and the estimated DR position at evening twilight is 35° 14' N, 74° 07' W, when a series of star and moon sights were taken. The date is March 24, 1985.

Four or five sights of *Regulus, Sirius,* and the lower limb of the moon were taken in rotation and plotted versus the corresponding watch times. A chosen sight time of 23:15:00 GMT (relative to the time set at LAN) was chosen and the following three observed heights were figured from the sextant heights read from the graph:

Sight data:	*Regulus*	H_o = 39°51.6'
	Sirius	H_o = 38°07.1'
	LL moon	H_o = 30°32.1'.

The first sight reduction from the DR position of 35° 14' N, 74° 07' W, at 23:15:00 GMT gave these lines of position:

Regulus	a = 265.2'	Toward	100.9°
Sirius	a = 11.6'	Toward	175.0°
LL moon	a = 266.8'	Away from	263.6°.

These lines plotted on a scale of 3 inches equal 6° of latitude gave the following results: Star fix at roughly 35° 26' N, 68° 37' W, with the moon line located about 12' to the west, indicating that the GMT used was slow by about 12' x 2 minutes = 24 minutes. These values are all fairly rough because a very condensed scale had to be used to plot these large a-values. This gives a longitude correction of 24m x (15'/1m) = 360' = 6° west of the star fix. Adding 24 minutes to the first GMT, adjusting the star-fix longitude 6° to the west, and assuming the star-fix latitude, we now do the second sight reduction.

The second sight reduction (see Figure 14-6) from 35° 26' N, 74° 37' W, at 23:39:00 GMT gave these lines of position:

Regulus	a = 4.8'	Toward	105.0°
Sirius	a = 15.8'	Toward	181.7°
LL moon	a = 6.2'	Away from	266.8°.

These lines plotted on a scale of 3 inches equal 6' of latitude gave the following results: Star fix at 35° 9.2' N, 74° 36' W, with the moon line located 7.7' to the east, indicating that the GMT used was fast by about 7.7' x 2 minutes = 15.4 minutes = 15 minutes and 24 seconds. This gives a longitude correction of 15.4m x (15'/1m) = 231' = 3° 51' east of the star fix. Subtracting 15 minutes and 24 seconds from the last GMT, adjusting the star-fix longitude 3° 51' to the east, and assuming the latest star-fix latitude, we now do the third sight reduction.

The third sight reduction from 35° 9.2' N, 70° 45' W, at 23:23:36 GMT gave these lines of position:

Regulus	a = 0.1'	Toward	104.8°
Sirius	a = 1.0'	Away from	181.7°
LL moon	a = 0.7'	Toward	263.6°.

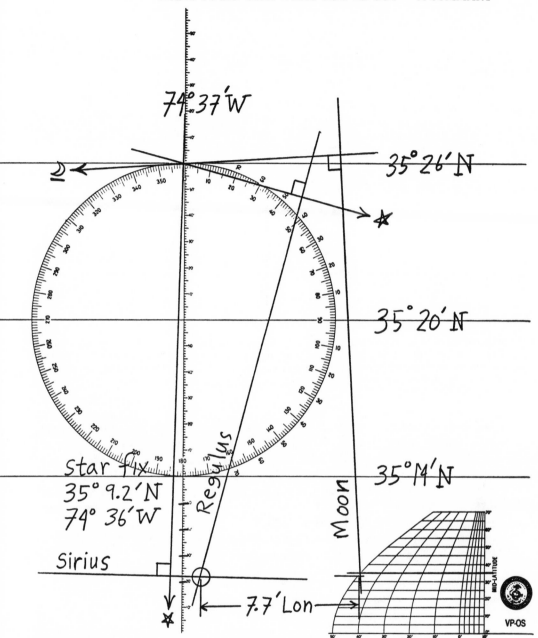

74° 37' W

35° 26' N

35° 20' N

35° 14' N

star fix
35° 9.2' N
74° 36' W

Regulus

Moon

Sirius

7.7' Lon

VP-OS

FIGURE 14-6. *Second plot of a star-moon fix for finding GMT. After plotting all three lines using the largest convenient expansion of the latitude scale, measure the longitude difference from the star fix to the moon line, equal to 7.7' in this case. Here the "moon is slow" (behind, or east of the star fix), so the "watch is fast." We must now reduce the GMT used for these sights by 7.7 × 2 minutes, or 15 minutes and 24 seconds, and do the sight reductions again. We repeat this process until the moon line crosses the star fix; then we know we have found the correct GMT, and with it our longitude. Note that all three LOPs are plotted from the same assumed position, which is only possible if the sight reductions are done with a calculator, as these were. Sight reduction tables will do the job as well, though this method takes more work. Using tables, each LOP will have a separate assumed longitude along the assumed latitude line.*

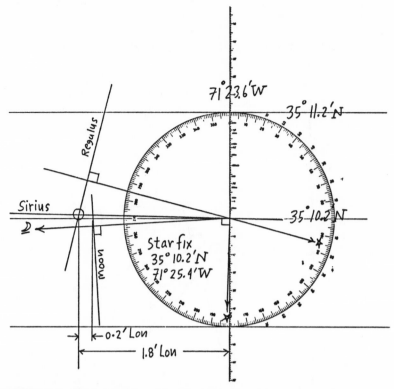

FIGURE 14-7. *Final plot of the star-moon fix to find GMT. This is as far as it is practical to go. The moon line agrees with the star fix to within 0.2' of longitude. Chances are the sextant heights of the stars and moon are not precise enough to carry this further. See Figure 14-6 for other notes on this type of plot.*

These lines plotted on a scale of 3 inches equal 0.6 of latitude gave the following results: Star fix at 35° 10.2' N, 70° 44.6' W, with the moon line located 1.3' to the west, indicating that the GMT used was slow by about 1.3' x 2 minutes = 2.6 minutes = 2 minutes and 36 seconds. This gives a longitude correction of 2.6m x (15'/1m) = 39' west of the star fix. Adding 2 minutes and 36 seconds to the last GMT, adjusting the star-fix longitude 39' to the west, and assuming the latest star-fix latitude, we now do the last sight reduction.

The fourth sight reduction (see Figure 14-7) from 35° 10.2' N, 71° 23.6' W, at 23:26:19 GMT gave these lines of position:

Regulus	a = 1.4'	Away from	104.8°.
Sirius	a = 0.0'	Toward	181.8°
LL moon	a = 1.3'	Toward	267.0°.

These lines plotted on a scale of 3 inches equals 6' of latitude gave the following results: Star fix at 35° 10.2' N, 71° 25.4' W, with the moon line located 0.2' to the east, indicating that the GMT used was fast by about 0.2' x 2 minutes = 0.4 minutes = 24 seconds. This gives a longitude correction of 0.4m x (15'/1m) = 6' east of the star fix. Subtracting 24 seconds from the last GMT and adjusting the star-fix longitude 6' to the east, we end up with our final longitude and GMT: 71° 19.4' W, 23:25:55. The watch is 10 minutes and 55 seconds slow — our longitude guess at LAN was quite a bit off.

The GMT accuracy ultimately depends on the accuracy of the measured heights, although you need accurate sight reductions and plotting to get any consistent answer at all. If the plotting is not accurate, it takes more sight reductions to find the

GMT that makes the lines all coincide. There are ways to shorten the procedure, but it is probably best to just remember the basic philosophy and then nail down the answer through sheer repetition.

If you work through this example as practice, you probably won't get the same a-values or the exact same star fixes, since these depend on the sight-reduction methods used and the precision in plotting — this example was chosen at random, reduced with a calculator, and plotted with no more than routine care — but you should come to about the same conclusions about longitude and time at each step, and definitely end up with the same final answer. To see how this works, try starting with a different first guess as to the time and longitude. Here is a summary that shows how position and GMT improve with successive sight reductions:

	Latitude	*Longitude*	*GMT*	*Watch Error*
DR	35° 14′ N	74° 7′ W	23:15:00	?
1st	35° 26′ N	74° 37′ W	23:39:00	24m slow
2nd	35° 9.2′ N	74° 45′ W	23:23:36	8m 36s slow
3rd	35° 10.2′ N	71° 23.6′ W	23:26:19	11m 36s slow
4th	35° 10.2′ N	71° 19.4′ W	23:25:55	10m 55s slow

Note that latitude improves quickly and the first sight reduction done here doesn't really count. We would have had to repeat that one even if we had known GMT, since the DR position was so far off.

It is good training in celestial navigation to practice this procedure. With some experience, you will see that it can also be extended to sun-moon sights during the day. With a known latitude from LAN, you can do this whenever the sun and moon have nearly the same or opposite bearings.

If you know the time but have lost only the date — which is not so unlikely as we might guess from land — then a single sight reduction of a star-moon or sun-moon fix for each day in question will do the job. The moon moves 12° each day, so only the right day will yield a fix near your DR position. Or just look at the night sky, as shown in Figure 7-1, it is easy to spot this 12° shift relative to the stars. To locate the moon's proper position among the stars on each of the days in question, figure its SHA at the time you plan to look from:

$$\text{SHA moon} = \text{GHA moon} - \text{GHA Aries},$$

and use this with the moon's declination to plot it on the star maps in the *Nautical Almanac*. A 2102-D Star Finder is also very convenient for this application.

14.4 Everything but a Sextant

If we should ever lose the only sextant on board, but still have GMT and all our other standard celestial navigation tools and books available, we still have an opportunity for, more-or-less, routine navigation — we can take "horizon sights" of the sun and moon. To do sun sights this way, note the time of sunrise or sunset to the second, call the sextant height of the sun's upper limb 0° 0′ at that time, and do a normal sight reduction for a line of position. Then do a conventional running fix between sunrise and sunset.

Using the sun alone this method is not highly accurate, but it is useful complement to other emergency procedures. You will have an uncertainty of 10 miles or so in each of the sun lines since they are so low, and some error in your all-day or all-night run that throws off the running fix.

If it happens that you can see the moon cross the horizon on the same day or night, bearing some 30° or more away from the sun's horizon bearing, then you might get a sun-moon fix that could be more accurate since it would reduce the uncertainty of the running fix. Narrow crossing angles should be avoided because the large inherent uncertainty in the sights will cause a large position uncertainty for narrow intersections.

In exceptional cases we might also do this with Venus or Jupiter, or perhaps even the two brightest stars, *Sirius* and *Canopus*. These opportunities will come during the night, so for rising sights the bodies must be precomputed or spotted one night and anticipated the next. However, exceptionally clear skies and smooth seas are required to see these bodies cross the horizon rising or setting.

A trick that might help verify nighttime rising or setting times has been suggested by Leonard Gray in his book *Celestial Navigation Planning* (Centreville, Md.: Cornell Maritime Press, 1985). Since we usually can't discern the horizon at night, try bobbing the star or planet when it first appears, just as you might do a light as you cross the geographic range (well within the nominal range) trying to get a rough check of distance off (Section 13.2). Watch for the body to rise from a high elelvation (standing on the boom, say) and when the object is first spotted jump down to bring the horizon forward. If the object was indeed just on the true sea horizon viewed from above, this should obscure it. Then go back up to verify the sight. If you wait from below, the object may be above the horizon when first detected. When watching a body set, watch from below, then bounce up when it disappears to see if you can bring it back. But you must move fast in either case; it only takes about 10 seconds or so for a planet to change altitudes by an angle that is too big to bob across. And remember, these nighttime sights, however they are done, could be way off. They must be treated as just another piece of data and fitted with their own uncertainties into the sum of the information you have.

Binoculars are a big aid to horizon sights, especially at night. Low clouds on the distant horizon are the big enemy, day and night. Horizon sights must be timed as the object crosses the true sea horizon, not just a low rim of clouds — and these clouds are there more often than not. During daylight you can see the clouds, and even make estimates of the time it takes for the sun or moon to move from cloud rim to horizon; at night you can't see the clouds which inhibits the value of moon sights. But if you can indeed, bob the upper limit of the moon or a planet (and be sure the waves aren't bobbing it for you), you can be reasonably confident that it is crossing the sea horizon at the time.

Sight reductions of horizon sights typically involve negative values of the observed altitude (Ho), calculated altitude (Hc), or both, so we must carefully reason through the required algebraic corrections and the subtraction of the two when figuring the altitude intercept (a-value). Otherwise, the sight reduction and plotting procedures are standard.

Publication 229 sight reduction tables, however, are awkward to use for this because of the way they record negative altitude data. Check the instructions for details. The procedure boils down to this: If the proper declination puts you across the C-S line (from the proper LHA end of the page), call the listed Hc negative, reverse the sign of the d value, and figure Z by subtracting the listed one from 180°. *Publication 249* tables are more convenient since negative Hc values with the proper d and Z are listed. The lower precision of the *Publication 249* numbers has little significance for these sights which are so uncertain to begin with. Pre-programed calculators should do the job adequately, though they may be off a few miles, depending on how they do the altitude corrections near 0°.

The big uncertainty in these sights comes from refraction, which is at a maximum for horizon sights. Refraction depends on the density of the air, which in turn depends on temperature and pressure. There is a special table in the *Nautical Almanac* for abnormal refraction corrections in various atmospheric conditions. These corrections can be as large as five or six miles for horizon sights. My feeling, however, is that the uncertainties in these extra corrections must be at least as large as the corrections themselves, so I typically ignore them in routine sights. Mirages are, after all, just abnormal refraction and if you've ever seen an impressive one you begin to appreciate how large the effect can be. I assume that all very low sights are uncertain by some 10 miles or so (meaning plus or minus 5' on the a-values), and do everything else in the standard fashion.

Dutton's Navigation and Piloting reports that Capt. P.V.H. Weems made 10 horizon sights on six occasions with an average error of two miles and a maximum error of four miles. Further details are not given. My own data (pieced together from logbook and plotting-sheet notes) for about the same number of sights are similar — about half were as good as I knew my position at the various times (two-to-five miles) but an equal number appear to be off by at least five miles and maybe more. Mine were all sunlines taken offshore, and only DR positions were available in most cases. More scientific results (even from a coastline) would be interesting, but it would take a lot of them before I would be more optimistic. Localized air masses well away from the vessel could influence the results, as could the prevailing air-sea temperature difference, the wind strength, and probably other factors.

Examples of the sight reductions and a plot of a sun-moon fix from horizon sights are shown in Figures 14-8 and 14-9.

14.5 Everything but Sight Reduction Tables

Latitude from *Polaris* or latitude and longitude from LAN do not require sight reduction, so these methods are available without sight reduction tables. You can also find latitude from any star that happens to be on the meridian at twilight, as covered in Section 11.5.

We usually avoid very high sights in celestial navigation because they are hard to take and require special sight reduction procedures. But these special procedures do not require sight reduction tables, so high sights are more attractive when we don't

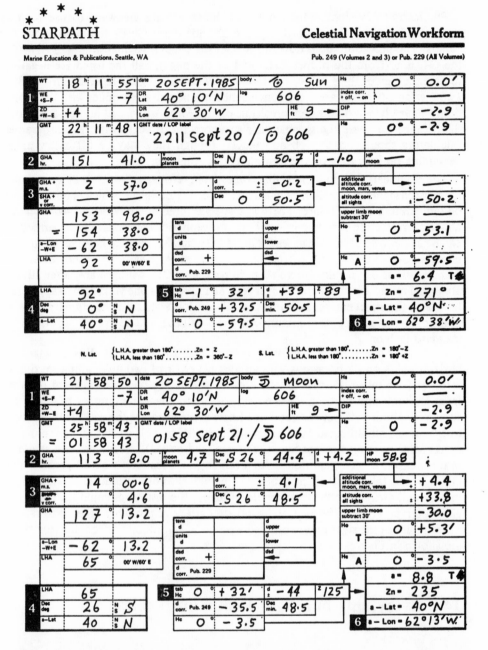

Above: FIGURE 14-8. *Sight reductions of horizon sights of the sun and moon. The procedure is standard, except that we end up with negative values of Hc and Ho. In the sun line, note that Hc = -59.5' is less than Ho = -50.2', since they are both negative, so the label for a is Toward. And in the moon line, the difference between Hc and Ho is numerically a sum of the two, since Ho is positive and Hc is negative, and here we want the angle between them. In contrast, applying a negative correction to a positive angle is still a difference, as in the d-corrections to Hc of each sight. These sight reductions were done with Pub. 249, which, for these sights, is more convenient than Pub. 229. The d-corrections to Hc were interpolated. For comparison, Pub. 229 answers would be: sun's Hc = -0° 59.4', Zn = 271.9, and moon's Hc = -0° 3.3', Zn = 234.0. Calculator solutions for Ho may be off by 2' or so, depending on their formulas for low-angle altitude corrections.*

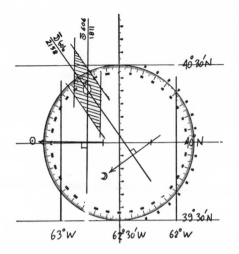

FIGURE 14-9. *Plot of a sun-moon fix from horizon sights. The sight reductions plotted here are from Figure 14-8. Note that the inherent uncertainty of plus or minus 5 miles, in each of the lines, can cause a large position uncertainty (shaded area) for narrow intersections. These sights were taken about four hours apart, so a running fix would have been required if the vessel had been moving. A more common fix of this type would be a running fix between sunrise and sunset. The intersection angle for such a fix would be twice the sun's amplitude, which means that this method would not work near the equinoxes, and, in general, works better at higher latitudes. Below: Examples of using SatNav or Loran units for sight reduction.*

Sight Reduction with Loran or SatNav Units

In a navigational emergency, Loran or SatNav units might prove useful even when not producing reliable electronic fixes. With broken antennas and useless position information, they will perform great circle sailing calculations which can be used for sight reduction.

Procedure:

(1) enter present position or an assumed position into Waypoint 1 (WP1)

(2) enter declination and GHA as Lat and Lon into Waypoint 2 (WP2)
(if GHA > 180°, enter 360° −GHA, and call it East Lon)

(3) ask for range and bearing from WP1 to WP2
(use great circle instead of rhumbline if given a choice)

(4) bearing or initial heading (Hi) answer is the azimuth, Zn

(5) range answer is the zenith distance in arc minutes. Find Hc by dividing this answer by 60 to convert to degrees; subtract this from 90° to get Hc in degrees and then convert to degrees and minutes.

Examples:

WP #1 DR-Lat/DR-Lon	WP #2 Dec / GHA	Loran Output GC Hi	GC range		
45° 20'N	03° 40.8'S	182.3°	2942.3'	= 49.038°	= z
124° 15'W	126° 01.2'W	Zn	40.962°	= 40° 57.7'	= Hc
45° 20'N	58° 22.1'N	346.7°	4454.9'	= 74.248°	= z
124° 15'W	279° 13.8'W use 80° 46.2'E	Zn	15.752°	= 15° 45.1'	= Hc
40° 00'N	26° 48.5'S	234.0°	5403.4'	= 90.057°	= z
124° 15'W	127° 13.2'W	Zn	−00.057°	= −0° 03.4'	= Hc

231

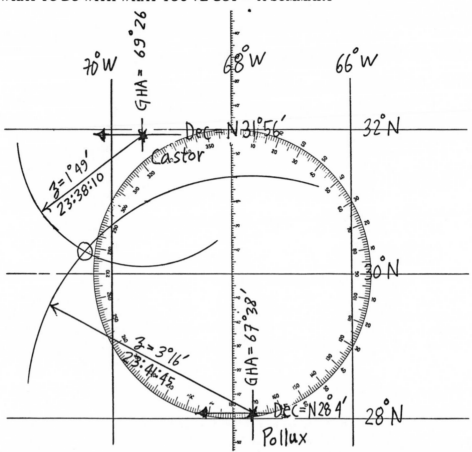

FIGURE 14-10. *Plot of a high-altitude fix from overhead stars done without sight reduction. Measure Hs for two high stars, convert them to Ho in the usual manner, and then figure the zenith distance (z = 90° - Ho) of each. Then plot the geographical positions (GP) of each star at the times of the sights on a plotting sheet with condensed scales. Each sight gives you a circle of position centered at the GP, with radius equal to the zenith distance. Here Castor and Pollux of Gemini are used (on March 30, 1985) as they pass overhead. The sights are difficult, but manageable in smooth seas. The trick is to stay oriented toward the star, and wait for it to reappear when the boat rocks it out of view. If you try to chase it around as the boat rocks, you will get poor sights. It also helps to start as early as possible and follow the star up, to get used to looking in the right direction. The sights don't have to be as high as those shown here to get a fix. Down a few degrees, the sights are much easier, but the plotting is less accurate. Even this fix is off (to the west) by about 5 miles, which represents typical plotting errors in this type of fix.*

have any way to do sight reductions. The method is based on the fundamental principle of celestial navigation. We measure and then correct the sextant height of a star to find its observed height (Ho). From its observed height we figure its zenith distance (90° - Ho), which is our distance from the geographical position (GP) of the star at the time of the sight. The almanac tells us where the GP was at the time of the sight, so now we know we are on a circle whose radius is equal to the zenith distance centered at the GP. With two such sights, we have a fix at the intersection of the two circles. For normal (lower) sights, we can't plot these circles because their radii are so large, but for very high sights we can.

To do the fix, take regular sextant sights of two stars that are above 85° or so.

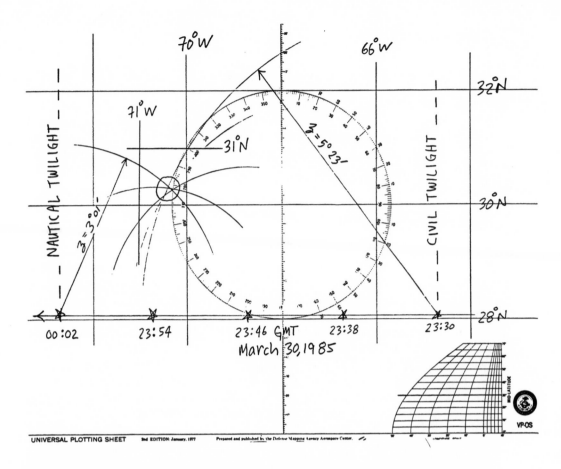

FIGURE 14-11. *A single-star, high-altitude fix done without sight reduction. The time and place are the same as in Figure 14-10, but now the fix is carried out using only Pollux. Note that the first sight taken (at 23:30) had an observed height of 84° 37', which, in reasonable conditions, is significantly easier than sights at, say, 88°. The true position was 30° 15' N, 70° 20' W.*

These are difficult sights, so we need several of each to get a good average, then figure observed height for each in the usual way. Then find from the almanac the precise location of the GP of each at the time of the sights, and plot these two points on a universal plotting sheet centered near your DR position. Use a condensed scale on the plotting sheets, such as 3 inches to 2° of latitude. The latitude of the GP is the star's declination and the longitude of the GP is the star's Greenwich hour angle (GHA), or 360° – GHA in eastern longitudes. Figure the zenith distance for each star and then draw the circles of position centered at the GPs. Figure 14-10 shows a fix done this way using *Castor* and *Pollux*. There will be two intersections, but your DR position or the observed bearings of the stars should rule out the wrong one if the stars are far enough apart.

Two stars at about the same height some 90° apart provide the best conditions for this, but you can plot the candidates ahead of time to pick the best available pair. For this method (or for latitude from stellar meridian passage), you will likely have to rely on stars from the back of the *Nautical Almanac*, where data are given for 173 stars. With a long twilight, you can sometimes do this fix with one star alone, since bearings change rapidly for very high stars. A single-star fix done this way is illustrated in Figure 14-11.

This plotting procedure and fix are most accurate for high stars at low latitudes. For lower stars at higher latitudes, a circle is no longer a good approximation of the "circle" of equal altitude on a Mercator plot. The proper elliptical shape of the circle of position must be figured from great-circle calculations — but these are usually done with sight reduction tables, which we don't have now. If you stick with stars above 85° or so, this won't be a problem.

14.6 Everything but a Compass

The loss of our compass makes storm steering more difficult, but general navigation in clear skies is not hard when we have all the rest of our routine celestial gear in place. Just do a series of sight reductions from your DR positions throughout the day and night for accurate sun and star bearings. Ways to steer without a compass, covered in Chapters 3 and 4, will be helpful. With sight reductions, they can be fine-tuned with accurate reference bearings.

If the "everything else" you have includes a 2102-D Star Finder — which it should — then finding reference bearings is especially easy. It takes a few minutes to set up every day or so, but then it gives you true bearings to all celestial bodies you might use throughout the day and night. You just read them from a scale as you rotate the dial to new times. See Figure 14-12.

14.7 Everything but an Almanac

With training in emergency navigation, we can do without an almanac, as discussed throughout this book. With makeshift prescriptions, we can figure the sun's declination to within 30' or so for latitude (Section 11.7) and the equation of time to within 1 minute or so for longitude (Section 12.2). The procedures are described earlier. We now add to this a makeshift rule for the sun's Greenwich hour angle (GHA), which will allow us to take conventional sun lines at any time of day without an almanac. With everything but an almanac, the accuracy of our position is determined by our precision in performing these makeshift prescriptions, including the altitude corrections of Section 11.2.

The sun's GHA can be figured as follows:

$$\text{Sun's GHA} = (\text{GMT} - \text{mer pass time}) \times 15°/\text{hr},$$

where "mer pass time" is the GMT of LAN at Greenwich that we figure from the equation of time prescription given in Section 12.2. Whenever the GMT is earlier than the mer pass time, add 24 hours to the GMT to maintain positive values throughout. For example, find the sun's GHA at 17:28:40 GMT on September 28.

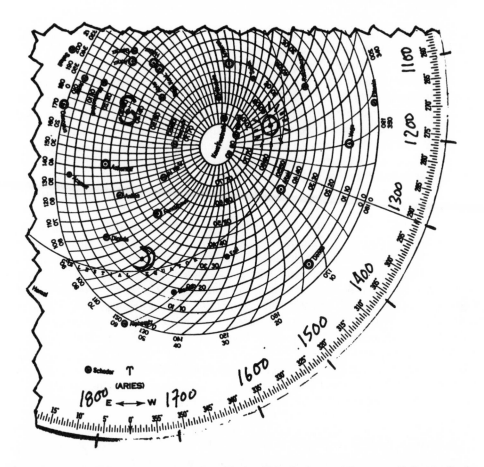

FIGURE 14-12. *Section of a 2102-D Star Finder. This device and the essentially identical British counterpart called N.P.323, are tremendously helpful aids to routine navigation, and a godsend in an emergency. Any long-term almanac is all that is needed to set them up, and, once you do, you have bearings to all celestial bodies, day and night. This one is set to local time 1300 at latitude 35°S. At this time the moon bears 080 True at a height of 25°, and the sun bears 330 True at a height of 60°. To find bearings at later times, just rotate the template grid to the new time, and read the new bearings. As you rotate the disk, the sun will set, the moon will rise, and the heights and bearings to all the brighter stars in this particular sky will be apparent. The author's book* Celestial Navigation with the 2102-D Star Finder *(Sausalito: Paradise Cay Publications, 1986) explains the full potential of this device with many practical examples.*

First figure the equation of time on September 28 and from it the GMT of LAN, as illustrated back in Figure 12-7. The answer is 11:50:30. So GHA = 17:28:40 – 11:50:30 = 5:38:10 = 5 hours and 38.2 minutes = 5.636 hours. Finally we convert this to arc units as GHA = 5.636 hr x 15°/hr = 84.542° = 84° 32.5′. The accuracy of this method of finding GHA is determined by the accuracy of the equation of time, which should be well within 1 minute in most cases, giving a GHA to within about 15′.

With the sun's GHA and declination, we can take sun lines, and from running fixes between sun lines, we can find our position. With careful reckoning of the declination and GHA, we should be able to achieve daily positions from the sun to within 30 miles or so without an almanac.

In the Northern Hemisphere, we can find latitude from *Polaris* without an almanac to within 60' or so, but we still need tricks or prescriptions if we are to reduce this uncertainty (Section 11.3). Other latitude methods of Chapter 11 can be carried out more precisely with a sextant and no almanac, but they generally require that we know a few star declinations. As for finding longitude, the sun is our only hope. There is simply no way to find longitude from the stars, moon, or planets without an almanac of some kind. Clearly, every vessel should carry a long-term almanac for sun and stars as a back-up. And even then, we should think twice before taking the only annual almanac on deck for a few sight reductions in the fresh air and sunshine.

A long-term almanac for stars alone is included in Pub. 249, Vol. 1. A long-term almanac for sun and stars is included in Bowditch (DMAHTC Pub. No. 9, Vol. 2) and other reference books on celestial navigation. Also remember you can do sun and star navigation with an outdated *Nautical Almanac*. The prescription is given in the almanac for the following year, and you can repeat this for another two years. Every fourth year, the sun and star data repeat (1986 should be the same as 1982, for example) — at least to well within the range of accuracy we need in an emergency. Other than pre-programmed calculators, there is no feasible long-term almanac for the moon and planets.

If you happen to recall the sidereal hour angles and declinations of a few stars from previous work (before the almanac was lost), you can do routine star sights of these once you figure the GHA of Aries. The formula is more involved, but it works.

$$\text{GHA Aries} = [DD + (GMT \div 24)] \times (360° \div 365d) + GMT \times 15°/\text{hr}$$
$$- 15' \text{ for each year past the last leap year,}$$

where DD is the number of days past September 21. The formula is accurate to within about 10'. For example, find GHA Aries at 17:28:40 on September 28, 1985. September 28 is 7 days past September 21, so DD equals 7. The GMT is 17:28:40 = 17 hours and 28.67 minutes = 17.478 hours, and 1985 is 1 year past the last leap year (the number of a leap year is divisible by 4, or 400 if it's a centennial number), so the correction is –1 x 15'. So,

$$\begin{aligned}
\text{GHA Aries} &= [7 + (17.478 \div 24)] \times (360° \div 365) + 17.478 \times 15° - 15' \\
&= 7.622° + 262.170° - 15' \\
&= 269.792° - 15' = 269°47.5' - 15' \\
&= 269°32.5'.
\end{aligned}$$

Obviously, it's a good idea to take a back-up almanac — it takes time to multiply and divide to three decimal places by hand. Nevertheless, regardless of our back-ups and their back-ups, we could still end up with nothing but our memory to go by, which we would soon hope included the sun's declination, the equation of time, and the declinations of a few prominent stars.

To figure the equation of time from a long-term almanac, first figure the sun's GHA at 1200 GMT. This will be either a small angle of 4° or less (LAN before 1200), or a large angle of 356° or more (LAN after 1200). The equation of time is the small angle converted to time at 15° per hour (4 minutes per 1°, 4 seconds per 1') in the first case, or 360° minus the larger angle converted to time in the second case.

14.8 Nothing but GMT

With nothing but GMT and the methods we have covered throughout, you should be able to find your way to safety from any point on earth. Greenwich mean time is ultimately the one thing to know to keep from getting lost. We can find latitude without time, but to find longitude we need GMT. With GMT, and nothing more than the makeshift rule for the equation of time, we can always find our position. Clearly then, it is very important to have a good watch and keep track of GMT.

And though some memory work and practice are needed to make full use of GMT, learning this and all the rest of emergency navigation can be quite a rewarding pastime for offshore sailors. It is good practice in navigation, even if we never need it. Sometimes we do better with what we've got if we know what we can do without it.

Bibliography

On Basic Marine Navigation

Bowditch, Nathaniel. *The American Practical Navigator*. Washington, D.C.: DMAHTC, Pub. No. 9: Vol. I, 1985, Vol. II, 1982.
  The encyclopedia of marine navigation on all waters. It includes a brief section on lifeboat navigation and valuable information on oceanography and weather.

Burch, David. *Self Study Course on Coastal Navigation*. Seattle: Starpath, 1984.
  Practical small-craft navigation explained in simple terms with extensive exercises. Topics limited to ones we need and use. Available from Starpath School of Navigation, 1900 N. Northlake Way, Seattle, WA 98103-9051. Includes a nautical chart.

Burch, David. *Self Study Course on Celestial Navigation*. Seattle: Starpath, 1984.
  A thorough course on small-craft ocean navigation with extensive practical exercises. Available from Starpath School of Navigation, 1900 N. Northlake Way, Seattle, WA 98103-9051. Includes all necessary materials and table selections.

Chapman, Charles F. *Chapman's Piloting, Seamanship, and Small Boat Handling*. 54th ed. New York: Hearst Books, 1979.
  The classic introduction to small-craft seamanship and navigation on inland or coastal waters.

Davies, Thomas D. *Concise Tables for Sight Reduction*. Centreville, Md.: Cornell Maritime Press, 1984.
  A 60-page booklet that includes both almanac and sight-reduction tables. Less convenient than having a *Nautical Almanac* and Pubs. 229 or 249, nevertheless it does the job nicely. Clearly the best bet for a back-up set of tables. Since 1989 called NOA tables and included as part of the *Nautical Almanac*.

Dunlap, G. D., and H. H. Shufeldt. *Dutton's Navigation and Piloting*. 14th ed. Annapolis: Naval Institute Press, 1985.
  The "other *Bowditch*," which many find a more readable alternative for an authoritative treatment of marine navigation. Subject matter restricted to navigation, with a short treatment of emergency procedures.

Eyges, Leonard. *The Practical Pilot*. Camden, Maine, International Marine Publishing Company, 1989.
  A basic navigation text with emphasis on short-cut estimates, especially small-angle navigation using kamal-like measurements.

Rousmaniere, John. *The Annapolis Book of Seamanship*. 2nd ed. New York: Simon & Schuster, 1989.
  A "new *Chapman's*" with a practical sailboat orientation.

On the Technical Side of Almanac Data

Almanac for Computers. Washington, D.C.: Nautical Almanac Office, U.S. Naval Observatory, 1985.
  An annual publication that lists equations and parameters for accurate almanac calculations on personal computers. The equations can be simplified for calculator usage with a tolerable loss in precision.

Explanatory Supplement to the Astronomical Ephemeris and to the American Ephemeris and Nautical Almanac. 3rd ed. London, WC1V 6HB, England: H.M. Stationary Office, 49 High Holborn, 1974.
  The official explanation of the mathematics behind almanac calculations.

Duffett-Smith, Peter. *Practical Astronomy With Your Calculator*. 2nd ed. New York: Cambridge University Press, 1981.
  Explains, in simpler terms, the equations used to calculate almanac data.

On Stars and Star Identification

Allen, Richard H. *Star Names Their Lore and Meaning*. New York: Dover Publications, 1963.
  The classic study.

Burch, David. *Celestial Navigation with the 2102-D Star Finder—A User's Guide*. Sausalito: Paradise Cay Publications, 1986.
  A comprehensive explanation of this important aid to celestial navigation with many numerical examples and a section on its use in emergency navigation.

Kyselka, Will, and Ray Lanterman. *North Star to Southern Cross*. Honolulu: The University Press of Hawaii, 1976.
  A brief summary of astronomy and the mythology of the constellations with unique star maps for each month. A helpful incentive to learning the stars.

"The Heavens." Washington, D.C.: National Geographic Society.
  A large, attractive, durable and useful map in the same format used for the round star maps in the *Nautical Almanac*.

On Finding Longitude without Time

Chichester, F. "Longitude without Time." *Journal of the Institute of Navigation* 19 (1966): 105.

Kerst, D. W. "Longitude Without Time." *Navigation: Journal of the Institute of Navigation* 22, no. 4 (1975–76): 283, and 25, no. 1 (Spring 1978): 87.

Letcher, John. *Self-Contained Celestial Navigation with H.O. 208.* Camden, Maine: International Marine Publishing Company, 1973.
  Although *H.O. 208* is not a popular means of sight reduction, this book remains an excellent treatment of practical celestial navigation. Among the several special topics covered are finding GMT from the moon and correcting LAN longitude sights for latitude changes during the measurement.

Luce, J. W., "Longitude Without Time." *Navigation: Journal of the Institute of Navigation* 24, no. 2 (1977): 112.

On No-Instrument Navigation

Burch, D. "Emergency Navigation Card." Sausalito: Paradise Cay Publications, 1988.
  Contains back-up sun almanac, world's shortest sight reduction tables, ways to figure sun's bearing, and brief reminders of star steering, finding position, and other methods covered in this book.

Creamer, Marvin. "Incredible Journey," "A Star to Steer Her By." *Cruising World.* May and September 1984. A two-part account of his 17-month circumnavigation without instruments. See also: "What Makes a Good Navigator" in *Navigator* magazine, August 1985. An article about Marvin Creamer and his voyage.

Finney, B. R., B. J. Kolonsky, S. Somsen, and E. D. Stroup. Submitted for publication in the *Journal of the Polynesian Society.* Auckland, New Zealand: 1985.
  Describes Nainoa Thompson's training in no-instrument navigation and his subsequent navigation of the sailing canoe *Hokule'a* from Hawaii to Tahiti and back.

Gatty, Harold. *Nature is Your Guide—How to Find Your Way on Land and Sea.* New York: Penguin Books, 1979.
  A "Raft Book for Land" with a summary of the Raft Book's marine methods. A unique source of natural guides in various parts of the world, though some of the reported ways of orientation on land are anecdotal.

Gatty, Harold. *The Raft Book—Lore of the Sea and Sky.* New York: George Grady Press, 1943.
  The pioneering first work devoted specifically to emergency navigation. It contains a wealth of information on emergency pathfinding, with a thorough compilation of the various signs of land at sea. The potential value of celestial methods included may be overestimated in some cases. Several methods rely on special aids provided with the book, intended as a liferaft companion.

Gladwin, Thomas. *East is a Big Bird—Navigation and Logic on Puluwat Atoll.* Cambridge: Harvard University Press, 1974.
  An interesting look at the society, psychology, and techniques of traditional navigators in this region.

Lewis, D. H. "An Experiment in Polynesian Navigation." *Journal of the Institute of Navigation* 19 (1966): 154.
  Gives navigational details of his no-instrument voyages from Tahiti to New Zealand.

Lewis, David. *We the Navigators—The Ancient Art of Landfinding in the Pacific.* Honolulu: University of Hawaii Press, 1975.
  The classic study of Polynesian navigation; includes a comprehensive bibliography.

Owendoff, Robert S. *Better Ways of Pathfinding.* Harrisburg, Pa.: The Stackpole Company, 1964.
  Covers orientation on land with an enthusiastic emphasis on the shadow-tip method.

On Emergency Seamanship

Coles, K. Adlard. *Heavy Weather Sailing*. 3rd ed. Clinton Corners, N.Y.: John de Graff, 1984.
Describes and analyzes many accounts of storms at sea and how the various skippers and vessels handled them.

Dowd, John. *Sea Kayaking—A Manual for Long-Distance Touring*. 3rd ed. Seattle: University of Washington Press, 1988.
Includes much sound seamanship. The author has covered thousands of miles offshore in a kayak.

Rousmaniere, John. *Fastnet Force 10*. New York: W.W. Norton, 1980.
The author sailed the race.

"1979 Fastnet Race Inquiry." Prepared by The Royal Yachting Association and the Royal Ocean Racing Club. Available from the United States Racing Union (P.O. Box 209, Newport, R.I. 02840) for $11.00.
An informative study of the effects of a violent storm that overtook an ocean racing fleet of 303 yachts. Fifteen lives were lost, 24 yachts were abandoned with five lost. Extremely valuable lessons on safety equipment and procedures are documented. Topics include yacht stability, storm procedures, heavy weather sails and rigging, safety equipment and use.

Periodicals of Interest to Emergency Navigation

Navigation—the quarterly journal of the Institute of Navigation available to members (Suite 832, 815 - 15th St. N.W., Washington, D.C. 20005, annual dues $24). Though mostly a technical journal, occasional articles on basics are of more general interest. Similar journals are published by the British Institute of Navigation and the Australian Institute of Navigation.

Ocean Navigator—bimonthly magazine devoted to navigational topics for sailors and other mariners (P.O. Box 569, Portland, Maine 04112).

Navigator's Newsletter—a quarterly publication of the Foundation for the Promotion of the Art of Navigation available to members (P.O. Box 1126, Rockville, Md. 20850, annual dues $25). A unique resource, available to any interested person, of information on practical details of celestial navigation and related topics.

On Meteorology and Oceanography

Bigelow, Henry B., and W. T. Edmonson. *Wind Waves at Sea, Breakers and Surf*. H.O. pub. no. 602. Washington, D.C.: U.S. Naval Oceanographic Office, 1977.
A non-mathematical, yet thorough treatment of waves.

Kotsch, William J. *Weather for the Mariner*. 3rd ed. Annapolis: Naval Institute Press, 1983.
A popular introduction to the facts and principles.

Mariner's Weather Log—a quarterly publication of the National Oceanographic Data Center, National Environmental Satellite, Data, and Information Service, NOAA, Washington, D.C. A detailed summary of marine weather with related articles. Best source of recent storm and hurricane statistics. (Available from Superintendent of Documents, U.S. Government Printing Office, Washington, D.C. 20402, $13 per year.)

Selected Worldwide Marine Weather Broadcasts—published periodically by NOAA and updated quarterly in the *Mariner's Weather Log*. Lists broadcast times, frequencies, content, and regions covered for English language weather broadcasts throughout the world (Sources in other languages are listed only when English ones are not available.). Also includes Morse code and weather fax schedules, and an explanation of the MAFOR code for weather reports.

Thomson, Richard E. *Oceanography of the British Columbia Coast.* Canadian Special Publication of Fisheries and Aquatic Sciences 56. Hull, Quebec: Canadian Government Publishing Center, 1981.

Although examples are all from British Columbia and the Northwest Coast, the book remains an outstanding introduction to coastal oceanography for readers in any part of the world. A wonderful book.

Walker, Stuart. *Wind and Strategy.* New York: W.W. Norton & Co., 1973.

Covers details of winds and wind shifts from various weather patterns. Racing oriented and not easy reading, but worth the effort.

Watts, Alan. *Weather Forecasting Ashore and Afloat.* London: Adlard Coles, 1968.

Written with sailors in mind, an excellent, non-technical book on weather with emphasis on shipboard forecasting from clouds and winds. *Instant Weather Forecasting* and *Instant Wind Forecasting* by the same author and publisher.

Published Aids to Navigation

Sailing Directions. Published annually by region for Canadian waters by the Canadian Hydrographic Service, available at authorized Canadian chart dealers. Similar format and content as the *U.S. Coast Pilots.* Outdated issues are still valuable for general information.

Light List. U.S. Coast Guard Publication CG-162.

Published annually by region in 5 volumes for all U.S. waters. Gives a full description of all lights, buoys, radiobeacons, and other aids in each region, as well as general information on navigation using these aids. This data supercedes that printed on any chart with an earlier date. Available from chart dealers or the U.S. Government Printing Office, Washington, D.C. 20402.

Sailing Directions for foreign and international waters published by region by DMAHTC and updated as needed. Similar format and content to the *U.S. Coast Pilots.* Outdated issues are still valuable for general information. Similar publications, called *Pilots,* are published by the British government.

U.S. Coast Pilots. Published by coastal region, annually, for American waters only, in 9 volumes by the National Ocean Survey, NOAA. Available at authorized chart dealers. Contains extensive navigational and related marine information throughout each of the regions covered. Required reading for all mariners. Outdated issues are still valuable for general information.

U.S. National Weather Service, NOAA. Marine Weather Services Charts.

Published annually in 15 regions for all U.S. waters. Explains all weather services available in the region, with notes on local weather. A valuable aid to all mariners. Available at $1.25 each from National Ocean Survey, Distribution Division (C44), Riverdale, Md. 20737.

Index

sight reduction, 225, 229; for sun's GHA, 234-235
Calculated altitude, 228, 230
Calibration lengths, 136-138
California Current, 132
Canopus, 51, 63-65, 166, 169, 228
Cape Breton Island, 71
Capella, 51, 54-56, 71, 167-169
Cassiopeia, 52-54, 56; for *Polaris* corrections, 158-160
Castor, 52, 232, 233
Cat's paws. *See* Ripples
Celestial Navigation (routine), 3, 12, 19, 112, 220; learning stars, 164 (*See Also* Star Finders); sextant sights in, 170, 222, 229, 232-233; workforms, 230-231
Celestial Navigation Planning, 228
Charts. *See* DR plots; Pilot charts
Chichester, Sir Francis, 223
Chiplog, 136-137
Chronometers, 11, 12. *See also* Watches
Circumpolar stars, 49, 50, 170
Clouds: color of, 202; on the horizon, 27, 29, 32, 37, 47, 88, 89; motion of 114, 116; obscuring horizon, 174, 182, 228; obscuring land, 198, 203; as signs of land, 104, 196-198; waves in, 24, 116, 117, 197
Coast Guard, 5, 220
Coast pilots, 5, 131
Color: of celestial bodies, 52, 58, 112; of clouds, 202; of lights, 205, 206; of ocean currents, 128
Compasses, 215, 234; back-up, 5, 7, 215; makeshift, 120-122. *See also* Sun compasses
Compass cards (portable), 209; construction of, 22; used as protractors, 173; relative bearings from, 21, 23, 47, 77, 83, 84, 114, 172; as sun compasses, 101
Compass checks (for errors), 18-21
Concise Tables for Sight Reduction, 5, 7, 215
Coriolis force, 148
Course, choosing. *See* Routes
Course made good, 146, 212-213
Creamer, Marvin, 162
Currents: accuracy of predictions, 127, 130, 131; California, 132; coastal, 130-132, 214; corrections for, 16, 144, 212-213; DR errors from, 138; effect on course, 15, 16, 126, 179, 195, 209, 211, 213; effect on sea state, 127, 132; equatorial, 127-130; jets in, 132; ocean, 127-130, 219; from pilot charts, 6, 33, 127-129; typical strengths, 27; and wind direction, 15, 27, 130, 131
Cygnus, 54-56

Date, finding, 227
Davison Current. *See* California Current
Davies Tables. See *Concise Tables for Sight Reduction*
Day, length of, 174-177

Dead Reckoning, 12, 133, 134, 137; accuracy of, 137-148, 179, 192, 215-219; cancellation of errors, 218-219; errors in, 133-135, 138-139, 143, 147-148, 215-219
Declination, 44, 45; star, 49, 50, 71-73, 152, 160-164; sun's, 10, 74, 98-99, 172-173
Deneb, 54-56
Deneb-Vega line, 55
Deviation (compass), 18-21
Dip, 156
Distance off, 196, 206-211
Dog Stars. See *Sirius; Procyon*
Doubling the bow angle, 209-211
Dowd, John, 206
DR. *See* Dead reckoning
DR plots, 8, 134, 135, 177-178, 193-194, 216
Dubhe, 45, 47, 48, 77
Dutton's Navigation and Piloting, 229

EPIRB, 4, 5
East-West, finding: from *Deneb-Vega* line, 55; from half-latitude rule, 66-70; from mid-day sun (see Shadow tip method); from *Mintaka,* 58, 59; from morning sun (see Sun, rising and setting); from planets, 113; from star lines, 55, 56, 68; from sun, time, and tide tables, 99; from tropics rule, 71-72; from winds aloft, 114-117
Easterly waves, 115
Emergency preparation, 4-6; knowing accuracy, 138; knowing compass checks, 19; knowing currents, 130; knowing equation of time, 191, 236; knowing GMT, 181-182, 192, 200; knowing position, 14, 135; knowing star distances, 180; knowing stars, 71, 236; knowing zenith stars, 164
Emergency, navigational, 2, 12; examples of, 12, 13, 130, 134
Equation of time, 185-191, 195, 236
Equator: currents near, 127; day length at, 174, 175; easterly waves at, 115; finding latitude near, 169, 171; longitude intervals, 11; *North Star* rarely visible from, 47; overhead stars, 44, 59, 66-67; star lines viewed from, 60; star motions viewed from, 9, 50, 63, 71; and sun's declination, 171-173
Equinoxes, 9, 10, 81, 82, 98, 231
Errors: accumulation of 133, 143, 215, 217; cancellation of, 42, 78, 217-219; combinations of, 139, 140; DR vs. celestial, 143, 215-219; in LOP's, 231; as percentages, 133, 217-219; in principle vs. practice, 26, 70; tendencies in angle measurements, 102, 162
Error current, 215-219
Evening stars (planets), 112-113

Falkland Islands, 65
Fallstreaks, 115, 116
Fathom, 137